INDIVIDUAL QUALITY OF LIFE

INDIVIDUAL QUALITY OF LIFE

Approaches to Conceptualisation and Assessment

edited by

C. R. B. Joyce,
Hannah M. McGee
and
Ciaran A. O'Boyle

 harwood academic publishers
Australia • Canada • China • France • Germany • India • Japan • Luxembourg • Malaysia
The Netherlands • Russia • Singapore • Switzerland

Amsteldijk 166
1st Floor
1079 LH Amsterdam
The Netherlands

British Library Cataloguing in Publication Data

Individual quality of life : approaches to
    conceptualisation and assessment
    1. Quality of life 2. Social sciences – Research –
    Methodology 3. Social service – Research – Methodology
    I. Joyce, C. R. B. II. McGee, Hannah III. O'Boyle, Ciaran A.
    362.1'0723

ISBN   90-5702-425-X (Softcover)

To those who have contributed so much to the quality of our lives, in the hope that we have not expropriated too much of theirs.

CONTENTS

FOREWORD

Almost four decades ago, in the first chapter of my doctoral dissertation, I began my inquiry with the observation that "There are almost as many definitions of health and illness as there are states of being. Every man [*SIC:* person] in the street, as well as health experts, humanists, scientists and philosophers has some notion of what is good health." While the dissertation rests on microfiche in the bowels of a dissertation archive, the book you are about to read explores the not-so-original observation of a young scientist and its implications for the definition and measurement of the even arger and more complex notion of quality of life. This is a truly daunting – task assigning value to individual experience – approached by the editors of this volume with a balance of humor, scholarly inquiry and a catholicity of approaches.

Taken from a phenomenological perspective, every person is indeed and 'island' and quality of life is inherently individual. Who else can experience the *n-of-1* trial that life represents but the individual herself or himself? Who else can report the deepest aspirations and fears, the fondest goals and fulfillment, the meaning of the winnings and the losings? These personal definitions and reports are individual quality of life, and they remain relentlessly personal and individual.

In the course of the cooperative human endeavor, however, we have found it useful in positivist fashion to assign numbers to the experiences and perceptions of individuals to represent the *quantity* of the *life quality* of individuals. Judgments of quality are made according to a predetermined rule that a higher (or lower) number represents a higher quality of life. Then, a very frightening step occurs: we aggregate across experiences and perceptions and across individuals and groups and we evaluate interventions or life circumstances to find out which treatments and which circumstances have a 'higher' or 'lower' quality of life.

This book challenges the widespread approach to conceptualization and measurement of quality of life using predetermined categories and predetermined values in the assessment. The editors, engaged in the practical conduct of research for many years, pose the question of to what extent and with what success can we measure the quality of life remaining true to the principle that individual definitions exist and individual values count. Drawing upon the contributions of a number of leading thinkers and researchers in the field, primarily from Europe and North America, they have put together a collection of writing that illustrates an illusive commonality across different applications, different cultures and different researchers in searching for the individual in quality-of-life assessment. From resource allocation and QALYs to individual patient response to palliative treatments, examples of inserting the individualized approach are offered and explored.

Many cherished values, such as autonomy, human rights, and the sacredness of human life, underpin the efforts to measure individual quality of life. As is observed in many different ways in this book, any life can be valuable to the one who is living it and the search for that individual expression of value is important in respect to those core values. Thus, it is not surprising that some of life's most difficult experiences, such as dying or the experience of living on the margins of society, can best be addressed using the individualized approach. Predetermined standards simply don't fit.

Once the concept is accepted, the challenges to measurement are myriad, and this book takes the major issues of going beyond content validity to measurement validity, scaling, and change over time. Several authors address the end result of all measurement efforts: what does the measure mean? Issues of causal sequence, preference weighting, provided versus elicited cues, cross-cultural similarity, relationship to personality and others are addressed. Many issues are common to all measures of quality of life, while others like cueing and assigning individual weights have specific relevance for individual measures.

Individual quality of life assessment is nearing its toddler stage, having moved out of its infancy with this collection of thoughts and advice. Individual measures have real strengths in that it is possible at different points of time to find out what individuals consider important in their lives and how they view their position in life within their culture, their historical moments and their goals and concerns. Many methodological and analytical challenges remain and these are exciting, complex in nature and difficult to explore. This book lays the groundwork. Now to take up the charge and push it forward.

Professor Donald Patrick
Department of Health Services
University of Washington, Seattle, USA

LIST OF CONTRIBUTORS

EDITORS

Professor C. R. B. Joyce,
Visiting Professor, Department
of Psychology, Royal College of
Surgeons in Ireland, Mercer
Building, Dublin 2, Ireland.

Professor Hannah M. McGee,
Director, Health Service Research
Centre, Department of Psychology,
Royal College of Surgeons in
Ireland, Mercer Building,
Dublin 2, Ireland.

Professor Ciaran A. O'Boyle,
Chairman, Department of Psychol-
ogy, Royal College of Surgeons in
Ireland, Mercer Building, Dublin 2,
Ireland.

CONTRIBUTORS

Professor Per Bech, Frederiksborg
General Hospital, Psychiatric
Institute, 48 Dyrehaverej, DK-3400
Hillerod, Denmark.

Professor Ann Bowling, Professor
of Health Services Research
University College London Medical
School, University of London,
London, UK.

Dr. John Browne, Surgical Audit &
Epidemiology Unit, Royal College
of Surgeons of England, 35–43
Lincoln's Inn, Fields, London,
WC2A 3PN, UK.

Professor Monika Bullinger,
Institute for Medical Psychology,
University Hospital Hamburg-
Eppendorf Kollaustr, 67–69 B
D-22529 Hamburg, Germany.

Mr. Robert F. Coen,
Neuropsychologist, Mercer's
Institute for Research on Ageing
(MIRA), St. James's Hospital,
Dublin 8, Ireland.

Dr. David Feeny,
Department of Clinical
Epidemiology & Biostatistics,
McMaster University, 1200 Main St
West, Hamilton, Ontario, L8N 3Z5,
Canada.

Dr. Andrew Garratt,
Department of Health Sciences
and Clinical Evaluation, Alcuir
College, University of York, York,
Y01 SDD, UK.

Professor Gordon H. Guyatt,
Department of Clinical
Epidemiology & Biostatistics,
McMaster University,
1200 Main St West, Hamilton,
Ontario, L8N 3Z5, Canada.

Dr. Matti Häyry,
Department of Philosophy,
University of Helsinki, Unionkatu
40B, SF-00170, Helsinki, Finland.

Dr. Anne Hickey, Lecturer in Psychology, Department of Psychology, Royal College of Surgeons in Ireland, Mercer Building, Dublin 2, Ireland.

Dr. Sonja M. Hunt, PO Box 1556, Pine, Arizona, USA.

Professor Michael E. Hyland, Department of Psychology, University of Plymouth, Plymouth PL4 8AA, UK.

Dr. Crispin Jenkinson, Deputy Director, Health Services Research Unit, Department of Public Health, University of Oxford, Institute of Health Sciences, Headington, Oxford OX3 7LF, UK.

Professor Robert M. Kaplan, Division of Health Care Sciences, Department of Family & Preventive Medicine, University of California, San Diegao, La Jolla CA 92093-0622, USA.

Dr. Yves Lacasse, Centre de Pneumologie, Hopital Laval, 2725 Chemin Ste-Foy, Ste-Foy, P. Quebec Giv 4G5 Canada.

Professor Donald L. Patrick, Department of Health Services, SC-37, University of Washington, Seattle, WA 98195, USA.

Dr. Dennis A. Revicki, (Banelle Institute)

Dr. Danny A. Ruta, Department of Health Sciences and Clinical Evaluation, Alcuir College, University of York, York Y01 SDD, UK.

Professor Stephen Senn, Department of Statistical Science and Department of Epidemiology and Public Health, University College London, Room 316, 1–19 Torrington Place, London WCIE 6BT, UK.

Dr. Dympna Waldron, Research Fellow, Department of Psychology, Royal College of Surgeons in Ireland, Mercer Building, Dublin 2, Ireland.

Dr. Evic Wong, Department of Clinical Epidemiology & Biostatistics, McMaster University, 1200 Main St West, Hamilton, Ontario, L8N 3Z5, Canada.

Dr. Sue Ziebland, Senior Research Fellow, ICRF General Practice Research Group, Institute of Health Sciences, Old Road, Headington, Oxford, OX3 7LF, UK.

I

CONCEPTUAL AND METHODOLOGICAL PRINCIPLES

1. INTRODUCTION: THE INDIVIDUAL PERSPECTIVE

C. R. B. JOYCE, CIARAN A. O'BOYLE and HANNAH M. McGEE

About ten years ago, one of the editors persuaded the multinational pharmaceutical company for which he was then working that the intention of its medical department to explore the value of quality of life (a so-called study of which had just been published by a competitor) (Croog et al., 1986) for its own clinical trials of new drugs would be better served by seeking new methods that focused on the individual, rather than the "epidemiological" methods then in vogue (Joyce et al., 1987). The original proposal of February 1987 noted that:

> "Until now, most attempts to study patients' quality of life have relied upon one or another form of questionnaire that describes the individual's state as seen from the outside; that is, in terms of signs and symptoms. The purposes of the present programme... are (a) to use methods derived from experimental and clinical psychology for the description by the patient of his/her own perception of health status and its personal meaning; (b) to determine which methods correspond best to quality of life statements with medical and personal value; (c) to examine the extent to which they capture information similar to/different from that found with current methods (convergent/divergent validity); (d) to explore the sensitivity of these measures to therapeutic interventions at both individual and group levels (discriminant validity)."

The other editors were becoming interested in similar problems at the same time, and a fortunate chain of circumstances brought all three into contact. The consequent fruitful collaboration continues. CIBA-Geigy, the company in question, provided generous financial support for a period of five years, and of the three techniques from experimental social psychology originally chosen for exploration (Judgment Analysis (JA), the Repertory Grid (RG) and Verbal Content Analysis), the first two have led to the JARGONS project (Judgment Analysis and Repertory Grid On New Systems) and many subsequent applications to the real-life study of individual quality of life. Meanwhile, other investigators have been developing other new approaches. There is now enough contrasting and complementary work to make it worthwhile to bring reviews and examples together under one cover, so that those who are interested can more easily compare the advantages and disadvantages, as well as the depth to which each method succeeds in penetrating the cloud of unknowing.

To change the metaphor, the black box of the individual person, which is both the student and studied of all psychological enquiry, though reluctantly yielding at last to the combined multidisciplinary attack of cognitive scientists, continues to present formidable methodological difficulties: of definition, of measurement, of stability and analysis, to name a few. Among the many examples of such methodological problems are those of psychological research to which Paul Meehl drew attention in 1973 (Meehl, 1973); Guy Claxton's demand for "a generic psychology... which is of practical use to ordinary folk in reflecting upon and ordering their daily lives" (Claxton, 1991) and the sober registration by a Lancet editorialist that the identical body of data yields very different conclusions if analysed with differing definitions of the target indication, changed analytical models or even a simple change in grouping by age (Lancet, 1991). While the deficiencies in such research at all levels are being pointed out and worried over it may seem paradoxical to some that the editors have concluded that much is nevertheless to be gained by returning as far as possible to the source of all difficulty: the individual himself.[1] La Bruyère pointed out 300 years ago, "Tout notre mal vient de ne pouvoir être seuls: de là le jeu, le luxe, la dissipation, le vin, les femmes, l'ignorance, la médisance, l'envie, l'oubli de soi-même et de Dieu." ("All our troubles come from inability to be alone: gambling, luxury, dissipation, drink, women, ignorance, lying, jealousy, neglect of oneself and neglect of God": la Bruyere, 1688–1694). This imposing list of behaviours seen as evil or at least undesirable would not be so regarded in its entirety today, a point that emphasises yet another strength of methods of intensively investigating the individual: that they do not restrict themselves, as do so many conventional methods, to negatives — limitations of movement, intellectual incapacities and moral uncertainties.

In introducing a book intended to present a comprehensive survey of its chosen field, it is necessary to apologise in advance for possible omissions. If these have occurred, they are certainly unintentional. As the title shows, methods that take the individual, rather than the group, as the unit of study, are our concern. Clearly there is no hard and fast dividing point; rather, any method (and there are by now several hundred) that investigates the area can be placed somewhere on a continuum that runs from Health Economics to Psychoanalysis. Our interest is in those methods which encourage each individual to represent his quality of life in his own terms, rather than being obliged to reply to some formal kind of questioning that has been based upon the decisions of others, no matter how expert, even if they have themselves been patients suffering from the same condition. Thus, some well-established instruments, such as the Sickness Impact Profile (Bergner et al., 1981) the Nottingham Health Profile (Hunt et al., 1991) or the Medical Outcomes Scale (Ware et al., 1992) are not included here, in spite of the undoubted contributions that they have made to knowledge about health

---

[1]   To make communication less clumsy, we use this apparently old-fashioned solution to what is in our view a non-problem. It has been sanctioned in the following terms by distinguished American authorities on style: "The use of *he* as a pronoun for nouns embracing both genders is a simple, practical convention rooted in the beginnings of the English language... It has no pejorative connotations." William Strunk and E. B. White. The Elements of Style. 3rd edn. New York: Macmillan, 1979. p. 60.

status in a wide variety of subject populations, healthy as well as sick. However, although our own interest began with the development of methods that could be used in clinical trials, and has therefore been greatly influenced by the problems associated with the study of phenomena that change with time, the majority of instruments that have been published so far have not had this restriction as a first concern. Moreover, although these and our own methods are mainly concerned with medical applications, there are good reasons for thinking that more attention should be paid than at present to the quality of life of "healthy" people, especially in developing countries or in the often no less disadvantaged communities to be found in so-called developed countries.

The desire that some of the work described here may find application in such circumstances as well as in the medical environment in which it usually had its origin decrees that we describe a further criterion for the present selection. In general, investigators have distinguished between "specific" and "general" methods. Specific measures such as the Rating Form of IBD Patient Concerns (Drossman et al., 1989) or the Arthritis Impact Measurement Scale (Meenan et al., 1992) were developed to provide information about a particular condition, inflammatory bowel disease and arthritis respectively. General measures such as the Sickness Impact Profile (Bergner et al., 1981), the Nottingham Health Questionnaire (Hunt et al., 1991) and the MOS-36 (Ware et al., 1992) are considered either to be applicable in a wide variety of indications or to tap into the more fundamental aspects of quality of life that are in some sense more fundamental. We believe that all methods of investigating true individual quality of life (IQOL) are general, and that there is no need to re-invent a method of studying quality of life in, say, diabetes if one has already been adequately established in hypertension. To paraphrase Gertrude Stein: "IQOL is IQOL is IQOL". Thus we believe that all the methods described here are not merely general but also permit the study of true, individual quality of life to be approximated.

With these general considerations in mind, the plan of the book can now be set out as follows. There are three sections. The first establishes the principles that are relevant to the study of individual quality of life, the second describes a number of methods that have been developed for the purpose by others as well as by our own group, and the third describes some practical applications of individual measures. Three of the 16 chapters have been reprinted from recent publications, because their authors, who had been invited to contribute to the book, felt that what they had already recently said could not be improved upon at present (an opinion with which the editors wholeheartedly agree).

In Section I, Matti Hayry lays out the kind of questions that have to be answered, Monika Bullinger describes the relationship of aspects of cognitive psychological theory to the assessment of individual quality of life; Michael Hyland follows with a considered formulation of a programme for research in this field. Next Bech draws attention to some methodological pitfalls that may be overlooked in studies of this kind. Then Senn outlines statistical considerations associated with n-of-1 trials particularly relevant to research on individual quality of life. Crispin Jenkinson and Sue Ziebland conclude the section with a discussion on problems in the interpretation of numerical observations.

Section II describes a number of instruments for the assessment of individual quality of life: the McMaster approach to individualising questionnaires is described by Yves Lacasse, E Wong and Gordon Guyatt, followed by Andrew Garrett and Danny Ruta's description of the Patient Generated Index. The Schedule for the Evaluation of Individual Quality of Life (SEIQoL) is described by Anne Hickey and her colleagues, and Robert Kaplan and his colleagues discuss so-called "preference" methods of assessing outcome. Finally, John Browne outlines briefly a number of other methods incorporating the individual perspective.

In Section III, Ann Bowling describes specific applications of the individual quality of life approach in population studies, Robert Coen writes about the assessment of quality of life by care-givers and the use of proxy judgements, and Dympna Waldron and Ciaran O'Boyle discuss quality of life in palliative care.

In Section IV, the editors offer the inevitable, but it is to be hoped, not cliché-ridden look towards the future, pointing out some deficiencies in current methods that need to be made good and possible extensions to other areas of interest, as well as frankly speculating about possible developments for individual quality of life research in the uncertain millennium to come.

The book concludes with an appendix by Sonja Hunt. This describes a kind of apotheosis, or apostasy, that has come to this leading contributor, originally, to the study of health status. Hunt now believes in the impossibility of studying quality of life although, paradoxically in its importance — not least because of the danger of its neglect in a world generally hostile towards the human right to a decent quality of life.

More than one investigator has been heard to utter an aphorism that is in danger of becoming a platitude: "I enjoyed an excellent quality of life until I began to study it !" The editors themselves will be content if the present volume helps to restore some of the pleasure to be found in such labours, rather than adding to the burden.

REFERENCES

la Bruyère, J. *Les Caractères: de l'Homme*. Paris, 1688–1694.

Bergner, M., Bobbitt, R. A., Carter, W. B. et al. (1981) The Sickness Impact Profile: development and final revision of a health status measure. *Medical Care* **19**, 787–805.

Claxton, G. (1991) Psychosophy: are we ready for a science of self-knowledge? *Psychologist*, 249–252.

Croog, S. H., Levine, S. and Testa, M. (1986) The effects of antihypertensive therapy on the quality of life. *New England Journal of Medicine* **314**, 1657–1664.

Drossman, D. A., Patrick, D. L., Mitchell, C. M., Murp, E. A., Zagomi, E. A. and Appelbaum, M. I. (1989) HRQOL in inflammatory bowel disease: functional status and patient worries and concerns. *Digestive Diseases and Sciences* **34,** 1379–1386.

Editorial. (1991) Subjectivity in data analysis. *Lancet* **337**, 401–402.

Hunt, S. M. and McKenna, S. P. (1991) *The Nottingham Health Profile User's Manual*, revised. Manchester, England: Galen Research and Consultancy.

Joyce, C. R. B. (1987) Quality of life: the state of the art in clinical assessment. In Assher, A. W., Walker, S. R. (eds) *Quality of Life: Assessment and Application*. Lancaster: M.I.T. Press.

Meehl, P. (1973) Some methodological reflections on the methodological difficulties of psychoanalytical research. *Psychological Issues* **8,** 104–117.

Meenan, R. F., Mason, J. H., Andersson, J. J. et al. (1992) AIMS2: the content and properties of a revised and expanded Arthritis Impact Measurement scales health status questionnaire. *Arthritis and Rheumatism* **35**, 1–10.

Strunk, W. and White, E. B. (1979) *The Elements of Style*. New York: Macmillan.

Ware, J. E. and Sherbourne, C. D. (1992) The MOS 36-item short-form health survey (SF-36). *Medical Care* **30,** 473–483.

2. MEASURING THE QUALITY OF LIFE: WHY, HOW AND WHAT?*

MATTI HÄYRY

In this paper three questions concerning quality of life in medicine and health care are analysed and discussed: the motives for measuring the quality of life, the methods used in assessing it, and the definition of the concept. The purposes of the study are to find an ethically acceptable motive for measuring the quality of life; to identify the methodological advantages and disadvantages of the most prevalent current methods of measurement; and to present an approach towards measuring and defining the quality of life which evades the difficulties encountered and discussed. The analysis comprises measurements both in the clinical situation concerning individual patients and in research concerning whole populations.

Three motives are found for evaluating the quality of human life: allocation of scarce medical resources, facilitating clinical decision making, and assisting patients towards autonomous decision making. It is argued that the third alternative is the only one which does not evoke ethical problems.

As for the methods of evaluation, several prevalent alternatives are presented, ranging from scales of physical performance to more subtle psychological questionnaires. Clinical questionnaires are found to fail to provide a scientific foundation for universally measuring the quality of life.

Finally, the question of definition is tackled. The classical distinction between need-based and want-based theories of human happiness is presented and discussed. The view is introduced and defended that neither of these approaches can be universally preferred to the other. The difficulty with the need approach is that it denies the subjective aspects of human life; whereas the problem of the want approach is that it tends to ignore some of the objective realities of the human existence.

In conclusion, it is argued that the choice of methods as well as definitions should be left to the competent patients themselves — who are entitled, if they so wish, to surrender the judgement to the medical personnel. Technical factors as well as the requirements of respect for autonomy and informed consent support this conclusion.

INTRODUCTION

When the quality of life, or rather *the good quality of human life*, is discussed in the context of modern medicine and health care, only one of the many aspects of the issue is usually addressed at a time. In reports prepared by practising physicians and clinical researchers, the methods of measuring quality of life in given clinical settings are often granted the focus of attention [1, 2]. Social scientists, on the other hand, tend to make questions of definition their primary concern [3, 4]. And if moral philosophers can be lured into discussing something as elusive as the quality of life, they can escape the more technical questions by concentrating on the interests behind defining and measuring human well-being [5].

Paralleling the three approaches, three questions can be formulated, namely:

(1) What is quality of life?
(2) How can quality of life be measured?
(3) Why do we need quality-of-life measurements?

---

* This article is reprinted with permission from *Theoretical Medicine*, 1991, **12**, 97–116.

These formulations account for the social scientist's question of definition, the clinical researchers quest for methods, and the moral philosopher's interest in the underlying reasons, respectively. From a purely formal point of view, it could be claimed that the first question is in fact the only one that requires philosophical scrutiny. The question concerning methods seems to be a theoretical scientific rather than a philosophical one. And the motives for measuring quality of life are presumably better known to administrators and medical practitioners than to academic philosophers. My point of departure is, however, that these three issues are too closely intertwined to be treated adequately in complete isolation from each other. In particular, I argue that responses to the question of definition will be much benefited by a prior understanding of the motives and methods of quality of-life-measurements. I shall, therefore, introduce and discuss the questions I have mentioned in the reverse order, starting from the issue of motives, and then working my way through the methods of measurement toward the problem of definition.[1]

WHY DO WE NEED QUALITY-OF-LIFE MEASUREMENTS?

Allocation of Scarce Medical Resources

One motive for estimating and comparing human lives that comes readily to mind is economic: recently there has been a lot of discussion about the scarcity of medical resources [8–10], and the quality of life preserved or produced is, obviously, a possible criterion for allocation decisions. The idea would be that in situations where not all those in need can be saved or otherwise treated, the medical personnel should choose to treat the patients who can benefit most, in terms of both the quantity and the quality of their remaining lives, from a given amount of resources allocated. More concisely, the matter can be expressed by employing the following formula:

$$Vi = (Ni \bullet Qi) - Ci \tag{i}$$

where Vi stands for the *Value of treatment i*, Ni for the *Number of expected life years after the treatment*, Qi for the *Quality of those years* and Ci for the *Cost of the treatment*. The value of a medical procedure, measured by the formula, is comparative, and when decisions concerning allocation are being made, the option with the highest value should always have priority over all others. This applies equally well to comparisons between treatments, patients, hospitals, physicians, branches of medicine, and different illnesses.

But although choices must be made where scarcity prevails, and although the formula just presented may be intelligible as such, its application to real-life medical situations is ethically problematic. To start with, the 'number of expected life years' is, owing to the uncertainties of prognosis, in many cases difficult to estimate, and it is therefore far from clear that doctors possess knowledge which is sufficient to make their choices legitimate. This problem is already manifest at the level of comparing individual patients, but it is particularly acute when larger units or categories such as hospitals or branches of medicine are evaluated. Even if the estimates were reasonably reliable, the problems of inherent ageism as well as implied racism and sexism would remain. Statistically speaking, the young would generally be preferred to the old, and as race, gender and social status are often distinct factors in the mortality rates, these factors could be directly employed as rules of thumb for efficient but inequitable decision making [5]. In the context of regional differences, moreover, the 'cost of the treatment' causes similar difficulties: quite regardless of the quantity or quality-of-life aspects of the matter, it is more economic to allocate certain complicated treatments to big city hospitals instead of smaller country clinics, since the cost of these particular medical services, if provided in the countryside, is considerably higher.

What these remarks amount to is that the 'quality of life' in the context of resource allocation seems to serve mainly as a camouflage for purely economic decision making — the actual problems of counting lives in money lie elsewhere, and questions concerning quality measurement do not even arise.

Facilitating Clinical Decision Making

The distribution of scarce medical equipment and services is by no means the only motive for the assessment and comparison of parallel human life spans. Another prominent candidate is the need to facilitate clinical decision making: a physician who knows what the expected values of alternative treatments in terms of the quantity and the quality of life are, is in a good position to make considered choices for her patients. Depending on the weight to be given to the number of expected life years, this idea can be interpreted in two ways.

According to the first interpretation, there is no value in survival as such — the quality of the prolonged life is always a factor in any evaluation of medical procedures. This can be expressed through the following simple formula:

$$Vi = Ni \cdot Qi \qquad (ii)$$

where the symbols have the same meanings as in formula (i) above. Given a few specifications, this reading comes close to one of the most debated recent attempts to create a workable index for health status, namely the QALY procedure developed in the University of York in England [11, 12]. The basic idea of QALYs, or Quality Adjusted Life Years, is to stipulate that one year lived in perfect health is worth one QALY unit, and years lived in less than perfect health are each worth less than one QALY unit. Assuming that it is possible to define in a satisfactory way 'perfect' and 'less than perfect' health, QALYs can then be used to count the comparative values of medical procedures by preparing QALY estimations for all the alternatives that are available to a decision maker at the time of the choice.

According to the second interpretation, quality of life is, as a value, hierarchically less important than the possibility of prolonging life. Put in a symbolic form, the point has to be expressed as a succession of two consecutive options:

$$Vi = Ni \tag{iii}$$

and only if this does not suffice to make a difference,

$$Vi = Qi$$

where the symbols are as in the above. In other words, the value of treatments is to be calculated by the expected life years alone, and only if this criterion fails to differentiate between two or more alternatives, the quality of the expected years may be taken into account.

The obvious initial appeal of such hierarchical ordering, as compared to a more straightforward multiplication of the two factors, can be easily explained. It derives from the intuitively sound assumption that underlies the model, stating that any life can be valuable to the one who is living it, and that, unless shown otherwise, decisions to alleviate suffering at the expense of saving lives are always ethically problematic. What the interpretation does not account for is that with the unprecedented development of life-sustaining technologies there is presently a growing need within Western health care systems to compare afresh certain treatments which prolong life to others which 'merely' relieve suffering. Clinical decisions based only on attempts to prolong life now seem in many cases positively inhumane [13, 14].

There are significant mutual differences in the approaches marked by definitions (ii) and (iii), but there are also serious difficulties of application that these approaches share. As regards comparisons across individuals or health care units or branches of medicine, both methods evoke most of the problems attributed to the economic model above: prognostic uncertainties, ageist tendencies, and other kinds of potential inequity are present regardless of the choice made between the two. And even if comparisons were limited to alternative treatments to one and the same person, ethical difficulties could not be completely avoided. Although clinical decision making based on, say QALYs, does not necessarily lead to inequity, it involves a set of questions related to *patient autonomy*.

In medico-ethical as well as medico-legal contexts, respect for the patient's capacity — and perhaps 'right' — to autonomous and self-determined decision making has during the last few decades gained a focal position. Especially the doctrine of *informed consent* has been much to the fore — according to this principle, it is the duty of medical personnel to inform patients about the alternatives open to them and about the risks inherent in these alternatives, after which the patients should themselves choose the line of treatment to be taken [15]. The implications of the doctrine in everyday medical practice have been challenged by physicians, but it does not seem likely that patient autonomy could be systematically ignored in discussions concerning morals and medicine.

Assisting Patients Towards Autonomous Decision Making

In the present context, the requirement of respect for autonomy makes it suspect that physicians could by themselves — basing their judgements on the QALY procedure or any other 'objective' indicator — legitimately decide about the treatment of competent patients. Even though the patients may make 'mistakes', in terms of QALY units or expected life years, in making choices concerning their own treatment, the choices and the ensuing mistakes are theirs to make, given that other people are not harmed in the process. Taking this aspect of the matter fully into account, the formula for assessing the values of alternative treatments can be put as follows:

$$V_i = (rN_i \bullet sQ_i) - tC_i \qquad\qquad \text{(iv)}$$

where the meanings of V_i, V_i, Q_i and C_i are as in formula (i), and r, s and t stand for ratings that the patient in question gives to the quantity, quality and cost factors, respectively. The patient must, of course, be well-informed, competent, emotionally stable and not under undue influences (such as economic pressures) at the time of the choice, but these points should not be exaggerated. Although there is often a real need in medical situations to protect patients from their own ill-advised choices, a 'reasonable degree' of autonomy must suffice to prove that the patient is capable of making her or his own decisions. Considerations concerning the quality of life are no exception to this rule.

There are, however, three specifications to the 'autonomy-respecting' model of medical evaluations.

First, concern for the patient's right to self-determination does not imply that the physician should psychologically abandon the patient: a doctor who merely spreads the options in front of the patient and then says 'Go ahead and choose, it's your life' is not anti-paternalistic but negligent [16]. Genuine respect for autonomy requires that doctors make sure that patients understand the options open to them — including the risks, the benefits and the side effects — as thoroughly as persons lacking medical training can be expected to understand such matters.

Second, despite the emphasis placed on autonomy, patients must not be deprived of the possibility of surrendering their final judgement to the medical professionals. Patients may feel that they are not capable of adequately grasping the situation no matter how thoroughly they are briefed, or they may hold the view that it is ultimately the doctor's duty to make the medical decisions for them. Under such circumstances, it is the physician's task to apply definitions (i), (ii) or (iii) to the patient's predicament in a manner that to the physician seems appropriate. The standards of 'appropriateness' employed by doctors in these assessments ordinarily derive from the prevailing professional consensus, or in hard cases sometimes from the moral sentiments of the surrounding community. It has recently been suggested, counter to this practice, that the doctor's decision should be based on *an estimate concerning the patient's wishes* rather than on the doctor's own values [17]. This, I think, is a commendable ideal: in situations where the patient has forgone the choice, a physician should indeed make an effort towards employing formula (iv), with the patient's own expressed or tacit ratings for the quantity, quality and (possibly) price factors. However, if the patient specifically wants the doctor to act on 'purely scientific' grounds, or if no information concerning the patient's preferences is available, then professional consensus may after all provide a safer basis for decisions than attempts to find out the patient's values through sympathetic guesswork.

Third, respect for patient autonomy is necessary and indeed desirable only when the patients in question are, in a technical sense, reasonably autonomous in the first place, i.e. they are capable of making consistent choices founded on their own preferences and beliefs. This condition is not always fulfilled in the cases of very small children, the mentally ill and the seriously demented. Moreover, unconscious and comatose patients lack, at least temporarily, the capacity to give their informed and valid consent to medical procedures.

HOW CAN QUALITY OF LIFE BE MEASURED?

Sanctity, Quality, and Measurability

The various motives for measuring life-quality, presented above, suggest three different guidelines for choosing methods for real-life clinical decisions or demographic research. These motives can be formulated as (a) respect for the sanctity of life, (b) respect for scientific efficiency, and (c) respect for human autonomy.

(a) The first directive emerged when the difference between definitions (ii) and (iii) was discussed. As noted in that connection, there are theorists who believe that human life is always valuable, or 'sacred', and that quality-of-life measurements are therefore in the majority of cases unethical. This moral conviction has obviously some validity, but there are, fortunately, two points that reduce its credibility as regards attempts to develop quality-of-life indexes for medical decision making. Firstly, even if all human life really were sacrosanct in some important sense, quality (and possibly cost) measurements would still be needed for situations in which the quantity factor of two or more alternative treatments is equal. And secondly, it is far from clear that the 'sanctity-of-life doctrine' should be understood as stating that prolonged life must *always* be preferred to the foreseen and intended hastening of death [18]. The fate of Ken, the sculptor paralysed in a road accident in Brian Clark's play *Whose Life Is It Anyway?* [19], gives a vivid, albeit fictitious, account of how the life of a competent adult human being can become genuinely miserable. If empirical evidence as to the existence of patently meaningless suffering is required, such evidence has been available since 1973, when Raymond Duff and Alexander Campbell 'went public' with their experience of having to let forty three seriously defective babies die in the Yale-New Haven Special Care Nursery [13]. It is now a widely recognised fact that the situation Duff and Campbell found themselves in is in no way unique, or even rare, and it is also evident that suffering infants with absolutely no prospect of meaningful life are being kept alive, in vain, in hospitals all over the world, due to a rigid interpretation of the sanctity-of-life doctrine.

(b) In sharp contrast to the religious and moralistic views, however, most motives for actually measuring life's value are quite antagonistic to the ideal of relentlessly prolonging lives. Health economists often emphasise that, in the name of efficiency and equity, scientific measurements of the quality and quantity factors of life and health should be employed, so as to facilitate decisions concerning resource allocation. But as the term "scientific" in the context of modern medicine and health care is mostly taken to refer to the exact and objective *natural sciences*, quality-of-life studies have since their advent in the 1940s mostly been based on the 'objective' requirements of reproducibility and measurability by external observation. The problem with these requirements — no doubt useful within their own domain — is that they may, owing to the inevitable subjective aspect of the quality of human life, produce quite unreliable·results [20].

(c) Respect for autonomy provides yet another contrast with the foregoing considerations. Seen from the viewpoint of personal self-determination, it is not necessary that the value of one's life is either absolute or objectively measurable. Rather, it seems natural to state that the quality, or value, of an individual's life is no more and no less than what she considers it to be. This way of thinking is, not altogether surprisingly, disagreeable to many interest groups: to many religious people who defy the idea that a person could himself decide that his life is worthless, to health economists who fear that people living 'objectively worthless' lives would be allowed to waste resources which could save 'better' lives, and possibly to medical professionals who wish to keep up the image that 'the doctor always knows best'. Interpreted strictly, the emphasis on autonomy renders external quality-of-life measurements impossible, since everything depends, in the last analysis, on the subjective judgement of the individuals themselves.

Asking the Patients

Despite the obvious theoretical problems stemming from the personal aspects of human experience, medical and social scientists have for more than forty years measured something that, according to their own vocabulary at least, is called the 'quality of life'. Underlying their practices is the assumption that the subjective and objective elements of life can somehow be reconciled by *asking the patients themselves* questions concerning their physical and mental health status. The idea of the model is that when people themselves assess the objective dimensions of their health and illness, the subjective factor is automatically included in the result. Moreover, it is usually presumed that when a sufficient number of people have answered the questions — i.e., when the sample is suitable for statistical purposes — the observations made about the sample group can be generalised to the population at large.

The questions that patients are required to answer in quality-of-life trials vary considerably, both in content and in form. As for the content of the researcher's inquiries, some questions are directly related to the patients' *condition* — to their physical and mental well-being as experienced by themselves [21]. Another set of questions concerns the patients' performance : their basic abilities to eat and sleep, wash, dress and go to the toilet themselves, as well as their more complex activities such as working, carrying out hobbies, communicating with other people and engaging in sexual practices [21, 22]. Finally, it can also be asked how the patients are coping with their present situation, i.e. how they are settling into everyday life, and how enjoyable they feel their life to be [22]. Obviously, questionnaires in the 'condition' and 'performance' categories can easily be supplemented by results of medical examination or behavioural observation. However, in quality-of-life assessments objective criteria such as state of health and observable behaviour must always, in the end, be submitted to the patient's own judgement. Amputation of a limb, for instance, obviously worsens someone's bodily condition, but the influence the operation has upon one's physical performance or enjoyment of life varies individually and over time.

As to the form of the questions, both very specific and very general approaches have been employed in clinical trials. The most general question is simply: 'How good is your quality of life?' [20]. Moving into different directions from this starting point, many kinds of specification are possible. One can take the comparative approach and ask, for example, 'How good is your quality of life, as compared to that of other persons of your own age?' [21] or, 'How good is your quality of life now, as compared to the situation before the operation?'. And if more specific questions than these are needed, standard practices include the asking of performance questions such as 'Did you get any sleep last night?' and 'Do you think you can eat by yourself today?' or coping questions such as 'Does it bother you to have to wear a wig?' and 'Do you get feelings of panic?' [1].

Some of the questions seem to presume a mere yes-or-no answer (the patient has either slept or not slept last night); some of them readily allow for at least three alternatives (the patient's quality of life can be better, equal or worse than that of other people); and there are also questions which are prone to invite linear rather than discrete estimations (e.g., 'Did you feel pain today? How much?' seems to permit any number of answers from 'Yes, the pain was intolerable' — to 'No, I felt no pain whatsoever'). When a clinical quality-of-life trial is designed, it is obviously important to formulate the questions and alternative responses so that the patients can understand them, and are willing and able to complete the questionnaire [20].

When all the questions have been asked and answered, the result can be expressed in many alternative forms. The popular and easy-to-use *Karnofsky scale*, for instance, presents the total performance status of the patient, which is based on answers to ten simple questions, in a rating from zero to one hundred points: the result 0 indicates that the patient is dead, the result 100 that the, patient's condition can be described as "normal; causing no complaints, and manifesting no evidence of disease" [1, 20]. The Karnofsky performance status scale was originally designed as an index for health status, and it is far from ideal as a quality-of-life measure: to name only two shortcomings, first, the questions are answered paternalistically by the physician, and second, all ten questions are supposed to have similar weight, which is highly unrealistic. But despite these problems, and despite the fact that better indexes such as the *Linear analogue self-assessment*, the *QL-index*, the *Cancer inventory of problem situations*, the *Psychological adjustment to illness scale*, and the *Hospital anxiety and depression scale* are available [23– 27], clinical quality-of-life measurements are almost invariably made by the Karnofsky method [1].

The theoretical criticism against the use of any of these indexes in measuring the quality of life is, however, that the researcher cannot know what it is that they measure and indicate [1, 20]. If the so-called objective indicators are employed, their connection with the subjectively felt quality of life remains unclear. Being poor or disabled, for instance, does not always imply that a person could not be happy; and material improvements in the living and working conditions have been reported, on a societal level at least, to coincide with a decrease in subjectively felt happiness [28]. The problem with subjective indicators, in turn, is that for all their primacy in the name of autonomy, they may contradict the objective realities too grossly to be relied upon as such. If, for example, a severely ill, disabled, poor and wretched patient who has no social support and who suffers from constant pain reports a quality-of-life level which is similar to that of perfectly healthy and well-off people who have all the social support they need, it is hard to believe that all research subjects have properly understood the aim of the researcher's questions.

Finally, even assuming that answers to individual questions could be obtained in a trustworthy manner, there would be the dilemma of priorities left to be dealt with [1]. As noted in discussing the Karnofsky method, quality-of-life scales which give equal weight to all items of the index are open to charges of unrealism. To give only one example, loss of mobility is presumably for the majority of humankind a more dreadful prospect than loss of appetite: to give equal weight to these aspects of life-quality would not only be scientifically untenable but contrary to common sense as well. On the other hand, although scales can be constructed by putting more emphasis on elements that are considered important, there are no unanimous interpersonal criteria that could be employed in doing so. Accordingly, every attempt towards prioritising the items is doomed to be, interpersonally, more or less arbitrary. In either horn of the dilemma, clinical questionnaires fail to provide a scientific foundation for universally measuring the quality of life.

Asking the Experts

Granted that asking the patients is not the solution the researchers are looking for, an alternative worth considering is that quality-of-life assessments could be made by people who are not at the time of the scoring in need of medical services. In the Karnofsky test, for instance, it is the physician instead of the patient who answers the questions, and there are other evaluation methods — viz. the QL-index and the Psychological adjustment to illness scale — in which the physicians as well as the patients may be the ones doing the rating. Moreover, it is possible to use an informed lay person as a 'control evaluator' for the assessments [29].

However, the ethical handicap shared by both these practices is that as long as the patients themselves are capable of judging — and feel that they are capable of judging — their own lives, estimates by other people are neither required nor desirable.[2] In actual bedside situations, the doctor or the benevolent lay person can legitimately determine the quality of another person's life only if that other person is unconscious or otherwise unable to formulate her or his own opinions. Competent patients, as emphasised in the above, ought to be given every chance to make up their own minds when important matters influencing their future are decided upon. Besides, even if it were possible to employ surrogate evaluators without arousing charges of immorality, one would have to make sure that the assessments made by them somehow correlate with the patient's own inner condition (cf. [29]).

Asking the Prospective Patients

In addition to physicians, patients and informed lay persons, there is still one group of people who have been regarded as the right ones to be subjected to quality-of-life interviews, namely *prospective patients*. It seems that this category is usually interpreted broadly, so that the class of possible respondents extends to all those who are not at the time of the survey actual patients or medical experts looking after them. The 'prospective patient' approach in this form is especially popular among the proponents of the QALY method.

There are four major types of questions which can be put to evaluators [11]. Firstly, in *time trade-off* the subject is asked to assess how many years she would give off her life, if in return she would be freed from certain specified kinds and levels of disability and distress attached to a longer life span. Secondly, in *standard gamble* the subject must evaluate the risk of death she would be ready to accept in an operation which would guarantee a complete recovery from a given disease. Thirdly, in *equivalence of numbers* the question is how many more people with a mild illness must be cured in order to gain more than by healing a given number of people with a more serious illness. And fourthly, in *direct ratio* the respondents should tell how many times more ill someone who suffers from a specified disease is, compared to someone who suffers from a milder disease.

Answers to these questions are then turned into combined quantity and quality-of-life ratings by transforming the percentages, numbers and ratios into QALY units. For instance, if the evaluators are willing to trade ten percent off their lifetime in order to avoid breast cancer, then the life-value of someone with breast cancer is 0.9 QALYs per annum. The same result will be reached by a standard gamble in which the evaluators judge a ten percent risk of death to be acceptable for an operation which is guaranteed to cure breast cancer entirely. The remaining methods — those of the equivalence of numbers and direct ratio provide the researcher with comparative values for the two conditions that are being assessed: given the QALY value of one of the conditions, the worth of the other can also be counted.

There are, however, some major problems with the employment of these methods [11]. In real life, studies conducted up till now have produced results that differ widely from each other, thus rendering the reliability of the methods questionable [30]. In the absence of sufficient consensus, it remains unclear which studies, according to the QALY theorists, ought to be trusted in clinical quality-of-life assessments. Theoretically, the variance is not in the least surprising: there are so many hidden premises in the questions that they are almost certain to distort the final result. It is assumed, for instance, that whatever their own health status, people always give the same comparative ratings to conditions which are described to them. If a healthy person predicts that breast cancer would reduce her yearly life-value to 0.5 QALYs, she is also supposed to hold on to the judgement after it is detected that she herself has contracted breast cancer. That such an assumption is psychologically problematic, even in principle, is obvious. Empirically, it has been demonstrated to be false in studies which show that, regardless of one's present condition, the QALY assessment of one's own life tends to 'creep' towards 1.0 per year [31]. As one might expect, people are reluctant to consider themselves unhealthy if they are not actually feeling ill [11].

Even the simple and innocent-looking point that the QALY value of one life year is usually supposed to vary from zero to one has its problems. The upper limit is awkward, because it renders it impossible to evaluate policy improvements in situations where people are reasonably content with their lives even before the changes. People who suffer from slight allergic reactions, for instance, are almost certain to assess that their lives are normal — worth a full QALY a year — but this cannot be interpreted to mean that their lives could not be improved by removing the symptoms. Similarly, it is not clear that the value of human lives should always be assessed above zero. If a terminal patient in great pain states that his life is positively evil for him, there seems to be little reason to claim that the patient is wrong and that the value of his life must be rated better than no life at all.

Yet another tricky assumption underlying the QALY method is that the questions posed in the interview are always supposed to make sense to the people answering them. However, it appears quite possible that many rational persons would prefer not to speculate on a choice, say, between a longer life span with breast cancer and a shorter one without it. And the same observation applies to comparisons between illnesses as well: although some people may find it informative to state that cancer is a thousand (or a million) times worse than influenza, there are others who find such a statement the purest nonsense. From the researcher's viewpoint the situation is embarrassing: if she excludes from the survey all those subjects who are not willing to cooperate, the original sample will be skewed; if she forces them to answer questions they think unanswerable, the validity of the study will suffer.

WHAT IS QUALITY OF LIFE?

Some Attempts Toward a Definition

As the foregoing considerations have shown, there are a variety of motives and methods for quality-of-life measurements, some of them ethically problematic or theoretically untenable. But what exactly is the entity that clinical researchers and social scientists are trying to discover in their observations and interviews? Can the concept of 'quality of life' be defined clearly and concisely, and in a way that would serve the motives and methods discussed?

Johanna de Haes and Ferdinand van Knippenberg in a review article [22] present six definitions which have been applied to the concept in the literature. These are:

(a) the ability of patients to manage their lives as they evaluate it;
(b) the degree of need satisfaction within the physical, psychological, social, activity, material and structural area;
(c) a function of the patient's natural endowment, and the efforts made on his behalf by his family and by society;
(d) the global evaluation of the good or satisfactory character of people's life;
(e) the totality of those goods, services, situations and states of affairs which are delineated as constituting the basic nature of human life and which are articulated as being needed and wanted; and
(f) the output of two aggregate input factors: physical and spiritual.

The problem with most of these characterisations is that they are neither clear nor, if one undertakes to analyse them properly, concise.

In fact, only definitions (a) and (b) are slightly more promising than the rest, as the point on which they differ from each other marks a dividing line in a philosophical dispute underlying practically all discussion on the value and quality of life. This debate between philosophers, theologians, reformers and scientists began long before the advent of modern medicine, and crucial to it is the following question: Is it more important to human happiness to achieve what one wants (roughly, the point of proposal (a)), or to be provided with what one needs (as suggested by (b))? Reasons have been given in favour of both options, but the issue still remains unsettled. (As Ingmar Pörn [32] and Lennart Nordenfelt [33, 34] have shown, the same question also applies to the analysis of the concept of *health*.)

An Early Example of the Need Approach: Thomas More

Let me give an example of the 'need' approach in early philosophical literature by citing a few passages on human happiness from Thomas Moore's *Utopia*, which was first published in 1516. Several contributions have been made, of course, since Moore's time within the same tradition. However, my point here is not so much to discuss the latest developments in need theory — which I think is not, ultimately, helpful in the medical quality-of-life discussion — as to show how elegantly philosophical classics sometimes describe the basics of contemporary discussion. (For more recent literature on the need and want approaches, see [32–34].)

More begins by pointing out that the ethical teaching in his ideal commonwealth is based on the concept of 'natural pleasures': the Utopians fail to understand the European notion of religious virtues in matters that only concern the agent herself, and "they judge it extreme madness to follow sharp and painful virtue, and not only to banish the pleasure of life, but also willingly to suffer grief without any hope to profit thereof" ([35], pp. 154–155). After a critique of asceticism, More goes on to give an account of the Utopian concept of physical (as opposed to intellectual) well-being:

> The pleasure of the body they [the Utopians] divide into two parts. The first is when delectation is sensibly felt and perceived: which many times chanceth by the renewing and refreshing of those parts, which our natural heat drieth up: this cometh by meat and drink, and sometimes while those things be voided, whereof is in the body overgreat, abundance. This pleasure is felt when we do our natural easement, or when we are doing the act of generation, or when the itching of any part is eased with rubbing or scratching ([35], p. 164).

This first part of the natural pleasures of the body could be called *active enjoyment* or *direct satisfaction* — by contrast to the second category, described by More as follows:

> The second part of bodily pleasure they say is that which consisteth and resteth in the quiet and upright state of the body. And that truly is every man's own proper

health, intermingled and disturbed with no grief. For this, if it be not letted nor assaulted with no grief, is delectable of itself, though it be moved with no external or outward pleasure. For though it be not so plain and manifest to the sense, as the greedy lust of eating and drinking, yet nevertheless many take it for the chiefest pleasure ([35], p. 165).

In the latter passage More introduces a type of pleasure which could perhaps be termed *passive enjoyment* — the quiet contentment deriving from bodily health and lack of pain. The Utopians are told to consider this kind of pleasure superior to active enjoyment, for two reasons: first, because human beings can experience health as such pleasurable, and second, because health is a necessary condition for the pursuit of more active and direct satisfactions. While good health alone can bring happiness to human beings, poor health in turn may prevent all natural and reasonable enjoyment of active pleasures.

Although More employs terms like "delectation" and "pleasure" which at first glance suggest a 'want' approach to the quality-of-life issue, his constant appeals to what is natural and reasonable, as well as the preference he gives to passive enjoyment, firmly place the Utopian theory in the 'need' category. Human life-quality, according to More's view, is dependent upon the satisfaction of certain basic needs, such as the needs for health (in the narrow sense as lack of disease), mobility, good physical performance, adequate nutrition and shelter. As one can easily detect, the Utopian theory is closely related to the many present-day attempts to measure quality-of-life in medicine by observing the patient's performance and symptoms.

The problem with the need approach is that it denies the purely subjective and psychological dimensions of human life and human experience. The basic needs of all human beings may well be roughly the same, but it is obvious that mere basic need satisfaction does not make (all) human beings content. Concepts which are more subjective and personal in nature are required to explain why people's happiness seems to depend on so many diverse and mutually incompatible factors.

The Want Approach: Calman's Theory

An example of the competing 'want' approach is provided by K.C. Calman, who in a recent article writes:

The quality of life can only be described and measured in individual terms, and depends on present life-style, past experience, hopes for the future, dreams and ambitions... A good quality of life can be said to be present when the hopes of an individual are matched and fulfilled by experience. The opposite is also true: a poor quality of life occurs when the hopes do not meet with the experience ([36], pp. 12–125).

In other words, Calman's claim is that life-quality can be maintained and improved by seeing to it that the individual, by and large, gets what he wants. However, this does not simply mean that the individual's hopes and expectations are registered and then fulfilled: Calman points out that the goals set by the agent must be *realistic* ([36], p. 125), and that the gap between hopes and their fulfilment can be quite legitimately narrowed "by making expectations more realistic or by encouraging the individual to develop and grow in other ways" ([36], p. 127). Thus, according to Calman's view, it is equally justifiable to improve a person's life-quality by thwarting his dreams as it is to work out the same effect by making those dreams come true.

In certain kinds of situation the elimination of desires, no doubt, is the only way to narrow the gap between what is expected and what is experienced. Consider, for instance, the case of a paralysed ballet dancer: if there is no prospect of recovery, previous hopes and ambitions simply cannot be fulfilled any more, and subsequently, their removal seems to be the correct method to restore the person's mental balance. This Stoic doctrine applies especially well to the *rehabilitation* aspect of monitoring life-quality — once the patient has already undergone an accident or a mutilating operation, it is natural to take the prevailing substandard situation as the measure of normality, and try to change the desires rather than the reality. Even here, of course, the Stoic solution must not be overemphasised, since genuine reinstatement of health is obviously preferable to mere passive adjustment to external circumstances. It is presumably better to learn to walk (talk, eat, read) again than to have one's related wishes gradually eliminated.

But the real difficulty within Calman's view is that rehabilitation is not the only medical function which employs quality-of-life considerations — these are also a factor in medical decision making *before* the patient is subjected to hazardous treatments. Suppose that a choice is being made between alternative treatments, and the doctor states self-confidently: 'Let's just perform the more radical operation — we can restore your life-quality afterwards'. In such a situation, the patient obviously has every right to assume that the physician refers to life-quality as the patient experiences it now, against the background of his present expectations and values. However, if one takes Calman's points seriously, all the doctor is saying is that either the patient's current wishes can indeed be fulfilled even after the radical procedure, or they can be modified to match reality by persuasion and therapy. Owing to this discrepancy, it seems questionable to regard Calman's solution as universally legitimate.

Besides, when the decision-aspect is fully taken into account, the Stoic approach seems to lose much of its legitimacy even when rehabilitation is concerned. Assuming that quality of life can be given values which rank below zero, then it is perfectly possible that the paralysed ballet dancer would rather not live at all if the only alternative is to live to be 'rehabilitated' to an entirely different life. 'Growing in other ways' is certainly commendable as long as it is reasonably voluntary, but forcing the ex-dancer to, say, enjoy and appreciate drawing with his teeth may come closer to torture than appropriate medical care.

CONCLUDING REMARKS

In the beginning of this paper I presented three questions. These questions can now be answered, to some degree at least, in the light of what has been discussed in the foregoing paragraphs.

Why do we need quality-of-life measurements? The motives for measuring life-quality include economic, clinical, and humanitarian reasons. I have shown that appeals to quality of life in the allocation of scarce medical resources are ethically suspect, due to latent injustices in the economic approach as a whole. Clinical decision making by physicians was found to be equally suspect, although partly for other reasons: if the current demand for patient autonomy is well-founded and if respect for the informed consent procedure is an important matter, then it is difficult to see how doctors could be permitted to judge the life-quality of their competent (and non-consenting) patients. Consequently, the only option that remains morally open is the attempt to use measurements as aids for the patients' autonomous decision making. It may be that a person is not adequately informed, in the sense required by the informed consent doctrine, unless she or he knows what the effects of alternative treatments on her or his quality of life would be.

How can quality of life be measured? There are religious moralists who are willing to argue that quality of life cannot be meaningfully assessed, since every human life, whatever the opinion of the one living it, has absolute — and hence equal — value. It was shown, however, that despite the initial appeal of the absolutist credo, it would, in the last analysis, be irrational to treat everybody with the same intensity regardless of all objective and subjective indications of life-quality. Attempts to evaluate physical performance and the inner aspects of human life are both legitimate and useful — provided, of course, that they can be made to meet the demands of reliability and validity. But the problem here is that as long as the theorists try to construct universal scales, their work is doomed to fail for technical and methodological reasons alone. The so-called objective criteria do not necessarily have any connection with experienced happiness, or life-quality. Subjective indicators, in turn, may produce grossly unrealistic results; and cannot therefore be universally relied upon. Moreover, in both cases the prioritisation of the various criteria proves to be a problem: all items of a questionnaire, for instance, can hardly be assumed to have equal weight, but if this is true, one needs to find a 'correct order' for the various elements, which is no easy task.

What is quality of life? Many attempts to define 'quality of life' once and for all can be found in the recent literature. Most of the attempts are, however, excessively complex or otherwise unclear. One of the more promising approaches states that good life-quality is closely linked to the concept of *need,* and that the fulfilment of our (objective) needs is both a necessary and a sufficient condition for our having a high quality of life. As far as this solution is connected with the idea that physicians know best what the needs of their patients are, there are definite ethical problems in its application. But the main alternative, namely the want approach, is equally problematic.

It is impossible to satisfy all desires — including the unrealistic ones — that people may have, but it cannot be assumed that the elimination or modification of desires would be the answer either.

Yet all these difficulties in defining and measuring life-quality can be evaded with a simple shift of emphasis. The main obstacle in all directions is, obviously, the fact that *universal interpersonal validity* cannot be claimed for any particular solution. But this kind of validity would only be needed if the motive for the evaluations were deemed to be exclusively economic or clinical. In these areas, it is true, one ought to have the 'correct' criteria for one's decisions, as otherwise many kinds of economic, medical and moral side effects could emerge. However, if the quality of human life were only defined and measured for humanitarian reasons, i.e. in order to assist patients towards informed, rational and autonomous decision making, the situation would be entirely different. It would then be up to the patients to accept or refuse definitions and methods of measurement, and to take the results of scientific research into account as they please. This could probably be accomplished in most physician-patient relationships, provided that the paternalistic attitudes among the medical profession could be removed, and information could be efficiently given to the patients as well as to the general public. In cases where informed consent is, for one reason or another, truly impossible to achieve, the physicians must, of course, continue to make the decisions as they see appropriate. Even in these situations, however, it would be praiseworthy if the doctors could try to learn as much as possible about the patient's own expectations and values, and to adjust their choices accordingly.

In a certain sense, then, it is indeed possible to define the good quality of human life in many individual cases. Given that the patients in question are competent and wish to choose for themselves, their quality of life is good if and only if their quality of life is good according to the criteria they themselves have chosen to employ. As regards attempts toward more extensive and general definitions, however, the chances of success seem to be bleak.

Acknowledgements — My thanks are due to Matti Hakama (University of Tampere) for his encouraging and helpful comments on an early draft of this paper, to Sakari Karjalainen (Finnish Cancer Registry), Timo Airaksinen, Martti Kuokkanen, and Heta Häyry (University of Helsinki) for their generous assistance and advice, to the Editor and two anonymous referees of *Theoretical Medicine* for advice and constructive criticisms, and to Mark Shackleton, Lecturer in English (University of Helsinki) for revising the language of the paper.

NOTES

1. This study is centred around the three questions (1–3), and in tackling these questions I have deliberately preferred philosophical argumentation to the mechanical reviewing of current literature. To achieve further

information about recent publications in the field, the reader may consult, e.g., references [6, 7].

2. Cf., however, the second specification to the 'autonomy-respecting' model of medical evaluations in the above. Estimates by medical experts are necessary and acceptable in two cases: first, when the patients are genuinely (physically or psychologically) unable to decide for themselves; and second, when they are competent but wish to surrender the judgement to the medical professionals. In these cases, doctors must estimate their patients' lives by employing whatever criteria their professional competence guides them to employ. In what follows, however, I shall be more interested in those cases where the patients are competent and wish to choose for themselves if they are allowed to do so.

REFERENCES

1. Clark, A. and Fallowfield, L. J. (1986) Quality of life measurements in patients with malignant disease: a review. *J R Soc Med* **79**, 165–9.
2. Daughton, D. M., Fix, A. J., Kass, I., Bell, C. W. and Patil, K. D. (1982) Maximum oxygen consumption and the ADAPT quality-of-life scale. *Arch Phys Med Rehabil* **63**, 620–2.
3. Hörnquist, J. O. (1982) The concept of quality of life. *Scand J Soc Med* **10**, 57–61.
4. Siegrist, J. and Junge, A. (1989) Conceptual and methodological problems in research on the quality of life in clinical medicine. *Soc Sci Med* **29**, 463–8.
5. Harris, J. (1987) QALYfying the value of life. *J Med Ethics* **13**, 117–23.
6. Lohr, K. N. and Ware, J. E. Jr, eds. (1987) Proceedings of the advances in health assessment conference. *J Chronic Dis* **40** (Suppl 1).
7. Neuhausser, D. (1989) Advances in health status assessment: conference proceedings. *Med Care* **27** (Suppl).
8. Callahan, D. (1987) *Setting Limits: Medical Goals in an Aging Society*. New York: Simon and Schuster.
9. Daniels, N. (1988) *Am I My Parents' Keeper?* New York: Oxford University Press.
10. Häyry, M. and Häyry, H. (1990) Health care as a right, fairness and medical resources. *Bioethics* **4**, 1–21.
11. Carr-Hill, R. A. (1989) Assumptions of the QALY procedure. *Soc Sci Med* **29**, 469–77.
12. Williams, A. (1985) The economics of coronary artery bypass grafting. *Br Med J* **291**, 326–9.
13. Duff, R. S. and Campbell, A. G. M. (1973) Moral and ethical dilemmas in the special-care nursery. *N Engl J Med* **289**, 890–4.
14. Shaw, A. (1973) Dilemmas of 'informed consent' in children. *N Engl J Med* **289**, 885–90.
15. Kirby, M. D. (1983) Informed consent: what does it mean? *J Med Ethics* **9**, 69–75.
16. Gillon, R. (1985) Consent. *Br Med J* **291**, 1700–1.
17. Hakama, M. and Holli, K. (1990) Millainen on oikea rintasyövan hoito? *Duodecim* **106**, 907–9.
18. Kuhse, H. (1987) *The Sanctity-of-Life Doctrine in Medicine : A Critique*. Oxford: Oxford University Press.
19. Clark, B. (1978) *Whose Life Is It Anyway?* London: Samuel French Ltd.

20. Fayers, P. M. and Jones, D. R. (1983) Measuring and analysing quality of life in cancer clinical trials: a review. *Stat Med* **2**, 429–46.

21. Drettner, B. and Ahlbom, A. (1983) Quality of life and state of health for patients with cancer in the head and neck. *Acta Otolaryngol* **96**, 307–14.

22. Haes, J. C. J. M. de and Knippenberg, F. C. E. van. (1985) The quality of life of cancer patients: a review of the literature. *Soc Sci Med* **20**, 809–17.

23. Priestman, T. J. and Baum, M. (1976) Evaluation of quality of life in patients receiving treatment for advanced breast cancer. *Lancet* **i**, 899–901.

24. Spitzer, W. O., Dobson, A. J., Hall, J. et al. (1981) The QL-index. *J Chronic Dis* **34**, 585–97.

25. Heinrich, R. L., Schag, C. C. and Ganz, P. A. (1984) Living with cancer. The cancer inventory of problem situations. *J Clin Psychol* **40**, 972–80.

26. Morrow, G. R., Chiarello, R. J. and Derogatis, L. R. (1978) A new scale for assessing patients' psychosocial adjustment to medical illness. *Psychol Med* **8**, 605–10.

27. Zigmond, A. S. and Snaith, R. P. (1983) The hospital anxiety and depression scale. *Acta Psychiatr Scand* **67**, 361–70.

28. Campbell, A., Converse, P. E. and Rodgers, W. L. (1976) *Quality of American Life Perceptions, Evaluations and Satisfaction.* New York: Russell Sage Foundation.

29. Lanham, R. J. and DiGiannantonio, A. F. (1988) Quality-of-life in cancer patients. *Oncology* **45**, 1–7.

30. Torrance, G. W. (1986) Measurement of health state activities for economic appraisal: a review. *Journal of Health Economics* **5**, 1–30.

31. Wright, S. J. (1986) *Age, Sex and Health: A Summary of the Findings from the York Health Evaluation Survey.* York: University of York.

32. Pörn, I. (1984) An equilibrium model of health. In: Nordenfelt, L., Lindahl, B. I. B., eds. *Health, Disease, and Causal Explanations in Medicine.* Dordrecht: D Reidel Publishing Co, 3–9.

33. Nordenfelt, L. (1984) On the circle of health. In: Nordenfelt, L., Lindahl, B. I. B., eds. *Health, Disease, and Causal Explanations in Medicine.* Dordrecht: D Reidel Publishing Co, 15–23.

34. Nordenfelt, L. (1987) *On the Nature of Health: An Action-Theoretic Approach.* Dordrecht: D Reidel Publishing Co.

35. More, T. (1908) *Utopia,* London: Chatto & Windus Publishers.

36. Calman, K. C. (1984) Quality of life in cancer patients — an hypothesis. *J Med Ethics* **10**, 124–7.

3. COGNITIVE THEORIES AND INDIVIDUAL QUALITY OF LIFE ASSESSMENT

MONIKA BULLINGER

Based on cognitive theories of personality and in reference to the ongoing debate about the situationist perspective in personality psychology, this chapter attempts to provide insight into the theoretical basis, methodological procedures and scientific implications of individual quality of life assessment by contrasting the individual approach with the prevailing group-oriented approach of psychometrically tested quality of life assessment (in the form of disease specific or generic instruments). It is proposed that individual quality of life assessments merit attention not only in clinical research, but also in regard to the clinical patient-physician interaction, especially for the purpose of adapting treatment to the individual.

INTRODUCTION

Since its introduction into the health field, the term quality of life has evoked vivid responses from proponents and opponents of patient-based health outcome assessment alike (Bullinger and Pöppel, 1988). While proponents such as Najman and Levine (1981) and Margolese (1987) have maintained that quality of life is a necessary supplement to the traditional clinical endpoints, opponents such as Gill and Feinstein (1994) have argued that the term is too subjective to be scientifically assessed. Since these early debates about the measurability of quality of life reflected, for example, in the work of the European Organisation for Research and Treatment of Cancer (EORTC: Aaronson and Beckmann, 1987), much has changed. Increased demand for quality of life measurements to be used in clinical studies has quickly generated a multitude of instruments to assess health-related quality of life (Spilker, 1990, 1996). Researchers have made use of health outcome measurement methods which were already available from Anglo-American epidemiological and public health research — so-called generic measures — as well as developing disease-specific measurements (McDowell and Newell, 1987). Many of these are now available in languages other than the original (Bullinger, Anderson, Cella and Aaronson, 1993; Bullinger and Hasford, 1991). In contrast to the flurry of practical activity in developing instruments, the theoretical background of quality of life assessment in medicine has remained astonishingly meagre. Few articles have dealt with definitions of quality of life (Calman 1987) and most that have done so make use of early sociological theories of life satisfaction (e.g. Campbell, Coverse and Rogers, 1976; Glatzer and Zapf, 1984).

The transition of the term "quality of life" from the social sciences to the medical field has been accompanied by a clear pragmatic priority, namely the construction of measures. The contribution of the social sciences in developing health-related quality of life assessments has mostly been in terms of methodological expertise (construction, testing and statistical analyses of questionnaires), rather than in conceptual reflections about quality of life in medicine. Although this has resulted in broad acceptance of the term in the medical community as well as an increasing number of health-related quality of life studies in different areas of medicine, the lack of theoretical foundation sets limits on progress for a number of reasons. Firstly, the normal epistemological sequence of a) formulation of a theory, b) its testing with the goal of falsification and c) its continuing examination against alternative theories has not been followed. Secondly, without a theoretical foundation, current quality of life measures are in danger of stating the obvious, i.e. providing tautological explanations of the phenomenon to be measured. Thirdly, current assessments unduly favour a single perspective on quality of life, namely that which is group-oriented.

Alternative conceptualisations of quality of life are difficult to propose because the pragmatism of current measures prevails without reflection. The challenge posed by alternative models is, in essence, the major criticism of current assessment methodology in quality of life. As vividly expressed by Thunedborg and colleagues (1993) and by O'Boyle et al. (1992), traditional quality of life scales imply that quality of life means the same to everybody and therefore can be defined in general terms. However, even if the items contained in such scales have been selected by studying an appropriate group of patients, the instrument may only strictly be applicable to a non-existent average individual (Bech, 1993). The present chapter attempts to examine the theoretical foundation of the quality of life field by contrasting the individually and group-oriented approaches against the background of contemporary theories of personality.

QUALITY OF LIFE AND THE THEORY OF PERSONALITY

The theory of science has dealt extensively with the question of how knowledge is gained. While the object of knowledge gain seems to be different in the natural and social sciences, the process of knowledge gain is not. It is characterised by explication of the phenomenon under study and of the methods by which it is researched, so that clear replications of the results are possible.

With regard to quality of life measurement, two basic approaches can be distinguished: the deductive and the inductive. The deductive approach implies the construction of an *a priori* conceptual model which governs the collection of data, while the inductive approach does not set any *a priori* restrictions but proceeds directly from data collection to theory construction. The deductive approach to knowledge gain in the social sciences has been associated with the nomothetic approach and the inductive with the ideographic. These are not of necessity mutually exclusive because an inductive approach may generate hypotheses about a certain phenomenon, which can then be formulated in a deductive manner and tested against further evidence. However, in the present context, it is fruitful to contrast inductive and deductive approaches as well as ideographic and nomothetic because they lead to conceptually very different paths to quality of life assessment: the group-oriented and the individual. These again reflect two other main themes in psychology: general psychology, focusing on the common principles of behaviour; and the psychology of individual differences, focusing on the specific conditions in which behaviour occurs.

Despite current confusion about the meaning of quality of life, it is clearly an attribute of the person. This attribute has been variously characterised as an attitude, a personality trait, a situational response, a feeling state, and a rational judgement. The multitude of descriptors of quality of life suggests that its definition is as difficult as is that of personality. In fact, personality theory provides a very appropriate ground for discussing conceptual approaches to the study of quality of life. Personality theory, in attempting to describe the causes and consequences of human behaviour, has evolved from basic typologies to complex models of person-environment interactions. Similarly, trait, cognitive and interactionist theories may all contribute to the theoretical formulation of quality of life. Other personality theories such as the psychodynamic or the behaviorist are only peripherally relevant to the discussion because they are more concerned with the aetiology of personality or its characteristics rather than their descriptive enumeration.

TRAIT THEORIES

Leading proponents of the trait theoretical approach such as Allport (1961) and Cattell (1967) propose that genetic or learned traits determine the behaviour of the individual in a stable and situationally invariant way. Personality denotes the total pattern of stable behavioural dispositions, and individuals differ by the intensity of trait endorsements; that is to say, by the extent to which they can be characterised by a certain personality dimension. Traits, as conceptualised within trait theories, differ both in content and structure. The pattern of traits seems necessary to describe personality comprehensively. It is assumed that behaviour is determined by generic characteristics relevant to a multitude of situations and that there are only few situationally relevant traits. Such invariant characteristics are identified by factor analysis. Consequently, most trait theoretical work as well as the psychodiagnostic tests resulting from it are empirically and statistically founded.

COGNITIVE PERSONALITY THEORY

Cognitive personality theories such as those developed by Lewin (1935) and Kelly (1955) maintain that behaviour is not the result of psychodynamic conflicts or behaviourally relevant environmental stimuli but comes about through perceptions of the physical, personally relevant, environment. Basically, cognitive personality theory assumes that cognitive processes structure the outer world and that behaviour is only elicited through such cognitive representations. Differences between persons exist with regard to the nature of this cognitive representation so that different persons react differently in the same situation. Lewin, one of the most widely known proponents of cognitive personality theory, explicitly rejected the concept of constant in-variant traits and regarded the person as part of the world which he[1] constructs by means of his inner psychological representation. Thus, the psychological environment is cognitively constructed, not necessarily in a manner directly proportional to reality, but modified by personal needs, wishes and perspectives. Without following Lewin's theoretical framework too closely, the distinction between needs and valence should be mentioned, the former being based on physiological states and the latter being of a learned social nature. When one considers the relevance of such factors as driving forces and future expectations, valence would appear to be a concept of special importance to the study of quality of life.

In Lewin's tradition, Kelly regards the person as a scientist in that he develops a personal theory of the world. Understanding a person thus requires knowledge of his individual cognitive system. The basic postulate assumes that the "processes of a person are psychologically channelled through the way in which he anticipates events" (Kelly, 1955). This system is said to be characterised by a variable number of personal constructs with which the person attempts to explain the world and to predict future events. Kelly maintains that it is important to recognise these cognitive hypotheses about the world and not to categorise the individual according to generally constructed categories such as traits. Rather, a construct system has to be developed and identified anew for each individual person. Kelly's theory resulted in a methodological procedure for the description of this inner world, the repertory grid test, also refered to as construct analysis.

Another proponent of the cognitive approach is Rogers (1961) with his self-theory of personality. This assumes that each person perceives himself in his environment in a unique way and that behaviour is the result of these individual perceptions, the inner frame of reference being only accessible to the person himself. The self is understood as a comprehensive psychological structure consisting of perceptions and evaluations concerning the person, her relationship to the external world and to other persons. The self governs and corrects behaviour which, according to Maslow's (1954) theory of needs, is oriented towards self-actualisation.

INTERACTIONIST THEORY

A third relevant personality theory is the social cognitive or interactionist theory. This assumes that personality can be explained neither through nature

---

[1] See footnote[1] to Chapter 1

nor nurture alone. Rather it is a result of the interplay between internal and external constellations in which the interaction between person and environment is of unique importance. One proponent of social cognitive learning theory places great emphasis on experience (Rotter, 1954), who states that the actual behaviour of an individual is the product of the experiences collected in his personal past. New experiences are integrated into the existing pool and contribute to its new structure as well as to stabilising the system, because former experience influences the formation of new ones. Rotter describes the behaviour of a person according to interacting forces ranging from behavioural potential to expectations. An essential influence on behaviour is ascribed to generalised expectancies, i.e. learned attitudes and competencies of the person with regard to his ability to solve problems in his world. On the basis of their learning and experiential history, persons differ in their expectations of coping with problems and attaining a goal. Thus, generalised expectations can be characterised as important cognitive construct systems determining behaviour — the most powerful being locus of control. Mischel (1946) explains human behaviour as resulting from the interactions between person and situation. Variables located within the person include competence, personal constructs and expectations. Although Mischel thus relates to Kelly's theory of personal constructs, he maintains that behaviour is largely determined by specific situations and that the person is able by applying regulatory mechanisms to change this environment. Mischel's typology of personal behaviour focuses on situations which he classifies as powerful if they elicit similar behaviours in almost every person, or weak if they allow a broad variety of individual behaviours. Behaviour thus results from an interaction between person and situation in which the person actively influences this process. The interactionist position as described by Magnusson and Endler (1977) argues that current personality theories neglect the importance of both the personal and the situational.

APPLICATIONS

So far, this brief review has suggested that trait theories and group-oriented psychometric methods to assess quality of life share a similar conceptual basis. The approach to individual quality of life assessment is reflected in the basic premises of the cognitive approach to personality. The interactionist perspective may also suggest a synthesis of group and individually oriented methods not only in personality but also in quality of life studies.

Group Allocation: The Trait Model

The description of the individual within a constellation of generic dimensions by the trait theories of personality is straightforward. The universe of personality characteristics is assumed to be inter-individually applicable, intra-individual specificity (individuality) being possible by allocating a space within a certain constellation of dimensions. Thus, personality is not unique in terms of inter-individually different dimensions, but it is unique in the particular pattern of constellations of generic dimensions that characterise a given individual.

In content as well as method of construction, group-oriented measures of quality of life are similar to the trait approach to understanding personality described above. In both cases, universal dimensions are assumed, and an individual patterning within these dimensions is allowed. Generic as well as disease specific quality of life measures adopt just such an inter-individually applicable set of dimensions. The items can be either deductively assumed or inductively collected and factor analysis applied to derive the underlying dimensions. In fact, most currently available quality of life instruments of the psychometric type have been developed from such an item pool, the subscale structure being derived from statistical methods such as factor analysis. Methodological rigour is usually high, because they have been developed and tested according to pertinent psychometric theory with regard to reliability, validity and also for responsiveness in longitudinal research. Early instruments such as the Sickness Impact Profile (Bergner, Bobbit, Carter and Gilson 1981) were relatively lengthy and time-consuming for the respondent, but more recent development tends towards shorter scales with comparable precision and psychometric power (e.g. SF-12 Health Survey as the short form of the SF-36 Health Survey: Ware and Sherbourne, 1992).

The dimensions reflected in the current generic as well as disease specific measures of quality of life show an astonishing degree of correspondence across instruments. In addition, drawing on research eliciting individual statements about quality of life with open questions these dimensions are neither inter-individually nor inter-culturally very different (Ludwig 1991, Sartorius 1990).[2]

Interestingly, recent research, using generic scales such as the SF-36 in the international quality of life assessment project (IQOLA, Aaronson et al., 1992) showed that international cross-culturally representative samples of a national population from Germany, Sweden, US, and UK shared almost identical profiles of the SF-36. The WHOQOL project, an inductive attempt to formulate quality of life questions for each culture, also resulted in an astonishing comparability of domains and facets of quality of life as developed within in each culture (WHOQOL Group, 1994). If one applies the

---

[2] NB: The editors of this book disagree with this and the following paragraphs of this section (which, indeed, runs counter to one of its major theses). It appears to them to be an inevitable consequence of providing cues to the respondent or forcing individual responses into externally determined categories. However, they would not for a moment dispute the fact that many, if not all, factors are manifested in different cultures as well as individuals. But even these differ greatly in the frequency with which they are alluded to. Discussion of this section with the author has led to understanding but not agreement.

WHOQOL experiences from the cross-cultural level to the individual level, it can be assumed that not much variance is explained by including purely individual specific measures or dimensions.

This is notable because it implies that there is inter-personal as well as inter-cultural common understanding of quality of life, also reflected in the dimensions of the generic and disease specific measures currently in use. Thus one can argue that individual quality of life may be adequately assessed by such group-oriented scales because their dimensions tap common constructs each person being individually characterised by a given cluster of those dimensions.

Research on the Individual — The Cognitive Model

Cognitive personality theories resemble individual quality of life assessment in maintaining that individuality has to be created anew within a measurement system for each person under study. This approach is dramatically different from the group-oriented approach depicted above, because universal dimensions are explicitly not assumed.

In formulations of individual quality of life, the perceived discrepancy between actual and intended state is often used as the basis of evaluation. Campell et al. (1976) proposed that quality of life pertains to the perceived discrepancy between ideal and real states; quality of life is higher if this discrepancy is small, and lower if the discrepancy is more pronounced. Cognitive theories thus assume that quality of life assessments are direct reflections of a perceived imbalance between the experienced and the projected self. Thus, any quality of life questionnaire has to be individual and relational and its measurements should be expressed as a difference score.

Methods such as those based on the repertory grid and social judgement theory allow the construction of a person's cognitive space without reference to dimensions relevant to others. Within the cognitive theories, individual quality of life assessment is possible, for example, by having the individual define the dimensions of quality of life relevant to their actual situation and assessing changes due to clinical or other interventions, or by using a more comprehensive and complex technique such as the repertory grid method to describe actual state and change over time of the quality of life perception.

Assessing change over time, however, is difficult because the individual's dimensions and their configuration change so that sophisticated statistical expertise is necessary to describe this changing configuration adequately (Guyatt, 1987). In addition, since individual statements are influenced by expectations, quality of life statements may be based on dimensions, changes in which cannot be assumed to be solely due to interventions. However, this is true of any measurement, not only quality of life assessment, and it is noteworthy that 'intention to treat' analyses *deliberately* ignore this. Thus the relationship between change in quality of life and intervention may be difficult to interpret. An example is a recent study by Porzsolt and colleagues (personal communication), in which patients with breast cancer were asked to describe in their own words before and after chemotherapy their expectations and problems with regard to quality of life. As expected, not only were the dimensions before and after treatment different as reported by each woman, but the relationship between the expectations and treatment was also difficult to trace. Calculation of difference scores is however possible if it is based upon identical measures such as those described above within the goal attainment approach.

Reconciling the Differences: The Interactionist Model

Just as generic and disease-specific measures may be reconciled, so also can the differences in individual and group-oriented quality of life assessments. The interactionist perspective in personality theory proposes that personality is the result of an interaction between the person and the situation. It can also be assumed that quality of life is a function of generic dimensions shared by a multitude of persons as well as highly individual aspects not thus shared. In this model, quality of life could be measured by assessing not only its generic components but also by including the actual and personal perceptions of the person represented in measures of individual specific components. Such a system would also enable the researcher to test empirically whether or not and in what way the individual-specific dimensions of quality of life as well as changes in them over time do in fact affect the generic dimensions. With the exception of group-oriented questionnaires that are supplemented by individual open questions, no such approach has been developed so far, although the idea of a modular system has been used in various group-oriented measurement systems such as the EORTC-8ORTC-QLQ-C30 (Aaronson et al., 1993).

A further model comes from facet theory, a mathematical model based on simularity ratings (Shye, 1989). This attempts to construct a definition which is both exclusive and exhaustive. Observational items are elicited that belong to conceptually different of dimensions. Basically, the term facet is used to denote clusters of quality of life items grouped together across theoretically defined areas. It is important that each individual as well as group can be localised in the multidimensional space, or facet, so defined. Another possible way to reconcile the group-oriented and individual approaches is to weigh each group-oriented item by an individual relevance score. This has been attempted in current research on life satisfaction and economic preference-oriented research (Spilker, 1990).

DISCUSSION

The question of how to assess individual quality of life can be posed at three levels — those of

a) the measurement instrument
b) the study design
c) the statistical analysis.

The present discussion focuses mainly on the types of instrument available for group-oriented or individual quality of life assessment. This emphasis may be misleading. As in all investigation, the results of assessment depend not only depend on the instrument used, but also on the study design and upon how the results are analysed. Statistical methods that compare groups of respondents can also be used to analyse person-specific cluster of quality of life statements. These can be compared with those at a later time point or can be contrasted with another person's cluster. Thus, the current use of distribution-oriented statistics (e.g. analysis of variance) is not the only way to analyse group-oriented data from quality of life questionnaires. It is also possible to apply structural analysis (such as cluster analyses or even structural equation models) to describe the individual in intra-individual and inter-individual dimensions.

With regard to design, individual quality of life assessment certainly has its place in a specific type of study. This is the individualised treatment situation, in which a patient's diagnosis includes her actual quality of life and an intervention is planned to positively influence the quality of life as well as clinical status. Applied in planning individual treatment and in physician-patient interactions, such assessments can also be used to explore expectations and possibilities for change as perceived by the patient. As in goal attainment scaling in psychotherapy, individual quality of life assessment is possible. However, clinical population studies that relate a certain treatment or intervention to changes in quality of life may not find it appropriate to use highly individualised quality of life statements, despite the availability of appropriate statistical methods, the most primitive of which is the formation of a difference score. Especially in randomised clinical trials in which the requirements of the study protocol are very strict, it may be difficult to include individual quality of life assessment as the only source of information about patients' well-being. It may be also difficult to make use of individual methods of quality of life assessment. In epidemiological studies in which different populations are compared with regard to the effect of illness upon their quality of life, as well as health economic studies in which quality of life changes are related to economic indicators, However, a specific subset of health economic studies might profit considerably from individual methods.

The questions of whether, how and on what theoretical basis to assess individual quality of life are not exhausted by the choice of method. They are included in the basic question of the trial design and the research questions being asked, as well as to the method of statistical analysis. Personality theories, as described above, help to explore the theoretical field of individual quality of life assessment methodology. However, the historical development of personality theories also suggests that the dichotomy into group and individual assessments may be too simple and that the future of quality of life assessment lies in studying constructive interaction between these approaches to the assessment of quality of life.

REFERENCES

Aaronson, N. and Beckman, J. (1987) Quality of life of cancer patients. New York: Raven Press.

Aaronson, N., Acquadro, C., Alonso, J., Apolone, G., Bucquet, D., Bullinger, M., Bungay, K., Fukuhara, S., Gandek, B., Keller, S., Razavi, D., Sanson-Fisher, R., Sullivan, M., Wood-Dauphinee, S., Wagner, A. and Ware, J. E. (1992) International quality of life assessment (IQOLA) project. *Quality of Life Research* **1**, 349–351.

Aaronson, N., Ahmedzai, S. and Bullinger, M. (1993) for the EORTC Quality of Life Group. Validation of the EORTC QLQ-C30, *Journal of the National Cancer Institute* **40**, 161–170.

Allport, G. W. (1961) Pattern and growth in personality, New York: Holt, Rhinehart & Winston.

Bech, P. (1993) The PCASEE Model: An approach to subjective well being In J. Orley and W. Kuyken (eds). *Quality of life assessment: International perspectives*. pp. 75–83. New York: Springer.

Bergner, M., Bobbit, R. A., Carter, W. B. and Gilson, B. S. (1981) The sickness impact profile: development and final revision of a health status measure. *Medical Care* **19**, 787–805.

Bullinger, M. and Hasford, J. (1991) Evaluating quality of life measures in German clinical trials. *Controlled Clinical Trials* **12**, 915–1055.

Bullinger, M. and Pöppel, E. (1988) Lebensqualität in der Medizin: Schlagwort oder Forschungsansatz. *Deutsches Ärtzeblatt* **85**, 679–680.

Bullinger, M., Anderson, R., Cella, D. and Aaronson, N. (1993) Developing and evaluating cross-cultural instruments from minimum requirements to optimal models, *Quality of Life Research* **2**, 451–459.

Calman, K. C. (1987) Definitions and dimensions of quality of life. In N. Aaronson, J. Beckman, J. Bernheim and R. Zittoun (eds) *The quality of life of cancer patients*. New York: Raven Press.

Campbell, A., Converse, P. E. and Rogers, W. L. (1976) *The quality of American Life*. New York: Russel Sage Foundation.

Cattell, R. B. (1967) *The scientific analysis of personality*. Harmondsworth: Penguin.

Gill, T. M. and Feinstein, A. R. (1994) A critical appraisal of the Quality of Life Measurements. *Journal of American Medical Association* **272**, 619–626.

Glatzer, W. and Zapf, W. (1984) *Lebensqualität in der Bundesrepublik Deutschland*. Frankfurt: Campus.

Guyatt, G. H. (1987) Measuring quality of life. A review of means of measurements in clinical trials of new medicines. *Pharmaceutical Medicine* **2**, 49–6.

Kelly, G. A. (1955) *The psychology of personal constructs*, Vol. I and II. New York: Norton.

Lewin, K. (1935) *A dynamic theory of personality*. New York: McGraw-Hill.

Ludwig, M. (1991) Lebensqualität auf der Basis subjektiver Theoriebildung. In *Lebensqualität bei kardiovaskulären Erkrankungen*, M. Bullinger, M. Ludwig, N. v. Steinbüchel (Hrsg.). pp. 24–35. Göttingen: Hogrefe.

Magnusson, D. and Endler, N. (1977) Interactional psychology: present status and future prospects. In *Personality at the cross-roads*, D. Magnusson and N. Endler (eds). New York: Wiley.

Margolese, R. G. (1987) The place of psychosocial studies in medicine and surgery. *Journal of Chronic Diseases* **40,** 627–628.

Maslow, A. H. (1954) Motivation and personality. New York: Harper & Row.

McDowell, I. and Newell, C. (1987) Measuring health: A guide to rating scales and questionnaires. New York: Oxford University Press.

Mischel, W. (1976) Introduction to personality. New York: Holt, Rinehart & Winston.

Najman, J. M. and Levine, S. (1981) Evaluating the impact of medical care and technology on the quality of life. A review and critique. *Social Science and Medicine* **15F,**107–115.

O'Boyle, C. A., McGee, H. M., O'Malley, K. M. and Joyce, C. R. B. (1992). Individual quality of life in patients undergoing hip replacement. *Lancet* **339,** 1088–1091.

Rogers, C. R. (1961) On becoming a person. A therapist's view of psychotherapy. Boston: Mifflin.

Rotter, J. B. (1954) Social learning and clinical psychology. Englewood Cliffs: Prentice Hall.

Sartorius, N. (1990) A WHO method for the assessment of health-related quality of life (WHOQOL). In *Quality of Life Assessment: Key Issues in the 1990s,* S. Walker & R. Rosser (eds.) pp. 201–207. Dordrecht: Kluwer Academic Publishers.

Shye, S. (1989) The systemic quality of life model. *Social Indicators Research* **21,** 343–378.

Spilker, B. (1990) Quality of life assessment in clinical trails. New York: Raven Press.

Thunedborg, K., Allerup, P., Bech, P. and Joyce, C. R. B (1993) Development of the repertory grid for measurement of individual quality of life in clinical trials. *International Journal of the Methods in Psychiatry Research* **3,** 45–56.

Ware, J. E. and Sherbourne, C. D. (1992) The MOS 36-item short form health survey (SF-36): I. Conceptual framework and item selection. *Medical Care* **30,** 473–483.

WHOQOL Group (1994) The Development of the WHO Quality of Life Assessment. Instruments (The WHOQOL). In J. Orley, W. Kuyken (eds). Quality of Life Assessment: International Perspectives. pp. 41–57. Springer Verlag, Berlin.

4. A REFORMULATION OF QUALITY OF LIFE FOR MEDICAL SCIENCE[1]

MICHAEL E. HYLAND

Current quality of life measuring tools are suited for economic decision making, not to investigate causal processes which lead to patients making evaluations of their lives. An alternative approach is presented based on research into positive versus negative life-satisfaction. Quality of life is a causal sequence of psychological states where perceived symptoms cause problems and the problems and symptoms cause evaluations, and where the causal sequence is a complex interaction between morbidity and psychological factors. Different types of medical intervention affect different stages in the causal sequence and so different types of quality of life instrument are needed for different kinds of medical research.

Despite the increasing acceptance that health related quality of life (QoL) is an important outcome measure in medicine,[1] this topic is characterized by a degree of diversity and multiplicity of approaches which is unusual in advanced sciences. Health related quality of life can be conceptualized in two distinctly different ways. The multifaceted approach is that QoL is an aggregation of several, conventionally agreed, health indices; the causal process approach is that QoL is a causal sequence resulting from an interaction between morbidity and psychological factors. The multifaceted approach is currently the dominant approach in medicine. In this article I show that the multifaceted approach may be appropriate for economic decision making where the aim is to allocate scare resources within a health-care system. However, the causal process approach is needed for medical science where the aim is to understand the causal processes underlying QoL change.

THE MULTIFACETED APPROACH

Writing within the context of health economics, Spilker[2] says "The major domains of quality of life generally (. . .) include the following categories: (1) Physical status and functional ability; (2) Psychological status and well-being; (3) Social interactions; (4) Economic status". Most QoL scales include one or more of these domains, and the decision to include a domain is agreed as a convention rather than being the outcome of scientific investigation. Consequently, different groups of researchers have different conventions about the domains that should be included in QoL assessment. For example, a recent review of scales measuring QoL for respiratory disease patients[3] concludes that although the scales differ in terms of whether symptom items and items

---

[1] This article is reprinted with permission from *Quality of Life Research* 1992, **1**, 267–272.

measuring limits to activities are included, each of the different types of scale can be justified in terms of the aims of the researchers, and hence each of the scales has content validity.

The multifaceted approach to QoL assessment provides a single score of QoL by aggregating across the items and domains which the scale measures. The method of aggregation often involves ascribing 'weights' to the different items so that items with a greater impact on QoL have a statistically greater contribution to the total score. Whether to use weights or not is a convention which varies between groups of reseachers. Tht majority view[4, 5] is that if items are weighted by the degree of distress caused by the problem described by that item, then an aggregation of weighted items provides a more accurate view of overal distress. Those who do not use weights[6] argue that it provides a spurious sense of accuracy. The conventionally accepted, multifaceted approach to QoL assessment has parallels with economic indices outside medicine. For example, as a measure of the costs of living, the price of a conventionally agreed shopping basket (e.g., retail price index) is calculated to see whether, on average, prices are rising or falling, and whether there are regional differences. The precise contents of this conventionally defined shopping basket is not questioned as it is merely a convenient approximation for examining price change and value for money. In the same way, by treating QoL as some conventionally defined aggregation of domains, it is possible to make broad statements about the advantages of different types of treat ment, and which types of treatment are the most cost effective.

The disadvantage of the multifaceted approach, however, is that information about specific domains is lost in the process of aggregation, and this has led some researchers to suggest that QoL outcomes should be disaggregated.[7, 8] In particular, information about causal processes is lost as causes operate on specific outcomes, not on conventional aggregations. Whereas economic decision making simply requires information about costs and outcomes, the medical objective of improving the QoL of patients is best achieved from knowledge not only of which treatments improve QoL but also the causal process whereby that improvement is achieved.

QUALITY OF LIFE AS A CAUSAL SEQUENCE

When used in clinical trials, QoL is commonly treated as an outcome measure which is independent of morbidity and mortality data. That is, the outcome measures of QoL and morbidity are analysed as though there were unrelated dependent variables. In reality, QoL must be affected by morbidity, and indeed one method of validating a QoL scale is to show that it correlates with morbidity. However, QoL is also affected by psychological factors. QoL scales (like other scales of life satisfaction) correlate with personality; depending on the study, dispositional mood can account for up to about 40% of the variance in QoL scales.[9] Thus, the outcome measures which are called QoL must represent some kind of causal interaction between morbidity and psychological factors.

Figure 4.1 provides a general model of causal processes involving different kinds of appraisal. As a first stage in the causal sequence, morbidity causes symptoms and anticipated symptoms (e.g., breathlessness, pain, inability to move limb). The patient reports not the objective symptomatology but the subjective experience of those symptoms, and these subjective, symptoms reports are affected by general mood, more specifically, negative trait affect.[10] People with depressive or anxious personalities perceive they have more symptoms due to bias associated with the recognition (encoding); mood accounts for about 10% of variance of symptom reports.[10,11]

The second stage in the causal sequence is for symptoms (or anticipated symptoms) to cause problems. However, symptoms do not always cause problems as the relationship between these two variables is moderated by other psychological factors, namely coping strategy. People vary in their ability to cope with negative events,[12] and patients who have developed effective coping strategies are less likely to experience a problem following a symptom.

The final stage in the causal sequence is for patients to evaluate their problems/absence of problems and symptoms/absence of symptoms on evaluative dimensions, such as 'distress', 'lack of control', 'anxiety' or 'happiness'. These evaluations (which are assessed by the 'mood' or 'emotion' items in current QoL scales) are affected by a variety of cognitive factors including the perceived cause[13] and outcome of the illness. Evans[14] reports that transplant patients, haemodialysis patients and peritoneal dialysis patients who (objectively and subjectively) experience a variety of problems are more likely to rate themselves as 'very happy' than the general population. These data illustrate an important feature of the evaluative stage. The presence of illness, particularly life threatening illness, can lead to patients re-evaluating

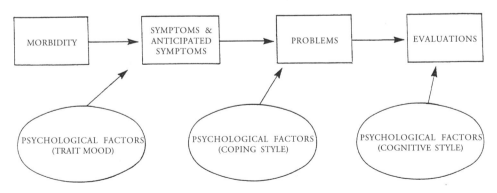

Figure 4.1 Quality of life represented as a causal sequence of symptoms, problems and evaluations.

their lives, so that events which were previously neutral (e.g., meeting family and friends, looking at flowers) are evaluated more positively. The relationship between problems and evaluations is therefore a complex one, and it should not be assumed that the presence of problems necessarily means an unhappy life — or that the absence of health problems means a happy life. Evans' data has implications for present QoL assessment: the potential complexity of the relationship between problems and evaluations means that a statistical aggregation of problems, with or without weights, is unlikely to provide an accurate representation of the patient's real level of distress.

In conclusion, the perception of symptoms, problems and evaluations are causally related, but the causal relationship is moderated by different psychological variables. Using a multifaceted approach, many QoL instruments provide a summation of symptoms, problems and evaluations. From the perspective of medical science, this kind of aggregation is unusual. For example, consider the causal sequence in asthma where eosinophils cause bronchial hyper-reactivity which causes diurnal variation in peak flow. Eosinophil levels can be measured by Eosinophil Cationic Protein analysis (ECP), bronchial reactivity can be measured by the inhaled histamine concentration required to produce a 20% fall FEV1 (PC20), and diurnal variation by the maximum percentage morning-evening difference, but no one has ever aggregated ECP, PC20 and morning-evening difference into a single measure of morbidity. Yet it is precisely this kind of aggregation that is carried out for measures of health, or more specifically QoL. If QoL, like morbidity, is a causal sequence of events, it makes sense from the perspective of medical science to try to measure each of those events independently as a way of investigating the underlying causal process.

POSITIVE VERSUS NEGATIVE QUALITY OF LIFE

There is a considerable evidence showing that positive evaluations represent different causal processes from negative evaluations. For example, research into life satisfaction[15,16] shows that positive life satisfaction (being satisfied with one's life) has a low correlation with negative life satisfaction (being dissatisfied with one's life); that is, people vary independently in their level of positive and negative life satisfaction. Evidence that positive and negative life satisfaction are the consequence of different causal processes comes from findings that negative life satisfaction is correlated with dispositional mood, whereas positive life satisfaction is correlated with extraversion. Negative ('hassles') and positive ('uplifts') evaluations of daily events are also relatively independent in terms of frequency; evidence that they have different causal consequences comes from the finding that hassles but not uplifts are predictors of somatic complaints.[17,18] Finally, research on daily mood variation shows that positive and negative mood are only weakly correlated, and that daily negative mood but not positive mood is associated with somatic complaints.[19]

Current QoL scales ask the patient whether and to what extent daily living has been adversely affected by health. QoL scales allow the patient to express a series of complaints about health, and as such provide a measure of negative life quality rather than positive life quality. However, research into life satisfaction, daily events and mood all suggest that such complaints are likely to be independent of positive life quality, that is, the extent to which the patient is enjoying life. Current QoL instruments measure only one kind of appraisal, a negative appraisal, which patients make of their lives.

COPING STRATEGY AND POSITIVE/NEGATIVE QUALITY OF LIFE

People use a variety of coping strategies to deal with problems, health or otherwise, one such strategy being avoidance.[12,20] For example, an anxious student will not enrol for a difficult course as a way of avoiding the possibility of failure; an asthmatic may avoid social contacts where there is the possibility of an asthma attack. The tendency to avoid potentially problematic situations is a personality trait; people vary in the relative tendency to engage in success seeking versus failure avoiding behaviour.[21]

One method of coping with chronic illness is to restructure one's goals and expectations to achieve very little, thereby avoiding the possibility of failure. For example, by staying at home every evening, the asthmatic avoids the problem of an asthma attack in a public place; by avoiding busy places, the sufferer of venous leg ulcers avoids the possibility of having a knock which will start another ulcer. This avoidant style of coping reduces the incidence of negative life events, and thereby improves negative life quality. However, an avoidant coping style also reduces the number of positive life events and therefore reduces positive life quality. Thus, a patient who adopts an avoidant coping style may have a good negative life quality — and appear to have a good QoL using existing instruments — but may also have poor positive life quality — which will not be detected by existing instruments. This trade off between the richness of experience and the avoidance of problems will be determined, in part, by the patient's coping style.

Figure 4.2 is an elaboration of Figure 1 but showing two independent causal sequences relating to negative and positive life quality. In terms of negative life quality, symptoms cause problem events, where problem events are discrete occurrences which occur at a point in time (for example, breathlessness causing the asthmatic to be late for an appointment, pain causing the leg ulcer patient to go home). The problem events and symptoms are then evaluated primarily on negative dimensions such as distress, bother or unhappiness. In terms of positive life quality, or life richness, evaluation of life occurs on positive dimensions such as the degree of happiness. Happiness is affected by a variety of factors including the extent to which the patient avoids positive situations as part of an avoidant coping strategy — as well as personality and social circumstances independent of the patient's

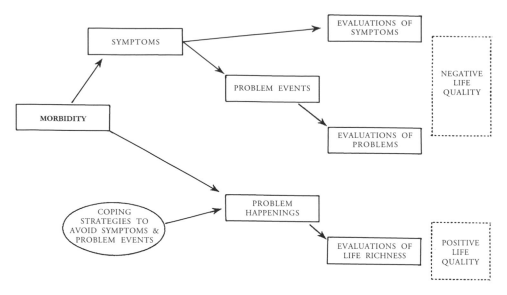

Figure 4.2 Different casual sequences for positive and negative life quality.

disease. I have called the avoidance of situations 'problem happenings' as they are not specific events which happen at a particular time but rather the absence of those positive events which typically occur in the well person. Thus, the antecedents of negative life quality evaluations are different from the antecedents to positive life quality evaluations, and, extrapolating from life satisfaction research, negative evaluations should correlate with dispositional mood and positive evaluations with extraversion. However, both positive and negative evaluations may be affected by cognitive factors such as re-evaluations or cognitive re-appraisals.

PURPOSE-SPECIFIC QUALITY OF LIFE ASSESSMENT

In order to understand the psychological reaction patients have to ill health it is necessary to conceptualise QoL as several causal sequences rather than as a multifaceted aggregation. If QoL is a causal process, what kinds of measurement are relevant to medical research?

First, let us suppose that researchers are interested in whether a new form of drug treatment improves QoL relative to some other treatment. Under such circumstances, the most direct, short term effect of a change in medication is a change in the frequency of symptoms and problem events. Thus the short term effect of morbidity reduction is a reduction in symptoms and problem events. In the longer term, reduction in morbidity may reduce the need for avoidant coping strategies and so lead to a reduction in problem happenings. However, any improvement in problem happenings depends on the patient altering his or her coping style, and as coping style is not affected directly by non-psychoactive drugs, this may take an as yet unknown length of time. Thus, for short term evaluations of drug treatments, greater sensitivity to the effects of treatments would be achieved by measuring symptoms and problems events, which can be measured either through questionnaires or, possibly more accurately, through symptom and problem daily diaries. For longer term evaluations it would also be useful to have a measure of problem happenings which could be assessed through a questionnaire.

The data reported by Evans[14] shows how evaluations can be poorly related to objective or subjective assessments of problems. The complex relationship between problems and evaluations suggests that evaluations are not a good outcome measure in clinical trials involving non-psychoactive drug treatments — though measures of happiness would be highly relevant to the evaluation of psychoactive drugs. On the other hand, improved styles of management on the part of the doctor may lead to greater perceptions of control by the patient, re-evaluations of life, or some other psychological factor which leads to improvement on evaluative dimensions. Thus, evaluations are a relevant outcome measure to assess the overall quality of care of a patient, and should therefore be included in patient audit. In particular, evaluations are relevant when making comparisons between patients having different diseases who have quite different types of problem. Comparisons of problems between types of patients is made difficult by the fact that like is not being compared with like, but it would be perfectly feasible to ask more general questions about the degree of happiness or unhappiness experienced by the patient across disease type. Thus, questionnaires which ask about the patient's general happiness and unhappiness with life — without referring specifically to disease related problems — may be a useful tool for cross-disease comparisons.

Guyatt et al.[22] have suggested that different instruments should be developed for cross-sectional (i.e., between types of patient) and longitudinal (e.g., clinical trials) research, but without suggesting that these different kinds of instrument should measure different kinds of QoL construct. The present proposal is consistent with Guyatt's in suggesting the need for purpose specific scales but goes further by suggesting that the different kinds of appraisal patients make about themselves vary in their relevance to different types of medical research. In general, cross-sectional research is best carried out with scales which measure evaluations whereas longitudinal research is best carried out with scales which measure problems and symptoms.

CONCLUSIONS

Existing QoL instruments measure a variety of psychological appraisals which are causally related. Although there may be merit in aggregating these different kinds of appraisal for economic purposes, such aggregations will not serve the purpose of medical science well. I propose that we should start a new chapter in QoL research where instruments are designed to measure specific constructs in the causal sequence that results from an interaction between morbidity and psychological factors.

REFERENCES

1. Editorial. Quality of life. *Lancet* 1991, **338**, 350–351.
2. Spilker, B. (1990) Introduction. In: B, Spilker., ed. Quality of Life Assessment in Clinical Trials. New York: Raven Press, 3–9.
3. Hyland, M. E. (1992) Quality of life assessment in respiratory disease: an examination of the content and validity of four questionnaires. *PharmacoEconomics* **2**, 13–53.
4. Bergner, M., Bobbitt, R. A., Carter, W. B. and Gilson, B. S. (1981) The sickness impact profile: development and final revision of a health status measure. *Med Care* **19**, 787–805.
5. Kaplan, R. M. and Bush, J. W. (1982) Health-related quality of life measurement for evaluation research and policy analysis. *Health Psychol* **1**, 61–80.
6. Juniper, E. F., Guyatt, G. H., Epstein, R. S., Ferrie, P. J., Jaeschke, R. and Hiller, T. K. (1992) Evaluation of impairment of health related quality of life in asthma: development of a questionnaire for use in clinical trials. *Thorax* **47**, 76–83.
7. Spilker, B. (1992) Standardisation of quality of life trials: an industry perspective. *PharmacoEconomics* **1**, 73–75.
8. Hyland, M. E. (1992) Selection of items and avoidance of bias in quality of life scales. *PharmacoEconomics* **1**, 182–190.
9. Jones, P. W., Baveystock, C. M. and Littlejohns, P. (1989) Relationship between general health measured with Sickness Impact Profile and respiratory symptoms, physiological measures, and mood in patients with chronic airflow limitation. *Am Rev Respir Dis* **140**, 1538–1543.
10. Watson, D. (1988) Intraindividual and interindividual analysis of positive and negative affect: their relation to health complaints, perceived stress, and daily activities. *J Pers Soc Psychol* **54**, 1020–1030.
11. Larsen, R. J. (1992) Neuroticism and selective encoding and recall of symptoms: evidence from a combined concurrent-retrospective study. *J Pers Soc Psychol* **62**, 480–488.
12. Carver, C. S., Scheier, M. F. and Weintraub, J. K. (1989) Assessing coping strategies: a theoretically based approach. *J Pers Soc Psychol* **56**, 267–283.
13. Turnquist, D. C., Harvey, J. H. and Anderson, B. L. (1988) Attributions and adjustment to life-threating illness. *Br J Clin Psychol* **27**, 55–65.
14. Evans, R. W. (1991) Quality of life. *Lancet* **338**, 363.
15. Costa, P. T. and McCrae, R. R. (1980) Influence of extraversion and neuroticism on subjective well-being: happy and unhappy people. *J Pers Soc Psychol* **38**, 668–678.
16. Heady, B. and Wearing, A. (1989) Personality, life events, and subjective well-being: toward a dynamic equilibrium model. *J Pers Soc Psychol* **57**, 731–739.
17. DeLongis, A., Coyne, J. C., Dakof, G., Folkman, S. and Lazarus, R. S. (1982) Relationship of daily hassles, uplifts, and major life events to health status. *Health Psychol* **1**, 119–136.
18. DeLongis, A., Folkman, S. and Lazarus, R. S. (1988) The impact of daily stress on health and mood: Psychological and social resources as mediators. *J Pers Soc Psychol* **54**, 486–495.

19. Watson, D. and Pennebaker, J. W. (1989) Health complaints, stress, and distress: exploring the central role of negative affectivity. *Psychol Rev* **96**, 234–254.
20. Roth, S. and Cohen, L. J. (1986) Approach, avoidance, and coping with stress. *Am Psychol* **41**, 813–819.
21. Raynor, J. O. and Entin, E. (1982) *Motivation, Career Stringing and Aging*. New York: Hemisphere.
22. Guyatt, G. H., Kirshner, B. and Jaeschke, R. Measuring health status: What are the necessary properties? *J Clin Epid* (in press).

5. METHODOLOGICAL ISSUES IN INDIVIDUAL QUALITY OF LIFE ASSESSMENT

PER BECH

INTRODUCTION

Quantifiers: Asking Questions to Quantify Meaning and Subjective Well-being

Questionnaires measuring illness severity are generally concerned with symptoms or behaviour whereas questionnaires measuring quality of life in relation to health are concerned with subjective experience, meaning or attitudes. Social adjustment scales should also be seen as attempts to measure things other than symptoms of illness by considering the individual's performance in various social roles, i.e. social interactions. However, subjective experiences of well-being or meaning are the domain of quality of life (McDowell and Newell, 1987; Bech, 1993).

A questionnaire is an instrument, often self-administered, containing a set of questions. Most questionnaires measuring attitudes or meaning have preselected quantifiers (closed questions) to which the respondents are offered a choice of alternative replies (answer categories). Such questionnaires with closed questions will in the following be referred to as group of epidemiological quality of life questionnaires; their objectives tend to be very simple and the instruments easy to complete, e.g., as screening instruments which can be distributed by mail or even by telephone. Table 5.1 shows examples of different quantifiers used in some epidemiological quality of life questionnaires (Bech 1993, 1996).

Table 5.1 Answer categories: Quantifiers in epidemiological quality of life questionnaires

PGWB intensity		PCASEE intensity		PGWB frequency		WHO (Ten) frequency	
Extremely	5	Good	5	All of the time	5	All of the time	3
Very much	4			Most of the time	4	More than half of the time	2
Quite a bit	3			A good bit of the time	3	Less than half of the time	1
Some	2			Some of the time	2	None of the time	0
A little bit	1			A little of the time	1		
Not at all	0	Poor	0	None of the time	0		

PGWB: Pychological General Well-being Scale
PCASEE: See text
WHO (Ten): World Health Organisation (Ten item)

51

Individual quality of life measurement is intended to help the respondent quantify meanings in his or her life. In this situation, open or free-response questionnaires are more appropriate. It is, however, often difficult to handle self-anchoring answer categories even when the respondents have understood or have been helped to understand the intent of the question. In the individual quality of life instruments to be discussed here, the visual analogue scale has been prefered as an open response quantifier.

A visual analogue scale is a continuous line, usually of 10 cm with the descriptive labels at each end. It is most unlikely that one respondent's 3.5 cm is equivalent to another's; thus the scale records self-anchoring responses, unlike the preselected (semantic) categories shown in Table 5.1. However, if a respondents is consistent, changes observed with visual analogue scales (e.g. expressed in percentage improvements) are valid indicators of change in the situation of the individual.

Visual analogue scales are also referred to as global scales because they are often used to provide overall assessment of a single dimension. The semantic-differential technique, originally developed by Osgood, Suci and Tannenbaum (1957), comprises bipolar graphic scales with the extremes defined by a pair of opposing adjectives, e.g, active and passive. Their continuous form can be considered as the original of various multi-point simplifications, such as seven-point rating scales. The global improvement scale developed by Guy (1976) is a seven-point semantic-differential scale with the extremes defined by 'very much improved' versus 'very much worse' and with the middle defined by 'no change'.

This kind of scale has a long tradition in clinical medicine (Bech, 1990). It is probably a unique measure for clinical medicine since it takes not only the symptom change into account, but also includes components of quality of life. It is in principle a scale tailored to the patient's individual situation (Bech, 1990).

Among the most widely used epidemiological quality of life scales is the Psychological General Well Being Schedule (PGWB, Dupuy 1984) which has questions both about intensity and frequency (Table 5.1). Such answer categories are traditionally referred to as Likert scales (Likert, 1932). The WHO (Ten) and the Well-Being Scale (Table 5.1) (Bech, Gudex and Staehr Johansen, 1996) have preselected categories of which only the poles are described. Finally, the PCASEE[1] scale poses bipolar questions, namely 'good' versus 'bad'. The original Likert attitude scale (Likert, 1932) was such a questionnaire (e.g., 'agree' versus 'disagree') and the visual analogue scales in the individual quality of life instruments to be discussed also use bipolar questions (e.g. 'best possible' versus 'worst possible'). The PCASE scale[1] (Joyce, 1987) was modified for the SmithKline Beecham Quality of Life Repertory Grid instrument (Bech, 1993) as an epidemiological questionnaire.

---

[1]   P: Physical; C: Cognitive; A: Affective; S: Social; E: Economic

Most epidemiological quality of life questionnaires have unipolar answer categories, as shown in Table 5.1 for PGWB and WHO (Ten). When measuring psychological well-being by means of epidemiological questionnaires, Sudman and Bradburn (1985) recommend unipolar answer categories, but for individual measurements, bipolar answer categories seem more valid.

Among individual quality of life methods, verbal content analysis should briefly be mentioned as an alternative scaling approach. This method was developed by Gottschalk three decades ago and he has recently published an updated review (Gottschalk, 1995). The content analysis of verbal behaviour is based on tape-recorded 5 minute samples of spontaneous speech in which the subject has been instructed to talk about "any interesting or dramatic personal experience..." (Gottschalk, 1995). A health-sickness scale counts the verbal statements the subject has made related to symptoms of illness and feelings of well-being. This method is an alternative to the other methods to be discussed in this chapter and, as mentioned in Chapter 1, was not considered further for the JARGONS project because of its various complexities (training, statistical analysis, etc). To date, it has only been used in pilot studies of quality of life (Gottschalk, 1995).

To summarize, closed questions with fixed or semi-fixed answer categories of the Likert type are important in epidemiological research to allow comparisons between large groups of persons. The number of questions in the questionnaire should be limited. Thus, the PGWB scale has 22 questions, the WHO (Ten) only 10 questions. In contrast, instruments for the study of individual quality of life should have self-anchoring answer categories; these are most appropriately covered by the use of visual analogue quantifiers.

In the following sections, the psychometric properties of the epidemiological quality of life questionnaires (especially the PGWB) and the individual quality of life instruments (especially with reference to the methods of repertory grid analysis (Kelly, 1955) and social judgment theory (Hammond, McClelland and Mumpower, 1980)) will be compared with regard to the three major issues: internal validity, reliability, and external validity.

INTERNAL VALIDITY

Both kinds of instrument are concerned with testable theories concerning health and well-being. This aspect is traditionally called content validity, the domain of which goes back to the three-dimensional model developed by the World Health Organisation (WHO, 1948: see below), based on a collection of epidemiological aspects under the concept of 'positive mental health' (Jadova, 1958). Psychometrically interesting contributions to the measurement of general psychological well-being were made by the *Affect Balance Scale* (Bradburn & Caplovitz, 1965). The content validity of this scale was reflected in its attention to various positive and negative affects and its construct validity in the extent to which these components varied on one dimension (with positive and negative affect labels for the poles). Bradburn developed a Likert scale in which each question was given equal weight, and the Likert categories were quantified by frequency (zero for 'never' and three for 'very often', i.e. four answer categories). The ABS has, in total, five questions for positive and five questions for negative affects. The psychometric problem, thus was whether the scale should be scored as two independent scales (from zero to 15 on each) or whether an index could be calculated, i.e. positive scores minus negative scores. Asymmetry, or bias, emerged in the frequency quantifiers. Being "excited" or "interested" (positive items) were scored generally higher than being "bored" (negative items). Because Bradburn has mainly been working with epidemiological questionnaires for quality of life, he concluded that in group comparisons individual differences were not too important given the advantages associated with a robust, brief, preselected Likert quantifier (Bradburn and Miles, 1979).

The scale that has gone furthest in dealing with the measurement of negative and positive well-being is the Psychological Well-Being Scale (PGWB: Dupuy, 1984). An epidemiological scale containing 22 items (11 positive and 11 negative) with six Likert response categories, with some questions having frequency quantifiers and others with intensity quantifiers (Table 5.1). The domains of the PGWB are mainly concerned with "mental health"; among the negative components are depression and anxiety, and among the positive components are well-being, and locus of control.

When discussing the content validity of health-related quality of life, what might be called the "top-down" approach is useful. At the top of the hierarchy is the disease with its associated biological impairment, underneath which is the clinical disability with its symptoms and behaviour disturbances. At the bottom comes the subjective experience, well-being, or quality of life. For a more detailed description of this general approach see the International Classification of Impairments, Disabilities and Handicaps (ICIDH: WHO, 1980).

Individual Quality of Life Measures

Table 2 compares an epidemiological questionnaire, the PGWB, and two individual instruments, the SEIQoL (O'Boyle, McGee, Hickey, O'Malley and Joyce, 1992: see Chapter 10) and the Repertory Grid (Thunedborg et al., 1993: see Chapter 12). Their terminologies differ: the content or domains of an instrument are traditionally termed components in epidemiological scales, and constructs or cues respectively in the others. The individual instruments employ either fixed or free constructs, or both. This is an important distinction, because the components may vary for each person or context. The individual's ability to provide his personal weights for the components is a further distinction.

From a measurement point of view, construct validity can be understood as the extent to which the domains (content validity) can be expressed in a

Table 5.2 Internal validity of epidemiological and individual quality of life scales

Type of instrument	Content validity (domains)	Qualifiers (frequency)	Qualifiers (intensity)	Construct validity (statistical models)	Target population	Outcome statistic Profiles	Index
Epidemiological instruments (e.g. PBWB)	Preselected components (negative and positive well-being)	Preanchored Likert scales (0–5)	Preanchored Likert scales (0–5)	Latent structure analysis or factor analysis	Epidemiological (n > 1000) Randomised clinical trails (n > 15)	Negative and positive subscales	Total score (normal values 80 ± 17)
Individual (Repertory Grid)	Fixed and free constructs		Visual analogue scales (0–100)	Factor analysis	The individual (n = 1)	Subjective weights	Percentage score (0–100) (normal values ≥ 75)
Individual SEIQoL	Free choice and interpretation		Visual analogue scales (0–100)	Multiple Regression Analysis	The individual (n = 1)	Subjective weights	Overall QoL index (0–100) (normal values ≥ 75)

descriptive statistic, either as one overall index (total score across the domain) or as a profile score (i.e. subscores for each of the included elements).
How can this be best evaluated? In the psychometric literature, Cronbach's
coefficient alpha has been the most frequently used test for the internal
validity or consistency of the items of a scale. This coefficient expresses the
average intercorrelations between the scale items, and values of 0.70 or
higher are usually considered acceptable (Nunnally, 1978). However, if many
items are highly intercorrelated, some may be redundant. Another disadvantage of using the alpha coefficient is that increasing the number of items
leads to higher coefficients. A more adequate statistical method for analysing
an index score (for example, to demonstrate the unidimensionality of scale
domains) is the requirement that each item should contribute information.
Some items that give information regarding the lower extreme of the dimension being measured will be answered by most respondents. Other items that
give information about the higher end will only be answered by a small
number (e.g., the most severely affected respondents). The most appropriate
coefficients for estimating the extent to which Guttman's requirement has
been met are the Loevinger and Mokken coefficients of homogeneity (Bech,
1993; Nunnally and Bernstein, 1994). A more sophisticated statistical analysis is that of latent structure or trait analysis (Allerup, 1986; Andrich, 1988;
Nunnally and Bernstein, 1994). Finally, factor analysis is a method of ensur-
ing unidimensionality if there are no *a priori* theories about the dimension in
a domain. Modern types of factor analysis, such as confirmatory factor
analysis, are comparable with latent structure or trait analysis (Nunnally and
Bernstein, 1994).

Developers of epidemiological scales have used factor analysis as an
argument for unidimensionality, identifying a general factor without using
factor loadings when calculated the overall index score. Thus, for example,
most studies using factor analysis with the PGWB have identified a general
factor explaining around 70% of the variance and have thereafter used the
total item score as an index. The coefficients of Cronbach and Loevinger
determined by Thunedborg et al. (1995) have confirmed that the PGWB
scale is unidimensional.

Multiple regression analysis can be applied to linear combinations of
weighted sums of items (Nunnally and Bernstein, 1994). Whereas epidemiological scales usually give all items equal weights, individual quality of life
scales have used either the individual factor loadings (repertory grid) or the
beta weights as found by a multiple regression analysis (SEIQoL). With the
repertory grid, factor analysis (Table 5.2) is used to integrate individual
results ($n = 1$). If a general factor emerges from a principal component
analysis that explains 70% of the variance or more, it is considered as
sufficient evidence that the factor loadings can be used in generating the
final factor score (index). In contrast to the epidemiological scales, such as
the PGWB, where a general factor derived from data from a large group of
persons (Table 5.2) is only an indication that the total score may be used as

a sufficient index, the repertory grid technique relies on the exact factor score. This score is then expressed as a percentage of the calculated distance between, for example, "when illness was worst" to "the ideal situation". The calculation of this statistical distance allows individual scores to be compared (Thunedborg, Allerup, Bech and Joyce, 1993).

In the SEIQoL (Chapter 10 and O'Boyle et al., 1992; 1993), the construct validity of the visual analogue scores is estimated by multiple regression analysis. If the analysis shows that the visual analogue scores capture at least 70% of the variance in the five cues, the overall quality of life score (Table 2) is considered to show adequate internal validity. The sum of the products of each cue rating multiplied by its weights derived from the multiple regression analysis forms the individual's quality of life score.

Thus the SEIQoL and repertory grid satisfy the methodological needs for an individual quality of life instrument. The content is tailored to the individual and the statistical methods used integrate content and construct validity. The cue profiles including the subjective weighting of the respective constructs or cues are considered essential when making meaningful evaluations of individuals. The calculated index, transformed to scores from 0 to 100, can be used when computing group differences, for example, in a randomised clinical trial (but see Chapter 10 for a discussion of certain problems in this regard). The two methods are apparently able to assess the quality of life of the individual (the idiographic principle) as well as to compare groups (the nomothetic principle). An acceptable individual quality of life index is one which has an internal validity for the scales of 0.75 or better (Table 5.2).

RELIABILITY

Reliability of a questionnaire refers to the stability of repeated measures; i.e. to whether the same, behaviourally consistent individual gives consistent responses to the scale at different points in time. This specific aspect of reliability is called test-retest reliability or stability. Concerning epidemiological questionnaires, high stability is often considered to be of importance. However, it may also mean that the questionnaire is insensitive as a measure of change over time.

The individual quality of life methods estimate reliability directly as part of the scoring system. Concerning the repertory grid, the individual's own assessment of the self is incorporated in the factor score across the elements (i.e. 'self now', 'self when your illness was worst', and 'how you would like to be'). With the SEIQoL, intra-subject reliability is elegantly evaluated at the same time as the internal validity. Thus, 10 of the 30 cases are duplicated, tenabling the direct calculation of intra-subject reliability (Chapter 10 and McGee et al., 1991; O'Boyle et al., 1992, 1993).

EXTERNAL VALIDITY

This aspect of psychometric analysis is, of course, the most crucial. The external validity of various quality of life instruments is described in more detail. External validity can be subdivided (Table 5.3) into convergent, discriminant, and predictive validity.

Convergent validity is the extent to which a scale correlates with other scales intended to measure the same construct or dimension. Table 5.3 shows that epidemiological scales correlated above 0.70, which is by convention accepted as representing adequate convergence. In contrast, both individual instruments have a very low correlation to the epidemiological scales, implying that they measure something else. In the case of the repertory grid this is further emphasised by its higher discriminant validity when treatments in a randomised clinical trial (Thunedborg et al., 1993). So far, however, few trials evaluate the discriminant validity of individual quality of life scales. This aspect of measurement is often refered to as responsiveness (Patrick and Erickson, 1994) but is in fact part of the validity issue (Hays and Hadorn 1991).

Predictive validity, too, has rarely been investigated. In a pilot study, Thunedborg et al. (1995) have shown that the PGWB, the PCASEE scale and the Smith Kline Beecham Repertory Grid were all able to predict relapse in patients with recurrent major depression.

APPLICABILITY

Brief questionnaires such as the PGWB are popular in epidemiological research, because they can be completed by the respondent within 5 to 10 minutes. However, the objective of individual-oriented scales is to give the respondent opportunity and time to communicate what is personally most important to him.

When evaluating the applicability, or acceptability, of an epidemiological scale, reliability is obviously important. People completing questionnaires may not be as literate as those who have written them. There are several formulae to assess *readability*, among them the Flesch formula (ranging from 'very easy' to 'very hard') or the Fog index (Todd and Bradley, 1994). Using the Fog index, an article in the British Medical Journal or the leader of a quality newspaper have very high Fog scores whereas articles in a tabloid newspaper have very low scores. The WHO well-being scale has obtained a Fog score at the level of the UK Sunday People newspaper (Todd and Bradley, 1994).

The translation of a questionnaire into another language seeks, of course, to maintain conceptual equivalence whilst allowing for necessary changes in word order and syntax. Among the epidemiological quality of life questionnaires, the Nottingham Health Profile (NHP) and the Medical Outcomes

Table 5.3 External validity: Convergent and discriminant validity of epidemiological and individual scales

Type of Instrument	Convergence on other scales	Discriminant validity	Predictive validity
Nomothetic instruments (PGWB)	0.77[1]	Superior to other epidemiological scales[4]	Relapse in recurrent depressive illness[5]
Individual instrument (Repertory Grid)	0.38[2]	Superior to epidemiological scales[2]	Relapse in recurrent depressive illness[5]
Individual instrument (SEIQoL)	0.21[3]	Superior to epidemiological scales[3]	Under investigation

[1] Dupuy (1984); [2] Thunedborg et al. (1993); [3] O'Boyle et al. (1992); [4] Croog et al. (1986); [5] Thunedborg et al. (1995).

Studies, Short Form 36 (SF-36) have been most widely translated from English to various European and other languages (Bjoerner, Thunedborg, Kristensen, Modvig and Bech, 1998; Hunt and Wiklund, 1987). There exist different translation procedures and their respective advantages and disadvantages are still hotly debated.

The *acceptability* of the individual quality of life scales is a major aspect of the procedure. This very important issue has been most clearly formulated by Joyce (1987): "If it is desired to quantify the effect of therapeutic interventions upon quality of life some kind of order, or pattern, must be discerned that will allow hypothesis testing. But instead of imposing this order to acquire data that can be easily manipulated but may be meaningless, even if results rich in meaning will require special ways to combine them. The key to this change of emphasis is to be found in the idea of helping, but not forcing, the patient with his definition, and in the use of 'self-anchoring' scales that allow one individual's judgements to be compared across time, as well as with others..."

Both the repertory grid and SEIQoL have high levels of applicability, or acceptability, in this sense. The complex analysis of the results is usually achieved by means of a computer. During the development of a new epidemiological scale very closed answer categories ('yes' versus 'no' or 'true' versus 'not true') have been used in order to diminish readability and translation problems (McKenna, 1994).

In regard to helping the respondent to communicate his or her feelings of well-being, Leff (1977), using the semantic differential rating scale developed by Osgood et al. (1957), showed that psychiatrists held concepts of anxiety, depression and irritability that were much more differentiated than the corresponding concepts held by neurotic patients. This problem has so far not been solved by other epidemiological scales. Individual quality of life seem more likely to be able to reduce the width of this gap between patients and their doctors.

CONCLUSION

Questions within the domains of quality of life are concerned with quantifying meaning and subjective well-being. Health-related quality of life measurements refer to health in its comprehensive range, including physical, cognitive, affective, social, economic, and ego or personality indicators.

Health-related quality of life instruments cover, between them, health in all its aspects and quantifiers of meaning and subjective well-being. The quantifiers can be closed questions with rather few categories, e.g., Likert scales. Epidemiological screening instruments measuring health-related quality of life usually consist of about 20 questions which can be completed by the respondents within 5 to 10 minutes. In this chapter the PGWB has been used as an example of a brief, epidemiological screening instrument in which the total score is the sufficient statistical index.

However, although the questions in epidemiological scales should be very easy to capture, they should not be like clichés, which might further insulate the person from communicating his or her real emotions or well-being.

In contrast to epidemiological screening instruments, individual quality of life methods have used quantifiers with open or free-response questions, as exemplified by the repertory grid and SEIQoL. Both have self-anchoring visual analogue scales as quantifiers.

The above psychometric evaluations have concentrated on the three main issues of internal validity and reliability, and external validity. Their applicability (including acceptability) has also been considered. Internal validity includes content and construct validity. The various types of instruments differ more or less in their content validity. The PGWB has predetermined weights for the cognitive and affective components of health-related quality of life, whereas the repertory grid and SEIQoL allow respondents to weight the different components, whether these are personally selected or provided by the investigator.

Construct validity has been considered in this chapter as the extent to which the content of the instrument can be transformed by the quantifiers into either a profile or a total score (index) based upon it. The statistical models associated with different instruments, e.g. factor analysis, have been outlined. These differ between the epidemiological and individual instruments. Thus, the general factor identified in studies with the PGWB has been interpreted as evidence for using the unweighted total score of the 22 items as a sufficient statistic (index). In contrast, factor loadings from the repertory grid have been used to maximise the individually weighted factor score (index).

The issue of reliability has been scientifically and elegantly treated with the individual instruments. In the repertory grid, the factor structure across the elements is part of the intra-subjective reliability analysis, the individual's own perception of himself being controlled. In the SEIQoL, duplicated cases directly measure the intra-subjective coefficient of reliability.

External validity is obviously an important aspect of validity. Comparisons between the epidemiological and individual instruments (Table 5.3) seem to show that the individual instruments have a better discriminant validity (*responsiveness* in clinical trials). These aspects, which are discussed in more detail in other chapters, emphasise that it is important to differentiate between various levels of examining health. Clinical symptoms have their own hierarchical level as indicators of illness, and social adjustment performances indicate disability. The quality of life level, at the bottom of the hierarchy, quantifies the meaning and subjective well-being of health. Although the screening instruments have a major role in epidemiological research, the individual methods, with their high discriminant validity, may eventually play a large part in controlled clinical trials.

The applicability of the instruments includes the extent to which a scale is acceptable to respondents. On one side, the brief epidemiological scales with their high readability should be highly acceptable. However, when applicability is defined as helping the respondent to express his own definitions of quality of life, individual methods are superior. In other words, the individual instruments are able to rank-order patients in terms of subjective well-being because statistical models control the underlying dimensions. Further research will determine the appropriate applications of both individual measures and epidemiological scales.

REFERENCES

Allerup, P. (1986) *Statistical Analysis of Rating Scales*. Copenhagen: Danish Institute of Educational Research.

Andrich, D. (1988) *Rasch Models for Measurement*. Beverly Hills: Sage.

Bech, P. (1990) Measurement of psychological distress and well-being. *Psychotherapy and Psychosomatics* **54**, 77–89.

Bech, P. (1993) *Rating scales for psychopathology, health status and quality of life*. Berlin: Springer.

Bech, P. (1996) *The Bech, Hamilton and Zung scales for mood disorders: Screening and listening*. Berlin: Springer. Second edition.

Bech, P., Gudex, C. and Staehr Johansen, K. (1996) The WHO (Ten) Well-Being Index: Validation in diabetes. *Psychotherapy and Psychosomatics* **65**, 183–190.

Bjorner, J., Thunedborg, K., Kristensen, T. S., Modvig, J. and Bech, P. (1998) Translation of the Danish SF-36: Preliminary validity and feasibility studies. *Journal of Clinical Epidemiology* (in press).

Bradburn, N. M. and Caplovitz, D. (1965) Report on happiness. *A pilot study of behaviour related to mental health*. Chicago: Aldine.

Bradburn, N. M. and Miles, C. (1979) Vague quantifiers. *Public Opinion Quarterly* **43**, 92–101.

Croog, S. H., Levin, E. S., Testa, M. et al. (1986) The effects of antihypertensive therapy on the quality of life. *New England Journal of Medicine* **314**, 1657–1664.

Dupuy, H. J. (1984) The Psychological General Well-Being (PGWB) Index. In *Assessment of quality of life in clinical trials of cardiovascular therapies*, N. K. Wenger, M. E. Mattson, C. D. Furberg and J. Elinson (eds). pp. 184–188. New York: Le Jacq Publishing.

Gottschalk, L. A. (1995) *Content analysis of verbal behaviour: New findings and clinical applications*. New Jersey: Hillsdale.

Guy, W. (1976) *Early Clinical Drug Evaluation (ECDEU) Assessment Manual*. Rockville: National Institute for Mental Health.

Hammond, K. R., McClelland, G. H. and Mumpower, J. (1980) *Human Judgement and decision making*. New York: Prager.

Hays, R. D. and Hadorn, D. Responsiveness to change: an aspect of validity, not a separate dimension. *Quality of Life Research* **1**, 73–76.

Hunt, S. and Wiklund, I. (1987) Cross-culture variation in weighting of health statements: A comparison of English and Swedish valuations. *Health policy* **8**, 227–235.

Jahoda, M. (1958) *Current concepts of positive mental health*. New York: Basic Books.

Joyce, C. R. B. (1987) Quality of life: The state of art in clinical assessment. In *Quality of life: assessment and application*, S. R. Walker and R. Rosser (eds). pp. 169–179. Lancaster: MIT Press.

Kelly, G. A. (1955) *The psychology of personal constructs*. New York: Norton.

Leff, J. P. (1977) Psychiatrists' versus patients' concepts of unpleasant emotions. *British Journal of Psychiatry* **133**, 306–313.

Likert, R. A. (1932) Technique for the measurement of attitudes. *Archives of Psychology* **140**, 1–55.

McDowell, I. and Newell, C. (1987) *Measuring health. A guide to rating scales and questionnaires.* New York: Oxford University Press.

McGee, H. M., O'Boyle, C. A., Hickey, A., O'Malley, K. and Joyce, C. R. B. (1991) Assessing the quality of life of the individual: the SEIQOL with a healthy and a gastroenterology unit population. *Psychological Medicine* **21**, 749–59.

McKenna, S. P. (1994) A new theoretical approach to the measurement of quality of life. *Drug Information Journal* **28**, 13–18.

Nunnally, J. C. (1978) *Psychometric theory.* New York: McGraw Hill.

Nunnally, J. C. and Bernstein, I. H. (1994) *Psychometric theory.* New York: McGraw Hill.

O'Boyle, C. A., McGee, H. M., Hickey, A., O'Malley, K. and Joyce, C. R. B. (1992) Individual quality of life in patients undergoing replacement. *Lancet* **339**, 1088–1091.

O'Boyle, C., McGee, H., Hickey, A., Joyce, C. R. B., Browne J., O'Malley, K. and Hiltbrunner B. (1993) *The schedule for the Evaluation of Individual Quality of Life (SEIQOL): Administration manual.* Dublin: Royal College of Surgeons in Ireland.

O'Boyle, C. A., McGee, H. and Joyce, C. R. B. (1994) Quality of life: Assessing the individual. In *Advances in medical sociology Vol. V. Quality of life in health care*, G. L. Albrecht and R. Fitzpatrick (eds). Greenwich, CT: JAI Press.

Osgood, C. E., Suci, C. J. and Tannenbaum, P. H. (1957) *The measurement of meaning.* Urbana, Ill: University of Illinois Press.

Patrick, D. L. and Erickson, P. (1993) *Health status and health policy: Allocating resources to health care.* New York: Oxford University Press.

Sudman, S. and Bradburn, N. M. (1985) *Asking questions. A practical guide to questionnaire design.* San Francisco: Jossey Bass.

Thunedborg, K., Allerup, P., Bech, P. and Joyce, C. R. B. (1993) Development of the repertory grid for measurement of individual quality of life in clinical trials. *International Journal of Methods in Psychiatric Research* **3**, 48–58.

Thunedborg, K., Black, C. and Bech, P. (1995) Beyond the Hamilton Depression Scale Scores in manic-depressive patients in long-term relapse-prevention: A quality of life approach. *Psychotherapy and Psychosomatics* **64**, 131–140.

Todd, C. and Bradley, C. (1994) Evaluating the design and development of psychological scales. In *Handbook of psychology and diabetes*, C. Bradley (ed.). pp. 15–42. Chur, Switzerland: Harwood Academic Publishers.

World Health Organisation (1948) *Construction in basic documents.* Geneva: World Health Organisation.

World Health Organisation (1980) *International Classification of Impairments, Disabilities, and Handicaps (ICIDH/WHO).* Geneva: World Health Organisation.

6. INDIVIDUALISING ASSESSMENT IN INTERVENTION STUDIES: N-OF-1 TRIALS[*]

STEPHEN SENN

To see a world in a grain of sand

William Blake

There are probably no two men in existence on whom the drug acts in exactly the same manner

Wilkie Collins, The Moonstone

If we could, this year, exactly reproduce, in your case, the conditions as they existed last year, it is physiologically certain that we should arrive at exactly the same result. But this — there is no denying it — is simply impossible.

Wilkie Collins, The Moonstone

This chapter describes a general methodological approach to study design which prioritises individual assessment. N-of-1 study designs have been widely used in learning disability settings and have been more recently used in clinical trials. The use of this methodology in quality of life studies provides the opportunity to focus on the status of the individual. Depending on the quality of life assessment format used, evaluation may be with individualised or generic measures. Methodological issues concerning the use of n-of-1 designs in research studies. To date these designs have not been used with quality of life assessment approaches. They provide however for the future an opportunity to combine both individualised study design and study assessment procedures.

INTRODUCTION

One man's meat is another man's poison. Simple and common medicines such as penicillin and aspirin are notorious for their ability to cause adverse reactions in a minority of patients. If their side-effects vary from individual to individual, might their main effects not also be expected to do so and is this not something which we should expect of all medicines? Patients come in different ages, sexes and sizes. They differ with respect to their ability to absorb, metabolise and eliminate drugs. They may have differing co-morbidity. Some may lack enzymes which most possess. The more we learn about genetics, the more we identify factors which can have an effect on health. Patients also differ with respect to lifestyle and severity of disease. These are all reasons to suspect that when it comes to therapy 'one size fits all' may be an inappropriate philosophy.

On the other hand, there appears to be a near universal human tendency to underestimate the effects of chance. Two apparently identical light-bulbs

---

[*] This is an amended version of Chapter 18 (N-of-1 trials) from Senn, S. *Statistical Issues in Drug Development*. London: Wiley, 1997. Reproduced with permission.

may have very different lifetimes. There may be nothing predictable about the eventual difference between the two yet, due to something we have little choice but to label 'chance', this may be large. In a similar way, with patients we find that they may differ considerably from day to day, even when given the same treatment. We should be cautious, therefore, when comparing two patients given the same treatment, in ascribing to individual factors a difference which may be transient and due to chance.

Both of these two opposing considerations are reflected in the chapter quotations from *The Moonstone* concerning the effect of opium. The plot of that novel hinges on the fact that the hero Franklin Blake takes a diamond, the Moonstone of the story, whilst under the influence of a dose of opium administered to him without his knowledge, and one of whose effects appears to be to erase all memory of the incident. In order to stage a reconstruction of his actions on the fateful night, he is to be given a second dose of opium. It is known from a physician's notes that he was given 'five and twenty minims of laudanum' on the night in question. However, various circumstances have changed in the meantime and there is no certainty that the same dose will reproduce the same effect, even though given to the same person. (In the end it is decided to give him 40 minims and this does the trick).

These two features are at the heart of this chapter. The fact that different patients respond differently to treatment suggests that individualising therapy may increase the utility of treatments considerably. That patients vary in their response from occasion to occasion suggests that establishing which treatments are best for which patients may be extremely difficult. For example, in a clinical trial we generally need a large sample of patients just in order to be able to say something about treatment effects in general. Even our ability to say something about the effect of treatments on sub-groups is limited. One might suppose, continuing the argument, that to say something definitive about an individual patient is almost impossible. There are, however, exceptions. The first is where the course of the untreated disease is so predictable, that there is little difficulty in establishing in a given patient whether the treatment has worked or not, by comparing the state of the patient after treatment to that which would have occurred. (Note the importance of our general notions of causality in all this). However, very few treatments fall into this category. A famous candidate, perhaps, is rabies, where the efficacy of Pasteur's vaccine was dramatically demonstrated in 1885 by treating a single boy. (Although note that not all who are bitten by rabid dogs and untreated develop rabies, so that the demonstration is short of being perfect). A second approach, which is possible for chronic diseases, is to turn the mechanism of the clinical trial inwards. Just as we repeatedly study different patients to determine the effects of treatments in general so we study repeated episodes of treatment in a given patient in order to establish the effects of treatment for him or her.

Such trials have been referred to as 'N-of-1' trials and may be defined as follows: an 'N-of-1' trial is a trial in which a number of episodes of treatment are studied in a single patient, usually with a view to making inferences about the effect of treatment on that patient. Where we run series of 'n-of-1' trials, we may regard ourselves as having run one experiment on at least two levels (patients and episodes). This means that many of the issues to do with n-of-1 trials are similar to those encountered in analysing multi-centre trials where the levels are centres and patients, or in carrying out a meta-analysis of a series of trials where the levels are trials and patients. By virtue of the fact that n-of-1 trials are within-patient studies, they also share many of the features of *cross-over* trials. (See Senn (1997) for a fuller discussion of these various trial design issues).

AT WHICH STAGE OF DRUG DEVELOPMENT SHOULD N-OF-1 TRIALS BE USED?

There is an opinion that n-of-1 trials should only be employed late on in drug development (Lewis, 1991). Indeed, it is an opinion I have expressed myself (Senn, 1993b). Essentially the argument is that establishing the effect on individual patients of treatment is a refinement of a more important question; 'does the treatment work?' If that is so, the broader question should be answered first. Furthermore, even where individuals react differently to treatment there is usually some value in using to some extent the results of others to predict the effects. Of course, given a large amount of data on a given patient we do not need results from others. However, even where we run n-of-1 trials it is rarely the case that we have very large amounts of data on individual patients. For example, in a series of trials run by March, Irwig, Schwarz, Simpson, Chock and Brooks (1994) each of a number of patients suffering from osteoarthritis was randomly allocated to receive either diclofenac or placebo in three pairs of periods. However, the individual trials had little power to detect appropriate treatment differences and it was necessary to look at the results in totality in order to interpret the trial correctly (Senn, Bakshi and Ezzet, 1995). In fact, it is a classic use of random effect models to 'shrink' individual effects close to the overall mean.

Furthermore, where there are true differences between patients, a more efficient way to gain information about the effect of a treatment with the object simply of establishing that it works, would be to run an AB/BA cross-over design. There is more information to be gained about the average effects of treatment under such circumstances by adding more patients rather than more periods. Hence in phase II clinical trials there is generally little point in running n-of-1 trials.

The above argument pre-supposes, however, that many patients can be obtained. For rare diseases, for example, Gilles de la Tourette syndrome, this may not be possible. Under such circumstances (and given that the condition is chronic), repeatedly treating the few patients available may be the only way to gain experimental material.

P-VALUES AND N-OF-1 TRIALS

It is almost never the case that we run a single n-of-1 trial. Usually we run a series using a number of patients. It has been suggested that such a series may be adequately analysed by calculating the p-value for the treatment effect for each patient and noting in which cases the treatment was significant and in which it was not. Of course, many statisticians (notable, but not exclusively, the Bayesians) think that p-values are generally inappropriate, whatever the context. There are, however, further reservations which may be applied to n-of-1 trials. First, there is the same problem which arises in trials of equivalence. Failure to find a significant difference does not imply that none exists. Many n-of-1 trials will have rather low power for individual patients. Therefore, there will be many false negative results. Figure 6.1 illustrates the distribution of a one-sided p-value for different n-of-1 trials on the assumption that the test statistic has a normal distribution. The case where the treatment is ineffective is illustrated. This leads to a uniform distribution. Cases are also illustrated where the power to detect a genuine treatment effect is respectively 0.1, 0.5 and 0.95. Second, we also have the general problem of multiplicity of p-values. Even where the treatment is ineffective it is likely that the odd patient will have a low p-value if we are treating many. Third, treating information on patients as completely independent is inefficient and runs contrary to general medical practice: how could we have medical handbooks describing the therapeutic effects of any treatments if we had to start from scratch with every new patient?

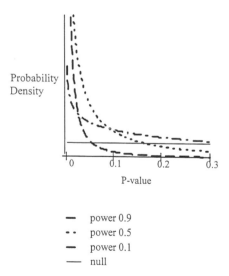

Figure 6.1 Distribution of a one-sided p-value given as a function of power given a nominal size of 0.025. (The range of p-values illustrated is restricted to 0.3 or less in order to produced a more readable graph).

RANDOM EFFECTS ANALYSIS

A way to use information from other patients together with information from an individual patient in a way which weights the two appropriately, for the purpose of producing treatment estimates for him or her, is to construct a random effect model. An alternative reason for using such a model might be to describe the true distribution of treatment effects in patients not studied. A fixed effects model cannot do this since either it makes the assumption that all patients react identically to treatment, or it can be regarded as a means of testing whether there is a treatment effect in at least some patients. (see Senn, 1997 chapter 14 for a discussion). If it is truly desired to say something about the distribution of treatment effects in patients in general, then the combination of a series of n-of-1 trials together with a random effects model is the most powerful available.

CORRELATED OBSERVATIONS

Any decent model used to analyse a series of n-of-1 trials will allow for at least three sources of variation: pure between patient variability, within patient *variability* and a random effect for patient by treatment interaction. Since a series of measurements are being obtained, however, it may be inappropriate to assume that within-patient errors are independent (or more formally that the correlations between them are equal). If patients are subject to spells of illness for example, then two measurements taken during two administrations of the same drug are more likely to be similar if the administrations are close together rather than far apart. This phenomenon can be referred to as serial correlation and is potentially a problem for the analysis of n-of-1 trials. (It would also be a problem for multi-period cross-over trials. The standard analysis of these however, ignore the even more serious problem of patient by treatment interaction.)

The practical experimenter's way to deal with this will include randomising the order of treatment given to the patient. An alternative approach, which exploits the correlation, would be to allocate the two treatments being compared in pairs but randomise the order within pairs. The paired differences can then be analysed using an appropriate random effects model. The alternative would be to introduce an explicit model for the correlation structure of repeated measures but this is unlikely to be simple.

BLINDING

The problems with blinding n-of-1 trials are particularly acute if the object is to say something about an individual patient. This is because the number of observations available for him or her alone will usually be small. Hence the probability of the patient correctly guessing the complete sequence used will be relatively large. For example if two treatments are to be allocated at random in three pairs using sequences such as AB AB BA, or AB BA AB and so forth, then there are only $2^3 = 8$ possible sequences in total. Hence, the probability of the patient correctly guessing a random sequence is 1/8. If all possible sequences are used subject only to the restriction that each treatment will appear three times, then there are $6!/(3!3!) = 20$ possible sequences. If the patient has a strong prejudice that one of the treatments is effective, and a strong belief (however irrationally based) that a particular sequence will be used, then (s)he may guess and report a series of biased numbers corresponding to the believed sequence. For example, the following visual analogue scale pain scores might be reported in a trial in arthritis in which patients received treatment. A three times and treatment B three times in random order and the patient assumed the sequence actually used was AA B A B B and wrongly believed B to be more effective: 63, 66, 24, 61, 27, 23. Now, there is a one in twenty chance that the patient guessed correctly, and if (s)he did then the mean difference between the two groups will be $(63 + 66 + 67)/3 - (23 + 24 + 27)/3 = 29$. The t-statistic will be 20.5 with 4 degrees of freedom corresponding to a p-value of 0.000033, which does not at all represent the true probability involved. Of course, a non-parametric test would get around the difficulty but these lack power for very small samples. As the *sample size* gets larger the problems caused by this sort of guessing strategy get less. The relevant sample size, however, is that of the episodes given to each patient. Increasing the number of patients will deal with this problem as regards the overall estimate of the treatment effect but individual patient estimates may still suffer and this will have an effect on the estimate of the variability of the treatment effect from patient to patient.

These problems should not be exaggerated but n-of-1 trials exemplify a particular general problem regarding blinding, randomisation and control which is often overlooked in clinical trials. Just because these elements have been used in designing and running a clinical trial does not mean that any conceivable analysis of the data is afforded the sort of protection they are designed to offer.

REFERENCES

Guyatt, G. H., Heyting, A. H., Jaeschke, R., Keller, J., Adachi, J. D. and Roberts, R. S. (1990) N-of-1 trials for investigating new drugs. *Controlled Clinical Trials* **11**, 88–100.

Lewis, J. A. (1991) Controlled trials in single subjects: 2 limitations of use. *British Medical Journal* **303**, 175–176.

Johannessen, T. (1991) Controlled trials in single subjects: 1 value in clinical medicine. *British Medical Journal* **303**, 173–174.

March, L., Irwig, L., Schwarz, J., Simpson, J., Chock, C. and Brooks, P. (1994) n-of-1 trials comparing a non-steroidal anti-inflammatory drug with paracetamol in osteoarthritis. *British Medical Journal* **309**, 1041–1046.

Senn, S. J. (1991) Controlled Trials in Single Subjects. *British Medical Journal* **303,** 716–717.

Senn, S. J. (1993a) *Cross-over Trials in Clinical Research*, Wiley, Chichester and New York.

Senn, S. J. (1993b). Suspended Judgement: N-of-1 Trials. *Controlled Clinical Trials* **14,** 1–5.

Senn, S. J., Bakshi, R. and Ezzet, N. (1995) 'N-of-1 trials in osteoarthritis: caution in interpretation needed' *British Medical Journal* **310,**11, 667.

Senn, S. J. *Statistical Issues in Drug Development*. London: Wiley, 1997.

II

SPECIFIC APPROACHES TO INDIVIDUAL QUALITY OF LIFE ASSESSMENT

7. INTERPRETATION OF DATA FROM HEALTH STATUS MEASURES: WHAT DO THE NUMBERS MEAN?

CRISPIN JENKINSON and SUE ZIEBLAND

A large number of medical interventions are primarily designed to improve the quality, rather than to extend the duration, of patients' lives. Despite much medical care being directed at improving patient well being, evaluation of the efficacy of this care has rarely been systematically undertaken from the perspective of those who actually receive the treatment. Medical interventions have been evaluated in terms of traditional mortality and morbidity statistics. However, over the last ten years there has been increasing consensus regarding the importance of subjective accounts of health in monitoring medical outcomes. Considerable effort has been expended to ensure such measures conform to statistical and psychometric criteria of reliability, validity and sensitivity to change yet relatively little has been written concerning how the data generated from such measures can be interpreted. Whilst a given questionnaire may reliably produce a certain number under certain conditions such information is of very limited use unless the number can be interpreted. The purpose of this paper, therefore, is to outline some of the problems associated with the interpretation of data gained from health status measures and suggest ways in which the data may be used to reflect more meaningfully the perceptions of the patient.

INTRODUCTION

The inclusion of a measure of subjective well being has, in recent years, become an increasingly standard feature in both clinical assessment of interventions and medical research. This has been welcomed as a potential method of gaining data which were once thought beyond measurement, or even irrelevant, but are now seen as imperative. However, the selection of measures of subjective well being is not always conducted with the care and attention due to a primary outcome measure. In part, this is due to methodological problems, such as measurement insensitivity or inappropriate questions being posed, but it is also due to philosophical problems, relating to what it is that should be measured. Terms such as 'health status' and 'quality of life' tend to be used interchangeably yet refer to quite separate phenomena. Bergner claimed that standardised measures such as the Sickness Impact Profile were measures of subjective health status and that 'quality of life' was a distinct phenomenon related to areas outside of the medical sphere (Bergner, 1989). On the other hand it has been suggested that quality of life, defined as "the extent to which hopes and ambitions are matched by experience" should be the very essence of subjective health measurement (Ruta et al., 1994). Such differences in viewpoints have contributed to a proliferation of measures with different measurement properties. As a consequence, those selecting measures for use in clinical trials and other studies designed to evaluate medical interventions find themselves faced with a plethora of instruments which have been demonstrated to be reliable and valid in conventional psychometric and statistical terms, yet there is little guidance about how to select an appropriate measure or how to interpret the data generated by such measures.

The use of subjective health measures cannot inform clinical practice, or those charged with the difficult decisions of resource allocation, if they are unable to interpret the data provided by the instruments. Despite this, little attention has been paid to what the numbers generated by these methods really mean. The purpose of this paper is to outline some of the problems associated with the interpretation of data gained from health status measures and suggest ways in which the data may be used to reflect more accurately the perceptions of the patient. The benefits of scoring schemes that are easily interpreted will be discussed taking as an example the Dartmouth COOP project (Landgraf et al., 1992).

THE PROBLEM OF INTERPRETING DATA FROM HEALTH STATUS MEASURES

In order to place some form on this large and increasingly disparate field a number of texts have documented existing validated measures (McDowell et al., 1996; Wilkin et al., 1992; Bowling, 1991; Bowling, 1995), chronicled the uses of such measures (Stewart et al., 1988; Stewart et al., 1993; Fallowfield, 1990; Teeling Smith, 1983) and outlined the methodological issues to be considered in developing (Streiner et al., 1989; Streiner et al., 1995), selecting and interpreting the data from such measures (Jenkinson, 1994; Brooks, 1995). However, despite these attempts to provide guidelines and assistance, most research projects tend to select the most popular instrument in use at any given time. Rarely do clinical trials or other medical studies report in any great detail why the particular measure chosen to assess health status was selected. For example, numerous studies include, at present, the Short Form 36 Health Survey questionnaire (SF-36). The SF-36 is a 36 item questionnaire which measures eight multi-item dimensions: physical functioning, social functioning, role limitations due to physical problems, role limitations due to emotional problems, mental health, energy/vitality, pain, general health perception, and health change (Ware et al., 1992). This measure has been shown to have high levels of reliability and validity (Ware et al., 1993). Its popularity has lead to its application throughout the world and its use in numerous studies (Bergner, 1989). However, it may not be appropriate for all ages or all illness groups. It has been suggested that the SF-36 may be an inappropriate measure of outcome for the elderly (Hayes et al., 1995; Brazier et al., 1992) and its face validity may be problematic for certain patients. For example women presenting with menorrhagia have found it difficult to disentangle issues relating to their overall health and their specific condition (Jenkinson et al., 1996). It is clearly important for researchers to state explicitly the reason for the choice of measure included in the research and, if necessary, to pilot the measure to ensure that it is acceptable and reliable within the respondent group.

In an attempt to make the data generated by health measures more intuitively meaningful it has been suggested that normative data (i.e. population norms) can act as a benchmark to facilitate interpretation in specific samples or illness groups (Ware, 1993). However, such benchmarks can provide only limited assistance. The data can indicate whether one group falls above or below the mean for persons of a given age, sex and/or social class but there is no way of further determining what a given score means, unless, of course, one goes back to the original questionnaires and looks up the items that have been affirmed. Put another way, does a population score of 82.8 on the SF-36 dimension of 'role limitations due to physical problems' indicate that this group of respondents were almost twice as ill (on this dimension) as another sample with a mean score of 41.4?

Unfortunately, no indication is given as to what the relative scores might mean, and such difficulties in interpretation could be a barrier to the clinical use of such questionnaires. If health assessment questionnaires are to be clinically useful then some indication must be given as to the significance of scores. One can sympathise with the clinician who poses the question 'But what do the numbers mean?' While the results may provide some indication of the relative impact of different treatment regimes, the criticisms made of medical measures such as, for example, Erythrocyte Sedimentation Rate (ESR) still apply. Thus the difference in scores between groups, or before and after treatment, may be visible and may even provide some insight into differences (e.g. in clinical trials where one group is given a drug, and the other a placebo, or where different treatments are given to patients with similar disease profiles) but such scores do not presently lend themselves to more accurate interpretation.

POWER CALCULATIONS

The problem of interpretation of scores is particularly relevant in deciding sample sizes based on power calculations. It is essential, when designing a trial, to ensure that the sample size is sufficiently large to detect differences between the treatment and control group. One could not, for example, conclude that a drug was efficacious if the study involved too few patients to achieve a statistically significant result. As a consequence, sample sizes are calculated to determine the numbers necessary in any given study. To determine what size sample is required one must put forward a hypothesis, postulating that one treatment is more efficacious than another and will lead to a superior outcome. This outcome may be a difference in proportions between the two groups (e.g. an effect may be expected to be three times greater in one group than another) or a difference in the mean scores on a given measure. This may be a clinical measure, or a subjective one such as quality of life.

As a consequence of the growth of interest in subjective assessments of well-being such outcomes are increasingly the basis for sample size calculations and tables exist to permit such calculations to be made relatively easily (Ware et al., 1993). The manual for the Short Form-36 Health Survey provides tables indicating what samples would be needed if one were attempting to gain 2, 5, 10 and 20 point differences over time and between groups (Jenkinson et al., 1996), yet very little indication is given as to what such differences may mean in practice. What would a 20 point difference on the 'role limitations due to emotional problems' or 'pain' dimensions of the SF-36 actually mean in terms of item responses? In Figures 7.1 and 7.2 we provide a more content based interpretation comparing scores and responses. Two points are worthy of note. Firstly, 2, 5, 10, or 20 point changes would not indicate any massive improvement in health status, at least in terms of the 'role emotional' or 'pain' scales. Secondly, and importantly, the scales, whilst both appearing to have the same range (from '0' for worse possible health state to '100' for best possible health state) manifest very different measurement properties. As a result, comparisons between the scales of the SF-36 is simply not possible. A score of 70 on one dimension of the SF-36 does not relate in any clear way to a score of 70 on another dimension. Consequently, it is essential that researchers attempt to provide some content based interpretation of scores to give them meaning. Table 7.1 provides such a content based

---

During the **past 4 weeks**, have you had any of the following problems with your

work or other regular daily activities **as a result of any emotional problems**

(such as feeling depressed or anxious)?

*(Please answer **Yes** or **No** to each question)*

	Yes	No
a) **Cut down on the** <u>**amount of time**</u> **you spent on work or other activities**	✗	✓
b) <u>**Accomplished less**</u> **than you would like**		✗ ✓
c) **Didn't do work or other activities as** <u>**carefully**</u> **as possible**		✗ ✓

✓ = 100   ✗ = 66.66

Figure 7.1 Responses needed to gain a perfect score (100) on the Role Emotional scale of the SF-36 compared with responses needed to gain a score of 66.66.

How much bodily pain have you had during the **past 4 weeks**?

*(Please tick **one** box)*

None	✓
Very mild	✗
Mild	
Moderate	
Severe	
Very Severe	

During the **past 4 weeks** how much did pain interfere with your normal work

(including work both outside the home and housework)?

*(Please tick **one** box)*

Not at all	✓
A little bit	✗
Moderately	
Quite a bit	
Extremely	

✓ = 100   ✗ = 77.78

Figure 7.2 Responses needed to gain a perfect score (100) on the Pain scale of the SF-36 compared with responses needed to gain a score of 77.78.

interpretation for the Physical Function scale of the SF-36 based on responses to the Oxford Health and Lifestyle Survey (Wright et al., 1992). This indicates that a change over time or difference between groups of, say, 10 points, does not *necessarily* indicate a great improvement in health. This apparently unremarkable assertion can be lost to view in statistical analysis and presentation of data.

Table 7.1 Content based interpretation of responses to the 'Physical Function' dimension of the SF-36

100	*No problems in physical function*. Respondents perform all types of activities without limitations in health
90	Very few problems in physical function. Respondents report *minor* limitations in a *small* number of areas, such as vigorous activities, walking more than a mile, or bending and kneeling.
80	Very few problems in physical function. Respondents report *minor* limitations in a number of areas, such as vigorous activities, walking more than a mile, or bending and kneeling.
65	*Respondents report severe limitations in one or two areas* related to physical function, such as vigorous activities, walking a mile or more and climbing stairs. Respondents may also report minor limitations in other aspects of physical function, like bending and stooping.
55	*Respondents report severe limitations in one or two areas* related to physical function, such as vigorous activities, walking a mile or more and climbing stairs. *They also report minor limitations in a number of other aspects of physical function*, like bending and stooping.
40	*Respondents report severe limitation in a number of areas* related to physical function, such as being severely limited in both moderate and vigorous activities, walking half a mile and bending. They may also indicate some limitation in other aspects of physical function such as bathing and dressing.
25	*Respondents report severe limitations in a large number of areas* related to physical function. In most areas in which they are not severely limited they will experience some limitation.
0	*Respondents report severe limitations in physical function, and are severely limited in both their mobility and daily routines.*

The regular use of the '*effect size*' statistic has lead to researchers believing that there is a standard available to them for assessing responsiveness (Kazis et al., 1989). Effect sizes are calculated by taking the mean change in a variable, and dividing it by the baseline standard deviation of the variable. An effect size of one indicates one standard deviation change since baseline. As a general rule of thumb effect sizes of approximately 0.2 are regarded as small, 0.5 as moderate and 0.8 as large. While the effect size takes account of the spread of responses (the standard deviation) as well as the mean score changes, there may still be problems in interpreting the size of the effect too literally since the suggested 'cut-off points' for small, medium and large effects are fairly arbitrary. For example, in one study (Jenkinson et al., 1995), large effect sizes detected on the basis of administration of a pain measure prior to and after treatment suggested that the instrument was highly sensitive. However, while the effect size statistic implied that the intervention had a substantial impact, the patients' direct ratings indicated only small improvements. This demonstrates the importance of considering the operating characteristics of a measure rather than relying on statistical indicators alone.

In the next section we consider strategies that may be used to overcome the problem of interpreting data from health status measures. These include methods which are applicable to both research and clinical settings (e.g. global assessments and transition scales) and those which have been designed for use with individual patients such as the pictorial COOP charts (Landgraf et al., 1992).

DIRECT ASSESSMENT OF CHANGE

Global Health Assessment

The problem of data interpretation in 'before and after' studies may be averted by asking respondents to provide simple, global health assessments. These require the respondent to describe their state of health by answering just one question, such as "Would you describe your health as very good, good, fair, poor or very poor?" There is evidence for the value of such simple global ratings (Rowan, 1994), although they will obviously only be sensitive to the more dramatic changes in a person's health state.

Changes over time can be successfully measured by simply asking the patient to make a direct judgement about the extent of improvement or deterioration (as in 'much better', 'slightly better', 'the same', 'slightly worse', 'much worse'). The use of transition items has been validated against other criteria (Ziebland et al., 1992), and it has been demonstrated that they do not seem to be contaminated by the patient's mood. (Fitzpatrick et al., 1993). One of their most useful features is that the units of change have the undeniable benefit of clarity. Although global *transition items*, such as those asking about overall changes in health, may be used to assess the outcome of a specific intervention there is a danger in more complex conditions of obscuring conflicting aspects of the course of an illness, whereby one aspect may have improved while another has deteriorated. It is also possible that global transition judgements may be dominated by variations in a particular symptom, such as pain.

TRANSITION SCALES

Multiple-item transition scales enable patients to rate the extent to which they have improved or deteriorated on a number of key variables, thereby allowing for the possibility that not all functions and symptoms will respond in the same manner. This method may also be considered where baseline measures are not plausible, such as in intensive care or accident and emergency outcomes research, although the respondent's reference point for the comparison would need careful definition.

There is evidence that patients can express the course of their health more accurately through these direct judgements, than by repeated use of the baseline questionnaire. In a study of patients with rheumatoid arthritis, a comparison was made between two approaches to measuring change using the Health Assessment Questionnaire (HAQ) (Jenkinson, 1995). The HAQ includes eight sections which cover various aspects of daily life, such as reaching, getting into and out of bed, dressing and climbing stairs. Respondents are invited to describe the amount of difficulty they have been experiencing with each task during the past week, selecting from a four point scale: 'without difficulty'; 'with some difficulty'; 'with much difficulty'; 'unable to do'. Three months later, the HAQ was administered again, but in addition to the conventional computation of the change score between the two assessments, respondents were also invited to complete an eight item transition index where specific tasks were rated as 'more difficult', 'less difficult' or 'stable' since the last interview. The data generated by the transition method were more highly correlated with clinical and laboratory measurements than those generated by conventional change scores. Such data are not only easily collected but easily interpreted. The use of a small set of transition items to measure changes as a follow-up to a full baseline assessment of health appears to have much to recommend it: it is quick to complete; it requires minimal scoring; it provides the opportunity for an unequivocal representation of changes which are relevant to the patient.

INDIVIDUAL LEVEL DATA FOR CLINICAL USE

Thus far, we have considered how it may be possible to make the data from health status measures more readily interpretable. However, this debate has been addressed at the level of aggregate data sets and not at the level of the individual. In this section the part played by measures that can be used at the individual level will be discussed.

Perhaps the most innovative approach to the measurement of health-related quality of life from the patient's perspective is that adopted by the developers of the Patient Generated Index (PGI; see Chapter 9) in the United Kingdom and the Schedule for the Evaluation of Individual Quality of Life (SEIQoL; see Chapter 10) in Ireland. These measures have the advantage of including the respondents' own priorities in which respect they are truly 'individualised'. However, both the PGI and SEIQoL developers have, for the most part, used the measures in aggregated studies in which many of the problems of data interpretation remain prominent.

An alternative use of individualised measures is as part of the clinical routine. The success of the consultation could be improved if patients were to complete a questionnaire which could be discussed during the appointment. It was this notion of health assessment that influenced the COOP chart developers. The COOP charts were developed by the Dartmouth Primary Care Co-operative Information Project. (Landgraf et al., 1992; Nelson et al., 1990; Wasson et al., 1992; Nelson et al., 1996). Pictorial charts are used to measure health status along nine dimensions (physical condition, emotional condition, daily work, social activities, pain, change in condition, overall condition, social support and quality of life). Each has a simply worded question with five response categories and each response category is linked to a drawing intended to represent that health state. Unlike many other measures, the COOP charts have been specifically developed for use in routine clinical practice, although the evidence suggests that research applications might also be considered.

The COOP charts have been assessed for validity and reliability and have compared well with longer measures. Whilst reducing respondent burden substantially when compared to long form measures utilised in the Medical Outcomes Study, the loss in precision was minor (McHorney et al., 1993). Similar results have been found with comparable dimensions of the SF-36 and COOP charts in a trial of open versus laparoscopic surgery (Jenkinson et al., 1995).

The designers have suggested that further research is required to determine the influence of the content and style of pictures on patients' responses. Other aspects which need further attention are their use in monitoring changes in health status for individual patients over time, their sensitivity to clinically important changes and (if research use is considered) their ability to detect small differences in health status between groups. Little evaluation has taken place outside America, nor outside the routine clinical practice for which they were originally designed. Despite these concerns, the charts are one of very few measures designed for the individual patient in a clinical setting. Research in America with the charts has so far been encouraging, with both clinicians and patients claiming that the inclusion of this questionnaire in the medical interview has improved the consultation and provided both sides with important information (Kraus, 1991). Physicians claimed that their clinical care was influenced by data from the charts which added new insights on patients functioning and well-being (Kraus, 1991). Their appeal lies in their simplicity: not only can they be completed easily and quickly but the data they generate is immediately interpretable without complex scoring algorithms or the need to combine scores.

CONCLUSION

Health status measures can provide a useful adjunct to the data traditionally obtained from mortality and morbidity statistics, or from traditional clinical and laboratory assessments. Measures must be selected to tap appropriate domains. Pilot work using semi structured interview techniques will often be necessary to establish which domains and models are appropriate for any specific purpose.

In the context of a well designed clinical trial, health status measures may permit scientific questions to be answered more fully and appropriately than has been possible in the past. If their use is to become more widespread and be informative to research and routine clinical practice, the results must be made intuitive and meaningful to potential users. In the absence of such clarification there is a danger that the data collection will consume resources and inform no-one.

We have suggested some ways in which the value of health status measures may be improved by using a content based interpretation: a transition scale to assess change or a brief measure designed to be used in the clinic. The results of the Dartmouth COOP research indicate the potential value of health status measurement to clinicians at the level of individual patient care. The message is clear: for health assessment data to be of use they must be easy to collect and interpret. Pictures, words and ordinal scales require less strained interpretation than do numbers, which suggests that where complex aggregated data are not required, there is nothing to be gained from abstracting them into numerals. Where aggregated data are required, ideally, there should exist benchmarks, such as content based interpretation tables, which can provide a meaningful explanation for statistically presented material. More research is required to address this fundamental, but hitherto largely unexplored, area.

REFERENCES

Aaronson, N. K., Acquadro, C., Alonso, J., Apolone, G., Bucquet, D., Bullinger, M., Bungay, K., Fukuhara, S., Gandek, B., Keller, S., Razavi, S., Sanson-Fisher, R., Sullivan, M., Wood-Dauphinee, S., Wagner, A. and Ware, J. E. (1992) International quality of life assessment (IQOLA) project. *Quality of Life Research* **1**, 349–351.

Bergner, M. (1989) Quality of life, health status and clinical research. *Medical Care* **27**, S148–S156.

Bowling, A. (1991) *Measuring Health: A Review of Quality of Life Measurement Scales*. Buckingham: Open University Press.

Bowling, A. (1995) *Measuring Disease*. Buckingham: Open University Press.

Brazier, J. E., Harper, R., Jones, N. M. B., O'Cathain, A., Thomas, K. J., Usherwood, T. and Westlake, L. (1992) Validating the SF-36 health survey questionnaire: new outcome measure for primary care. *British Medical Journal* **305**, 160–164.

Brooks, R. G. (1995) *Health Status Measurement: A Perspective on Change*. London, Macmillan.

Fallowfield, L. (1990) *The Quality of Life*. London: Souvenir.

Fitzpatrick, R., Ziebland, S., Jenkinson, C., Mowat, A. and Mowat, A. (1993) A Comparison of the Sensitivity to Change of Several Health Status Measures in Rheumatoid Arthritis. *Journal of Rheumatology* **20**, 429–436.

Hayes, V., Morris, J., Wolfe, C. and Morgan, M. (1995) The SF-36 Health Survey Questionnaire: Is it suitable for use with older adults. *Age and Ageing* **24**, 120–125.

Jenkinson, C. (ed.) (1994) *Measuring Health and Medical Outcomes*. London: UCL Press.

Jenkinson, C., Carrol, D., Egerton, M., Frankland, T., McQuay, H. and Nagle, C. (1995) Comparison of the sensitivity to change of long and short form pain measures. *Quality of Life Research* **4**, 303–357.

Jenkinson, C., Lawrence, K., McWhinnie, D. and Gordon, J. (1995) Sensitivity to Change of Health Status Measures in a Randomized Controlled Trial: Comparison of the COOP Charts and the SF-36. *Quality of Life Research* **4**, 47–52.

Jenkinson, C., Peto, V. and Coulter, A. (1996) Making sense of ambiguity: An Evaluation of the internal reliability and face validity of the SF-36 in patients presenting with menorrhagia. *Quality in Health Care* **5**, 9–12.

Kazis, L. E., Anderson, J. J. and Meenan, R. F. (1989) Effect size statistics for interpreting changes in health status. *Medical Care* **27** (Supplement): S178–S189.

Kraus, N. (1991) The InterStudy Quality Edge, Volume 1, Number 1. Excelsior, MN: InterStudy.

Landgraf, J., Nelson, E., and the Dartmouth COOP Primary Care Network. (1992) Summary of the WONCA/COOP international health assessment field trial. *Australian Family Physician* **21**, 269.

McDowell, I. and Newell, C. (1996) Measuring Health: A Guide to Rating Scales and Questionnaires, Second Edition. New York: Oxford University Press.

McHorney, C. A., Ware, J. E. and Raczek, A. E. (1993) The MOS 36-Item Short-Form Health Survey (SF-36): II. Psychometric and Clinical Tests of Validity in Measuring Physical and Mental Health Constructs. *Medical Care* **31**, 247–63.

Nelson, E., Wasson, J., Johnson, D. and Hays, R. (1996) Dartmouth COOP functional health assessment charts: brief measures of clinical practice. In *Quality of Life and Pharmacoeconomics in Clinical Trials*, B. Spilker (ed.) Philadelphia: Lippincott-Raven.

Nelson, E. C., Landgraf, J. M., Hays, R. D., Wasson, J. H. and Kirk, J. W. (1990) The Functional Status of Patients: How can it be Measured in Physicians' Offices? *Medical Care* **28**, 1111–26.

O'Boyle, C. A., McGee, H., Hickey, A., O'Malley, K. and Joyce, C. R. B. (1992) Individual quality of life in patients undergoing hip replacement. *Lancet* **339**, 1088–91.

Rowan, K. (1994) Global questions and scores. In *Measuring Health and Medical Outcomes*. C. Jenkinson (ed.) London: UCL Press.

Ruta, D. and Garratt, A. Health status to quality of life. In *Measuring Health and Medical Outcomes*, C. Jenkinson (ed.) London: UCL Press.

Ruta, D., Garratt, A., Leng, M., Russell, I. T. and MacDonald, L. (1994) A new approach to the measurement of quality of life: The Patient Generated Index. *Medical Care* **32**, 1109–1123.

Stewart, S. R. and Rosser, R. M. (eds) (1988) *Quality of Life: Assessment and Application*. Lancaster: MTP.

Stewart, S. R. and Rosser, R. M. (eds) (1993) *Quality of Life: Key Issues in the 1990's*. London: Kluwer.

Streiner, D. L. and Norman, G. R. (1989) *Health Measurement Scales: A Practical Guide to their Development and Use*. Oxford: Oxford University Press.

Teeling Smith, G. (1983) *Measuring the Social Benefits of Medicine*. London: Office of Health Economics.

Ware, J. and Sherbourne, C. (1992) The MOS 36-Item Short-Form Health Survey 1: Conceptual Framework and Item Selection. *Medical Care* **30**, 473–483.

Ware, J. E. (1993) Measuring Patients' Views: The Optimum Outcome Measure. SF36: A Valid, Reliable Assessment of Health from the Patient's Point of View. *British Medical Journal* **306**, 1429–1430.

Ware, J. E., Snow, K., Kosinski, M. and Gandek, B. (1993) *SF-36 Health Survey: Manual and Interpretation Guide*. Boston: The Health Institute, New England Medical Center.

Ware, J. E., Snow, K. K., Kosinski, M. and Gandek, B. (1993) *SF-36 Health Survey: Manual and Interpretation Guide*. Boston: The Health Institute.

Wasson, J., Keller, A., Rubenstein, L., Hays, R., Nelson, E., Johnson, D., and the Dartmouth Primary Care COOP Project. (1992) Benefits and obstacles of health status assessment in ambulatory settings: the clinician's point of view. *Medical Care* **30,** Supplement, MS42–MS49.

Wilkin, D., Hallam, L. and Doggett, M. (1992) *Measures of Need and Outcome for Primary Health Care*. Oxford: Oxford University Press.

Wright, L., Harwood, D. and Coulter, A. (1992) Health and Lifestyle in the Oxford Region. Oxford: Health Services Research Unit, University of Oxford.

Ziebland, S., Fitzpatrick, R. and Jenkinson, C. (1992) Comparison of Two Approaches to Measuring Change in Health Status in Rheumatoid Arthritis: The Health Assessment Questionnaire (HAQ) and the Modified HAQ. *Annals of the Rheumatic Diseases* **51,** 1202–1205.

8. INDIVIDUALISING QUESTIONNAIRES

YVES LACASSE, ERIC WONG and GORDON H. GUYATT

This chapter examines the use of individualised questionnaires as evaluative health status measurement instruments; those designed to measure longitudinal changes within persons over time. We review the measurement properties required of an evaluative instrument. We emphasise the limitations and pitfalls of individualised questionnaires in a discriminative role, to detect cross-sectional differences between persons at a single point in time. The Chronic Respiratory Disease Questionnaire illustrates the applications of individualised health status measurement instruments and offers the opportunity to compare properties of both "fixed" and "self-generated" items within the same disease-specific questionnaire.

INTRODUCTION

Assessment of quality of life has gained wider recognition in the medical community over the last decade, mainly in clinical trials. However, defining "Quality of life" remains a difficult task as demonstrated by a survey of the dimensions assessed by a representative group of quality of life instruments, which ranged from burden of symptoms to social functioning (McSweeny and Creer, 1995). Whatever the instrument, the concept of quality of life has consistently referred to the performance in at least one of four domains: (1) physical and occupational function, (2) psychological state, (3) social interaction, and (4) somatic sensation (Schipper, Clinch and Powell, 1990).

Two definitions of quality of life best apply to the intent of individualised questionnaires. Calman (1984) stated that quality of life pertains to the difference between the patients' expectation and what they can actually achieve. Schipper et al. (1990) added that quality of life represents the functional effect of an illness and its therapy upon a patient, as he perceives it. The term "health related quality of life" is often used when widely valued aspects of life not directly related to health, such as income and freedom, are not considered (Guyatt, Feeny and Patrick, 1993).

A questionnaire designed to measure quality of life may contain individualised items, items that are selected by the patient. Individualised questionnaires may be particularly useful in situations where respondents are at opposite extremes of the disease spectrum, and may therefore have very different limitations. For example, in chronic lung disease, patients with mild disease may be able to do vigorous activities whereas patients with severe disease may be able to perform only basic care activities. Important differences in approach in individualising questionnaires exist among the investigators who have adopted this technique, depending on whether they intend to measure overall quality of life or health-related quality of life. In the Schedule for the Evaluation of Individual Quality of Life (O'Boyle, McGee, Hickey, O'Malley and Joyce: see Chapter 10), patients are asked to list the five areas (domains) of life that they judge to be most important to their overall quality of life, without any specific reference to their medical condition. In the Patient-Generated Index (Ruta, Garratt, Leng et al., 1994; see Chapter 9), patients are asked to think of the different areas or activities (domains or items) of their lives that have been affected by their health condition. In the Chronic Respiratory Disease Questionnaire (Guyatt, Berman, Townsend et al., 1987a), patients are asked to think of the activities (items) performed during the last two weeks that have made them feel short of breath. The focus of each of these individualised questionnaires is thus different and might affect their measurement properties.

Proper clinical use of an individualised questionnaire must be put in the context of the three broad categories of potential applications of health status measures: discrimination, evaluation, and prediction (Kirshner and Guyatt, 1985). A discriminative instrument is one which can distinguish between groups of patients. An evaluative instrument is one that measures changes in individuals or groups over time. A predictive instrument classifies individuals or groups into categories as defined by a gold[1] or criterion standard. The requirements for maximising any one of the functions of discrimination, prediction, or evaluation may impede the others (Kirshner and Guyatt, 1985). This observation constitutes the thesis of this chapter: our objective is to describe the use and limitations of individualised questionnaires as evaluative and discriminative instruments.

INDIVIDUALISED QUESTIONNAIRES AS EVALUATIVE INSTRUMENTS

Evaluation is a longitudinal process aimed most often at the quantification of treatment benefits after clinical interventions (Kirshner and Guyatt, 1985). The ability of a questionnaire to detect small but important change in any aspect of a patient's quality of life has been referred to as itˢ "responsiveness". Because disease-specific questionnaires focus on the areas of function that are relevant to a particular condition, they are more likely to be responsive to small but important changes (Feeny, Guyatt and Patrick, 1991).

Over the last few years, a number of evaluative instruments have been developed at McMaster University, most of them in a disease-specific context: chronic lung disease (Guyatt et al., 1987a), breast cancer (Levine, Guyatt, Gent et al., 1988), heart failure (Guyatt, Nogradi, Halcrow et al., 1989b), inflammatory bowel disease (Guyatt, Mitchell, Irving et al., 1989a), rhinoconjunctivitis (Juniper and Guyatt, 1991), asthma (Juniper, Guyatt, Epstein et al., 1992) and myocardial infarction (Hillers, Guyatt, Oldridge et al., 1994). For the purpose of each of these instruments, the major issue in selecting items has been that patient status is likely to change after an

---

[1] See Chapter 16

appropriate intervention (Kirshner and Guyatt, 1985). Individualisation of items in at least one domain of four of these questionnaires has best served this purpose (Guyatt et al., 1987a; Guyatt et al., 1989a; Juniper et al., 1991; Juniper et al., 1992). We shall refer to the Chronic Respiratory Disease Questionnaire (CRQ; Guyatt et al., 1987a) along with some other selected instruments in order to illustrate our thesis.

The Chronic Respiratory Disease Questionnaire (CRQ)

The CRQ is an interviewer-administered instrument that measures patients' dyspnoea, fatigue, emotional function and mastery (the extent to which they feel they can cope with the disease and its manifestations). Only the dyspnoea domain is individualised; that is, patients choose five activities during which they experience shortness of breath, and which they perceive as important in their daily lives. During the development of the CRQ, the decision to individualise the dyspnoea dimension was based on the observation that the items varied significantly depending on age, gender and level of disability of the patients (Guyatt, Townsend, Berman et al., 1987c). Therefore, to make this dimension applicable to a broad array of respondents suffering from chronic lung disease of varying severity, patients are asked to identify the activities that make them short of breath. To aid in the identification process, the interviewer asks the patients to list those activities associated with shortness of breath which they perform regularly and are important to them in their day-to-day lives. A list of 23 activities is given as an aid. The five most important activities are included in the dyspnoea dimension, and the patients rate each activity on a 7 point scale (see Appendix).

In the other 3 dimensions, the questions are in the traditional "fixed" format. Each domain includes 4–7 items and each item is scored on a scale of 1–7 (for example: Extremely short of breath; Very short of breath;...Not at all short of breath). To measure change in health status, the items first selected by the patients in the dyspnoea domain are presented and scored on the same 7-point scale. The questionnaire can be administered with respondents aware (the "informed" condition) or unaware (the "blind" condition) of their previous responses. Results from one observational study (Guyatt, Berman, Townsend et al., 1985c) and one randomized trial (Guyatt, Townsend, Keller et al., 1989c) suggest that informed administration may enhance the questionnaire's measurement properties.

Face and Content Validity

The item selection process is important to ensure both face and content validity of a questionnaire. Face validity refers to the capacity of an instrument to measure what it is intended to measure as it is perceived by its users. Since its development, the CRQ has been used in over 20 clinical trials in patients with chronic lung diseases. It has also been translated into different languages for use in clinical trials. This suggests that clinicians have accepted CRQ as a useful evaluative measure for chronic lung disease and suggests that the instrument meets criteria for face validity.

Content validity refers to the comprehensiveness with which an instrument represents the domain which it is intended to measure. Accordingly, items must reflect areas that are important to patients and should be derived from what patients say about how the illness affects their lives (Guyatt, Bombardier and Tugwell, 1986). Asking patients what problems they experience most frequently, and are most important in their daily lives, has proved useful in many respects, mainly in maximising content validity of the questionnaire. Individualisation of items guarantees their importance to every participant in the study.

Longitudinal Construct Validity

For an evaluative instrument, validity is demonstrated by showing that correlations of change in different measures conform with what would be expected if the instrument under study is measuring what it is supposed to measure (Kirshner and Guyatt, 1985). In the absence of a reference standard, the validation process requires a series of predictions about how changes in instrument score should correlate with changes in other related measures (Guyatt et al., 1986). If the observed correlations do not conform to *a priori* predictions, either the instrument being tested is not valid or the investigator's understanding of the independent measures is imperfect (Juniper et al., 1992).

To test the longitudinal construct validity of CRQ, twenty-eight patients with COPD entering a multidisciplinary respiratory rehabilitation programme completed the questionnaire before and after the intervention. The CRQ was administered as one part of a series of physiological and health status measures. *A priori* predictions were generated about how closely changes in each of these measures would correlate with changes in the four domains of the CRQ. Results are presented in Table 8.1.

Table 8.1 Longitudinal construct validity : correlations between Chronic Respiratory Disease Questionnaire (CRQ) dimensions and other measurements #

	CRQ dyspnoea	CRQ fatigue	CRQ emotional function
Walk test	**0.46***	**0.35***	0.19
Patient global rating dyspnoea	**0.37***	**0.62***	0.37*
Patient global rating fatigue	**0.36***	**0.42***	0.27
Patient global rating emotional function	0.35*	**0.36***	**0.35***

*   p<0.05.

Bold type indicates that moderate correlation was anticipated.
From Guyatt, G. H., Berman, L. B., Townsend, M., Pugsley, S. O. and Chambers, L. W. (1987) A measure of quality of life for clinical trials in chronic lung disease. *Thorax* **42**, 773–8.

Correlations related to the individualised domain of the questionnaire (the dyspnoea dimension) were not different from those of the "fixed" domains because longitudinal construct validity is evaluated by correlating *within-patient* changes in quality of life scores with *within-patient* changes in other indices.

Signal to Noise Ratio: Responsiveness

Evaluation (as well as discrimination) may be thought of in terms of measurement of "signal" and "noise". In the case of an evaluative instrument, the "signal" is the true change in patients' status over time; the "noise" is the measurement error over which the true difference must be detected (Guyatt, Kirshner and Jaeschke, 1992). An evaluative instrument thus aims at the detection of the true difference over time within patients. Conversely, the purpose of a discriminative instrument is to detect a "signal" which comes from between patients at a point in time. Random within-patient differences over time contribute to "noise".

To be useful, any health status measure should demonstrate a high signal to noise ratio. For evaluative instruments, the term "responsiveness" refers to this ratio; the corresponding term for discriminative instruments is "reliability". Responsiveness is the ability of an instrument to detect real change, even when it is small and is, along with validity, an important property of an evaluative instrument (Guyatt et al., 1993). Demonstrating reliability and the validity is necessary for concluding that a discriminative instrument is useful; the validity and responsiveness of an evaluative instrument must be demonstrated before it can be used with confidence (Kirshner and Guyatt, 1985).

Individualisation of questionnaires maximises responsiveness mainly because (1) it taps important areas related to perceived change in health status (high content validity); (2) consequently, it facilitates the detection of the "signal"; and (3) it minimises, and may eliminate floor- and ceiling-effects. Proper item scaling is also important to ensure responsiveness.

Ceiling and floor effects: "Ceiling effect" refers to the situation in which patients with the best score on a health status measure may nevertheless have significant quality of life impairment which is open to further improvement over time; "floor effect" refers to that in which patients with the worst score may deteriorate further (Guyatt et al., 1993; Ganiats, Palinkas, and Kaplan, 1992; Bindman, Keane and Lurie, 1990).

To illustrate the concepts of ceiling and floor effects and how they can be avoided by individualising questionnaires, let us consider Patients A and B who both suffer from moderate chronic obstructive pulmonary disease, but perceive differently the effect of their disease. They are both subjected to a trial of oral theophylline, a bronchodilator drug. Two questionnaires (one with "fixed" items, the other with "self-generated" items) are administered before and after the intervention. The first questionnaire containing "fixed" items asks, among others, how short of breath climbing stairs makes them. Even before getting the treatment, Patient A was not bothered by climbing stairs (Not at all short of breath). However, oral theophylline benefits Patient A during vigorous activities, but he keeps answering "Not at all short of breath" when asked after the trial about climbing stairs — a ceiling effect.

In contrast, Patient B perceives dyspnoea differently and claims that climbing stairs has made him "Extremely short of breath" for years. As a side effect, theophylline provokes atrial fibrillation leading to heart failure in this patient. When asked again, Patient B remains "Extremely short of breath" while climbing stairs, even though his condition has worsened — a floor effect.

The second questionnaire is an individualised one. Both patients are asked to select dyspnoea-generating activities which they do frequently and which are important in their day-to-day life. Patient A selects "running" as an activity, and Patient B, "having a bath". Both grade their shortness of breath as "moderate". Improvement of Patient A and deterioration of Patient B are thus both likely to be captured on the second administration of the questionnaire.

Item scaling: For an evaluative index to be successful, it must be able to register any clinically important change. Self-generated items are not sufficient to ensure responsiveness, for inappropriate choice of item scaling may compromise the instrument's responsiveness. 'Yes-no' questions must be avoided since the only way of appreciating any change in health status is to make it perfect: no room is left for in-between situations, in which the symptom associated with the item has improved but not disappeared. Multi-item ordinal scales or visual analogue scales best serve this purpose. Visual analogue and 7-point scales have shown comparable responsiveness as methods to present response options (Guyatt, Townsend, Berman et al., 1987b; Jaeschke, Singer and Guyatt, 1990).

Selected Examples

Responsiveness of CRQ in respiratory rehabilitation trials: comprehensive respiratory rehabilitation programmes that include exercise therapy and psychological support improve exercise capacity without any change in expiratory flow rates. Health-related quality of life has been measured in some trials using a variety of health-status indices, including the CRQ. Table 8.2 presents the experience with the CRQ in selected trials of respiratory rehabilitation.

In general, the CRQ has proved responsive in detecting rehabilitation effects, not only in uncontrolled before-after studies but also in randomised control trials. Rehabilitation programmes have generally led to small to moderately important changes in health-related quality of life. Even with small sample sizes, the CRQ was able to exclude chance as an explanation of the differences.

In only one trial of rehabilitation did the CRQ fail to detect a difference between treatment and control (Busch and McClements, 1988). In this study of a 6-week duration home-based rehabilitation programme, the investigators used the dyspnoea domain of the CRQ as the sole health status index. Seven patients in each of the rehabilitation and conventional community care group

Table 8.2 Chronic Respiratory Disease Questionnaire (CRQ) in selected respiratory rehabilitation trials

Reference	Design/ length of folow-up	Sample size	Use of CRQ and statistical handling	Results
Busch and McClements, 1988	Randomised controlled trial, 18 weeks	Treatment: 7 Control: 7	Dyspnoea domain of CRQ only; Non-parametric analysis of variance	No change in dyspnoea during the activities of daily living
Simpson, Killian, McCartney et al., 1992	Randomised controlled trial, 8 weeks	Treatment: 14 Control: 14	Four domains of the CRQ considered separately; two-way analysis of variance with repeated measures	Significant effect of treatment in the dyspnoea domain
Wijkstra, van Altena, Kraan et al., 1994b	Randomised controlled trial, 12 weeks	Treatment: 28 Control: 15	Four domains of the CRQ considered separately; unpaired t-test between the changes in both groups	Change between groups for the dyspnoea domain is statistically significant
Goldstein, Gort, Stubbing et al., 1994	Randomised controlled trial, 24 weeks	Treatment: 40 Control: 40	Four domains of the CRQ considered separately; unpaired t-test between the changes in both groups	Change between groups for the dyspnoea domain is statistically significant

completed the trial. As for any negative trial, explanations include the treatment not working, the outcome measure not being responsive, or the study, by virtue of its sample size, not being powerful enough to detect an underlying treatment effect. Given the positive results of all the other trials, the very small sample size seems the most likely explanation in this study.

Head-to-head comparison: The ability of the dyspnoea dimension of the CRQ to measure change over time was examined in a controlled trial of inhaled salbutamol and oral theophylline (two bronchodilator drugs) in 24 patients with chronic obstructive pulmonary disease (Guyatt, Townend, Keller et al., 1989c) and compared to two established instruments which measure dyspnoea in chronic lung diseases: the Oxygen Cost Diagram (OCD) (McGavin, Artvinli and Naoe, 1978) and the Medical Research Council dyspnoea questionnaire as modified by the Rand Corporation (the Rand Instrument) (Rosenthal, Lohr, Rubenstein et al., 1981). The OCD is a 10 cm line with day-to-day activities placed along the line in proportion to their required oxygen uptake. Patients are asked to mark the line at the level of activity they can undertake without limiting breathlessness. The Rand Instrument categorizes patients according to whether they are dyspneic on dressing, walking at their own pace, walking with others, and climbing stairs.

To explore the validity of the three instruments, a regression analysis was used to determine their ability to predict patients' global rating of change in

Table 8.3 Results of regressions of functional status measures (Chronic Respiratory Disease Questionnaire, Oxygen Cost Diagram and Rand Instrument) on a global rating of change in dyspnoea

	Order of entry			
	Rand, CRQ	CRQ, Rand	OCD, CRQ	CRQ, OCD
Global rating of change in dyspnoea	$F(1, 46)=90.7$ $p < 0.001$	$F(1, 46)=1.24$ $p > 0.25$	$F(1, 46)=99.1$ $p < 0.001$	$F(1, 46)=0.10$ n.s.

F and p represent the statistical significance of the additional variance explained when the second variable is added to the first in an attempt to predict outcome.
Adapted from Guyatt, G. H., Townsend, M., Keller, J. L., Singer, J. and Nogradi, S. (1989) Measuring functional status in chronic lung disease: conclusions from a randomised controlled trial. *Respir Med* **83**, 293–7.

dyspnoea. In succession, each of the three measures was entered first into the regression, and whether the other instruments explained additional variance was determined (Table 8.3). In each case, the additional variance explained when the CRQ dyspnoea score was added to the other instrument in an attempt to predict outcome was statistically significant, suggesting superior validity for the CRQ.

INDIVIDUALISED QUESTIONNAIRES AS DISCRIMINATIVE INSTRUMENTS

A discriminative instrument is one which can distinguish between groups of patients; for instance, to determine which patients have more severe dyspnoea on daily activities, and which have less severe dyspnoea. To be useful, a discriminative instrument must be reliable and valid. Reliability and validity of individualised questionnaires have been the focus of much controversy. The following discussion aims at the clarification of this situation.

Signal to Noise Ratio: Reliability

Reliability is the ability of the instrument to consistently discriminate among more disabled and less disabled patients. In this case, the signal is the between-patient difference, and the noise, the within-patient difference. In the simplest form of reliability assessment, Pearson's correlation coefficient fails to take into account variability in results attributable to systematic differences in test scores (Kramer and Feinstein, 1981). Reliability is thus best measured by an intraclass correlation coefficient that examines the ratio of the variability between patients (the signal) to the total variability (the noise — that is, the variability within patients over time — and the signal).

Investigations also sometimes look at an instrument's internal consistency, the extent to which different items in an instrument are measuring the same thing. The higher the correlation between items (and thus the higher the chosen statistic, often Cronbach's alpha), the greater the internal consistency (Kramer and Feinstein, 1981).

The reliability and internal consistency of individualised questionnaires or domains are likely to be low in comparison to traditional questionnaires with "fixed" questions because of the tendency to use mid-range responses. Consider the dyspnoea domain of the CRQ: patients are asked to "think of the activities that you have done during the last 2 weeks that have made you feel short of breath. These should be activities which you do frequently and which are important in your day-to-day lives". Thus, a wide spectrum of activities, regardless of the work-load associated with them, will be chosen,

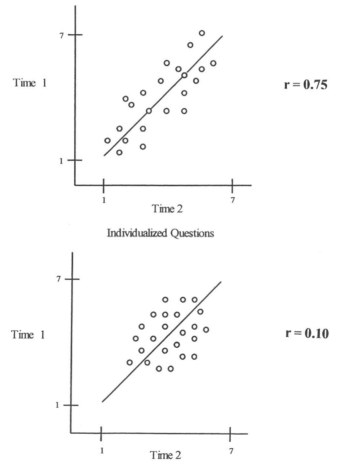

Figure 8.1 Consequence of self-generated items on test-retest reliability of a questionnaire: (a) high between-subject variance and low within-subject variance lead to high reliability as expressed by a Pearson's coefficient of correlation; (b) low between-subject variance and high within-subject variance lead to lower reliability.

so that each respondent will answer a different set of questions. Since patients are asked to choose activities that make them short of breath, it is likely that one end of the 7-point scale ("Not at all short of breath — a little shortness of breath") will be under-represented in their selection of answers. Similarly, since patients are asked to choose activities that they are still able to undertake, it is likely that the other end of the 7-point scale ("Extremely short of breath") will also be under-represented. Consequently, the between-patient variance in scores will be diminished (Figure 8.1). The low test-retest reliability and internal consistency is thus a direct and predictable consequence of the self-generated items of the dyspnoea dimension.

The numerator of the reliability coefficient (the between-patient difference) is not, however, relevant to either the longitudinal validity or the responsiveness of an individualised questionnaire. Therefore, the usual methods of quantifying reliability are not appropriate for the evaluative role of a questionnaire. The low reliability of individualised questionnaires reflects a limited ability to discriminate between patients, but does not bear on their ability to measure within-patient change over time.

To further clarify this matter, consider an hypothetical situation where four new instruments (A, B, C and D) have been developed with an evaluative purpose. All four questionnaires yield a single score on a 0–20 scale. Prior to using them, an investigator decides to measure their reliability, administering them to eight stable patients two weeks apart. Then, eight patients are randomly submitted to an intervention of known efficacy: half of the group (patients 1 to 4) receive the active drug; the other half (patients 5 to 8) receive placebo. The four questionnaires are readministered after the trial. Results are presented in Table 8.4.

Instrument A is not reliable but is responsive to change. Instrument B is reliable but not responsive. Instrument C is hopeless: it shows neither reliability nor responsiveness. Instrument D shows both reliability and responsiveness. These selected examples represent extreme situations. However, it is apparent that conventional measurement of reliability that relates between-person variance to total variance may be misleading if one forgets the different requirements of an evaluative and a discriminative instrument.

These theoretical concepts have been verified in clinical conditions. Wijkstra et al. (1994a) administered the CRQ to 40 patients with stable chronic obstructive pulmonary disease two days apart. Cronbach's coefficient alpha was used in order to assess internal consistency of the four domains of the questionnaire. Cronbach's coefficient alpha greater than 0.7 was taken as acceptable. Test-retest reliability of each domain was then also investigated by the Spearman-Brown reliability coefficient p; p greater than 0.7 was also considered as reliable. Test-retest reliability was found to be good (>0.7) for all four domains of the CRQ, though substantially lower for dyspnoea than for the other three domains (dyspnoea: 0.73; fatigue: 0.90; emotion: 0.93; mastery: 0.91). Internal consistency was however found to be unacceptable

Table 8.4 Reliability and responsiveness: assessing the usefulness of evaluative instruments (see text for details)

Instrument A	Time 1	Time 2	Intervention	Time 3	Difference score
Subject 1	8	9		15	+6
Subject 2	9	8		15	+7
Subject 3	8	9		15	+6
Subject 4	9	8		15	+7
Subject 5	8	9		8	−1
Subject 6	9	8		9	+1
Subject 7	8	9		8	−1
Subject 8	9	8		9	+1

Instrument B	Time 1	Time 2	Intervention	Time 3	Difference score
Subject 1	5	5		5	0
Subject 2	9	9		9	0
Subject 3	7	7		7	0
Subject 4	11	11		11	0
Subject 5	5	5		5	0
Subject 6	9	9		9	0
Subject 7	7	7		7	0
Subject 8	11	11		11	0

Instrument C	Time 1	Time 2	Intervention	Time 3	Difference score
Subject 1	8	9		9	0
Subject 2	9	8		8	0
Subject 3	8	9		9	0
Subject 4	9	8		8	0
Subject 5	8	9		9	0
Subject 6	9	8		8	0
Subject 7	8	9		9	0
Subject 8	9	8		8	0

Instrument D	Time 1	Time 2	Intervention	Time 3	Difference score
Subject 1	5	5		11	+6
Subject 2	9	9		16	+7
Subject 3	7	7		13	+6
Subject 4	11	11		18	+7
Subject 5	5	5		6	+1
Subject 6	9	9		8	−1
Subject 7	7	7		8	+1
Subject 8	11	11		10	−1

Adapted from Guyatt, G., Walter, S. and Norman, G. (1987) Measuring change over time: assessing the usefulness of evaluative instruments. *J Chron Dis* **40**, 171–8.

for the dyspnoea dimension (Cronbach's coefficient alpha: 0.51 and 0.53 on successive administration of the questionnaire), while Cronbach's coefficient alpha for all other domains was greater than 0.7 (ranging from 0.71 to 0.88). The authors made the incorrect conclusion that the dyspnoea domain of the CRQ should not be used. The conclusion that it should not have been used as a discriminative measure is reasonable; to suggest that these results demonstrate that the dyspnoea domain as an outcome in clinical trials should not be used is unreasonable.

Concurrent Validity

According to the previous considerations, individualised questionnaires may not necessarily be valid instruments for discriminative purposes. This defect is built into the design of the questionnaire. When patients are asked to choose items which affect them most significantly, those with less severe disabilities will choose different items from those who are more severely affected. However, the response option they assign to the items may be identical.

An example: concurrent validity of the CRQ:- Wijkstra et al. (1994a) administered a Dutch translation of the CRQ and Symptom Checklist (SCL-90) to 40 patients with chronic obstructive pulminary disease participating in a rehabilitation programme on the day of admission to hospital and repeated them one day later. The Cronbach's alpha for the anxiety, depression, somatisation, obsessive-compulsiveness, sensitivity, and sleeping disturbances dimensions of SCL-90 were good (ranging from 0.73 to 0.85). These dimensions were related to the four dimensions of CRQ. Moderate, statistically significant cross-sectional correlations (0.40 to 0.55) were seen between fatigue, emotional function and mastery domains of CRQ with anxiety, depression and somatisation domains of SCL-90. On this evidence, CRQ has again shown construct validity with 3 of the 4 domains having discriminative ability (Table 8.5).

Table 8.5 Pearson correlation coefficient between the dimensions of the Chronic Respiratory Disease Questionnaire (CRQ) and comparable dimensions of the Symptom Checklist (SCL-90)

CRQ	SCL-90			
	Anxiety	Depression	Somatisation	Sensitivity
Dyspnoea	–	–	0.09	–
Fatigue	–	0.53**	0.55**	–
Emotion	0.50**	0.49**	0.52**	0.24
Mastery	−0.55**	−0.48**	−0.40*	−0.27

* $p < 0.01$;** $p < 0.001$.
From Wijkstra, P. J., Tenvergert, E. M., VanAltena, R., Otten, V., Postma, D. S., Kraan, J. and Koëter, G.H., (1994a) Reliability and Validity of the chronic respiratory questionnaire (CRQ). *Thorax* **49**, 465–7.

Given what has been said, it is not surprising that the dyspnoea domain did not show discriminative ability. A possible reason was that the domains of SCL-90 did not measure anything related to dyspnoea at all. Even if they did, the results showing low cross-sectional correlations would be anticipated.

CONCLUSION

The required measurement properties of any evaluative or discriminative health status measurement instrument are encompassed within two major concepts: validity and high signal to noise ratio. Because they focus on specific and important aspects of the patient's quality of life, individualised health status measurement instruments are likely to demonstrate high content validity. As a consequence, individualised questionnaires have the potential to serve as powerful evaluative health-status indices. The signal to noise ratio of an evaluative instrument (responsiveness) assesses the extent to which the instrument is able to detect true within-patient difference over and above within-patient differences not related to true within-patient change. Reliability, which relates between-patient variance to total variance, may be misleading when applied to individualised instruments, because detection of between-patient differences is not relevant to the evaluative role of the questionnaire. It is possible for an instrument to be responsive but not reliable; conversely, an instrument may show poor responsiveness but high reliability. Proper use of evaluative, individualised, disease-specific questionnaires is gaining wider acceptance as appropriate outcome measures in clinical trials and should serve both clinicians and patients in focusing on important aspects of quality of life and allowing more efficient measurement of outcomes in clinical trials.

REFERENCES

Bindman, A. B., Keane, D. and Lurie, N. (1990) Measuring health changes among severely ill patients. The floor phenomenon. *Medical Care* **28**,1142–52.

Busch, A. J. and McClements, J. D. (1988) Effects of a supervised home exercise program for patients with chronic obstructive pulmonary disease. *Physical Therapy* **68**, 469–74.

Calman, K. C. (1984) Quality of life in cancer patients — an hypothesis. *Journal of Medical Ethics* **53**, 2316–23.

Feeny, D., Guyatt, G. H. and Patrick, D. L. (1991) Proceedings of the International Conference on Quality of Life as an Outcome in Clinical Trials. *Controlled Clin Trials* **12**, 79S–280S.

Ganiats, T. G., Palinkas, L. A. and Kaplan, R. M. (1992) Comparison of Quality of Well-Being Scale and Functional Status Index in patients with atrial fibrillation. *Medical Care* **30**, 958–64.

Goldstein, R. S., Gort, E. H., Stubbing, D., et al. (1994) Randomised controlled trial of respiratory rehabilitation. *Lancet* **344**, 1394–7.

Guyatt, G. H., Berman, L. B., Townsend, M., Pugsley, S. O. and Chambers L. W. (1987a) A measure of quality of life for clinical trials in chronic lung disease. *Thorax* **42**, 773–8.

Guyatt, G. H., Berman, L. B., Townsend, M. and Taylor, D. W. (1985a) Should study subjects see their previous responses? *Journal of Chronic Diseases* **38**, 1003–7.

Guyatt, G. H., Bombardier, C. and Tugwell, T. X. (1986) Measuring disease-specific quality of life in clinical trials. *Canadian Medical Association Journal* **134**, 889–95.

Guyatt, G. H., Feeny, D. H. and Patrick, D. L. (1993) Measuring health-related quality of life. *Annals of Internal Medicine* **118**, 622–9.

Guyatt, G. H., Kirshner, B. and Jaeschke, R. (1992) Measuring health status: what are the necessary measurement properties? *Journal of Clinical Epidemiology* **45**, 1341–5.

Guyatt, G. H., Mitchell, A., Irving, E. J., Singer, J., Goodacre, R. and Tomkins, C. (1989a) A new measure of health status for clinical trials in inflammatory bowel disease. *Gastroenterology* **96**, 804–10.

Guyatt, G. H., Nogradi, S., Halcrow, S., Singer, J., Sullivan, M. J. J. and Fallen, E. L. (1989b) Development and testing of a new measure of health status for clinical trials in heart failure. *Journal of General Internal Medicine* **4**, 101–7.

Guyatt, G. H., Thompson, P. J., Berman, L. B., Sullivan, M. J., Townsend M., Jones, N. L. and Pugsley, S. O. (1985b). How should we measure function in patients with chronic heart and lung disease? *Journal of Chronic Disease* **38**, 517–24.

Guyatt, G. H., Townsend, M., Berman, L. B. and Keller, J. L. (1987b) A comparison of Likert and visual analogue scales for measuring change in function. *Journal of Chronic Disease* **40**, 1129–33.

Guyatt, G. H., Townsend, M., Berman, L. B. and Pugsley, S.O. (1987c) Quality of life in patients with chronic airflow limitation. *British Journal of Diseases of the Chest* **81**, 45–54.

Guyatt, G. H., Townsend, M., Keller, J. L., Singer, J. and Nogradi, S. (1989c) Measuring functional status in chronic lung disease: conclusions from a randomized control trial. *Respiratory Medicine* **83**, 293–7.

Guyatt, G., Walter, S. and Norman, G. (1987d) Measuring change over time: assessing the usefulness of evaluative instruments. *Journal of Chronic Disease* **40**, 171–8.

Hillers, T. K., Guyatt, G. H., Oldridge, N., Crowe, J., Willan, A., Griffith, L. and Finney, D. (1994) Quality of life after myocardial infarction. *Journal of Clinical Epidemiology* **47**, 1287–96.

Jaeschke, R., Singer, J. and Guyatt, G. H. (1990) A comparison of seven-point and visual analogue scales: data from a randomized trial. *Controlled Clinical Trial* **11**, 43–51.

Juniper, E. F. and Guyatt, G. H. (1991) Development and testing of a new measure of health status for clinical trials in rhinoconjunctivitis. *Clinical and Experimental Allergy* **21**, 77–83.

Juniper, E. F., Guyatt, G. H., Epstein, R. S., Ferrie, P. J., Jaeschke, R. and Hiller, T. K. (1992) Evaluation of impairment of health-related quality of life in asthma: development of a questionnaire for use in clinical trials. *Thorax* **47**, 76–83.

Kirshner, B. and Guyatt, G. (1985) A methodological framework for assessing health indices. *Journal of Chronic Disease* **38**, 27–36.

Kramer M. S. and Feinstein A. R. (1981) Clinical biostatistics. LIV. The biostatistics of concordance. *Clinical Pharmacology and Therapeutics* **29**, 111–23.

Levine, M. N., Guyatt, G. H., Gent, M., DePauw, S. and Goodyear, M. D. (1988) Quality of life in stage II breast cancer: an instrument for clinical trials. *Journal of Clinical Oncology* **6**, 1798–1810.

McGavin, C. R., Artvinli, M. and Naoe, H. (1978) Dyspnoea, disability and distance walked: comparison of estimates of exercise performance in respiratory disease. *British Medical Journal* **2**, 241–3.

McSweeny A. J. and Creer, T. L. (1995) Health-related quality of life assessment in medical care. *Disease-a-Month* **41**, 1–71.

O'Boyle, C. A., McGee, H., Hickey, A., O'Malley, K. and Joyce, C. R. B. (1992) Individual quality of life in patients undergoing hip replacement. *Lancet* **339**, 1088–91.

Rosenthal, M., Lohr, K. N. and Rubenstein, R. S. (1981) *A conceptualization and measurement of physiologic health for adults: Congestive heart failure.* Santa Monica, CA. Rand Corporation.

Ruta, D. A., Garratt, A. W., Leng, M., Russell, I. T. and MacDonald, L. M. (1992) A new approach to the measurement of quality of life: the Patient-Generated Index. *Medical Care* **11**, 1109–26.

Schipper, H., Clinch, J. and Powell, V. (1990) Definitions and conceptual issues. In: *Quality of Life Assessments in Clinical Trials.* Spilker, B. (ed) pp. 11–24. New York: Raven Press.

Simpson, K., Killian, K., McCartney, N., et al. (1992) Randomised controlled trial of weightlifting exercise in patients with chronic airflow limitation. *Thorax* **47**, 70–5.

Wijkstra, P. J., Tenvergert, E. M., VanAltena, R., Otten, V., Postma, D.S., Kraan, J. and Koeter, G. H. (1994a) Reliability and validity of the chronic respiratory questionnaire (CRQ). *Thorax* **49**, 465–7.

Wijkstra, P. J., van Altena, R., Kraan, J., et al. (1994b) Quality of life in patients with chronic obstructive pulmonary disease improves after rehabilitation at home. *Eur Resp J* **7**, 269–73.

APPENDIX

Summary of the Dyspnoea Dimension of the Chronic Respiratory Disease Questionnaire

The questionaire begins by eliciting five activities in which the patient experiences dyspnoea during day to day activities:

1. I would like you to think of the activities that you have done during the last 2 weeks that have made you feel short of breath. These should be activities which you do frequently and which are important in your everyday life. Please list as many activities as you can that you have done during the past 2 weeks which have made you feel short of breath.
[*Circle the number on the answer sheet list adjacent to each activity mentioned. If an activity mentioned is not on the list, write it in, in the respondents own words, in the space provided.*]
   Can you think of any other activities you have done during the past 2 weeks that have made you feel short of breath?
[*Record additional items.*]

2. I will now read a list of activities which make some people with lung problems feel short of breath. I will pause after each item long enough for you to tell me if you have felt short of breath doing that activity during the last 2 weeks, just answer << No >>. The activities are:
[*Read items, omitting those which respondent has volunteered spontaneously. Pause after each item to give respondent a chance to indicate whether he/she has been short*

of breath while performing that activity during the last week. Circle the number adjacent to appropriate items on answer sheet.]

1. Being *angry* or upset
2. Having a *bath* or shower
3. *Bending*
4. *Carrying*, such as carrying groceries
5. *Dressing*
6. *Eating*
7. *Going* for a walk
8. Doing your *housework*
9. *Hurrying*
10. *Lying* flat
11. *Making a bed*
12. *Mopping* or scrubbing the floor
13. *Moving* furniture
14. *Playing* with children or grand children
15. *Playing* sports
16. *Reaching* over your head
17. *Running*, such as for a bus
18. *Shopping*
19. *Talking*
20. *Vacuuming*
21. *Walking* around your own home
22. *Walking* uphill
23. *Walking* upstairs
24. *Walking* with other on level ground
25. *Preparing* meals
26. While trying to *sleep*

[*If more than five items have been listed, the interviewer then helps the subject determine the five activities which are more important in the subject's day to day life.*]

3(a). Of the items which you have listed, which is the most important to you in your day to day life? I will read through the items, and when I am finished I would like you to tell me which is the most important.
[*Read through all items spontaneously volunteered and those from the list which patient mentioned.*]
        Which of these items is most important to you in your day to day life?
[*List them on response sheet.*]
This process is continued until the five most important activities are determined. The interviewer then proceeds to find out how much shortness of breath the subject has experienced during the prior two weeks. Throughout the questionnaires, response options are printed on different colour cards with which the subject is presented.

4. I would now like you to describe how much shortness of breath you have had during the last two weeks while [*Interviewer : insert activity list in 3(a).*] by choosing one of the following options from the card in front of you [*green card*] :

    1. Extremely short of breath
    2. Very short of breath
    3. Quite a bit short of breath
    4. Moderate shortness of breath
    5. Some shortness of breath
    6. A little shortness of breath
    7. Not at all short of breath

This process continues until the subject's degree of dyspnoea on all five of his or her most important activities has been determined.

9. THE PATIENT GENERATED INDEX

ANDREW M. GARRATT and DANNY A. RUTA

This chapter introduces an individualised approach to quality of life assessment and is composed of three sections. In the first, problems with current approaches to measuring quality of life are discussed and an argument is made for a "working" definition of quality of life — the extent to which hopes and expectations are matched by experience. Using this definition as a conceptual base we describe, the developments of a quality of life instrument — the patient generated index (PGI). In the second section, the empirical work that has been undertaken in the development of the PGI is summarised. In the third and final section, we consider the directions for future research in this field.

INTRODUCTION

In recent years measuring health or "quality of life" has received a great deal of attention as an endpoint in clinical and health services research. A review of medical literature that uses the search term "quality of life" between the years 1989–93 will generate some 1500 publications. However, quality of life is frequently used as a blanket term that can cover anything from crude clinical and laboratory markers through to instruments developed using psychometric theory. Recent studies have given greater consideration to instruments based on more sophisticated measurement techniques. However, even these have been criticised for focusing on something much narrower than quality of life (VanDam et al., 1981; Bergner 1989; Siegrist and Junge, 1989).

Such instruments usually measure concepts such as health status or health-related quality of life (HRQL) (Bergner et al., 1981; Hunt et al., 1985; Ware and Sherbourne 1992). Generic instruments, such as the Medical Outcomes Study Short-Form-36 item (SF-36) health survey, the Nottingham Health Profile, and the Sickness Impact Profile, measure HRQL across several dimensions. For example, the SF-36 includes eight dimensions that cover physical functioning, social functioning, role limitations, mental health, energy and fatigue, pain and general health perception (Ware 1992). The choice of these dimensions is predetermined, however, and their relative importance will differ across individuals. Dimensions that are valued highly by some individuals may be of little or no importance to others. These differences are not taken account of in the scores which such instruments generate. Furthermore, they may fail to incorporate aspects of health and functioning that make an important contribution to individual quality of life. To have meaning and relevance to the individual, therefore, a truly valid measure of quality of life must be defined in individual terms. It must focus less on functional disability, and incorporate dimensions or aspects of life that sustain life and hence give it meaning and purpose.

THE PATIENT GENERATED INDEX

In recognising the subjective and individualistic nature of quality of life, Calman (1984) has defined it as "the extent to which our hope and ambitions are matched by experience." We took this definition, which as been used before in clinical research (Cohen 1982; Presant 1984; Dupuis 1988; Nordenfelt 1989), as a conceptual basis for a patient-centred approach to measuring quality of life — the Patient Generated Index (PGI). Our aim was to develop an instrument that could be used to quantify the difference between individual's hopes and expectations and reality in a way that has meaning and relevance in their daily lives. To be useful as an evaluative tool that could be administered routinely to patients the PGI must possess several important attributes:

- It must describe the effect of a condition on those areas of individual patients' lives that they consider to be of greatest importance.
- It must allow individual patients to rate how badly affected they are in areas of their lives impacted by the condition.
- It must be reliable.
- It must be responsive to changes in quality of life and allow individual patients to rate those changes.
- It should be suitable for a wide variety of patients in different settings.
- It should be brief and simple for patients to complete.

ADMINISTRATION OF THE PGI

The PGI is completed in three stages. These are illustrated in Table 9.1, using as an example the responses for a 30 year old man with back pain.

Table 9.1 Stages in the completion of the Patient Generated Index (PGI) for a thirty year old man with low back pain

STAGE 1 Nomination of area or activity affected	STAGE 2 Score out of 100	STAGE 3 Spend your 60 points	Score × Points Columns 2×3
1 Work suffers	10	10/60	1.7
2 Makes me moody	30	10/60	5.0
3 Always thinking	30	5/60	2.5
4 Can't play with kids	50	20/60	16.7
5 My sex life suffers	70	10/60	11.7
6 All other aspects of your life not mentioned above	90	5/60	7.5
		TOTAL	45.1

The first stage asks the patient to list up to five of the most important areas of his life affected by his condition. In the second stage the patient is asked to rate each of these areas on a scale of 0 – 100, where 0 is the worst he can imagine and 100 the best possible he can imagine for himself. To assist recall patients are provided with a trigger list of areas most frequently mentioned by other patients. The patient is also asked to rate how badly affected they are in the remainder of their lives. This can include other areas of their lives affected by the condition but not as important as the other five areas. It can also include areas of life unrelated to their particular condition, or even to their health. In the third and final stage the patient is given 60 'points' to distribute between the different areas to represent the relative importance of potential improvements in the chosen areas. Multiplying the ratings for each of the areas by the proportion of 'points' and summing generates an index between 0 and 100.

The PGI scores of two women suffering from varicose veins, aged 30 and 37 respectively are shown in Figure 9.1. Both patients have the same PGI score of 40, but the Figure serves to highlight the differences in the aspects of their lives affected by varicose veins, the extent to which they are affected as measured by their ratings, and the values that they attach to improving each area as measured by the distribution of the 60 'points'. The two patients share areas, such as "tiredness", but these are affected to a different extent. Patient A give a score of 70 to "tiredness", while patient B gives a score of 40, which suggests that patient B is further from the best she could imagine for herself in this area of her life. They also have different priorities with respect to desired improvements, as indicated by differences in the distribution of 'points' representing potential improvements in the areas affected. Patient A gives all 60 'points' to removing "the aching and bruising of legs" while patient B distributes her 'points' more evenly across her chosen areas.

APPLICATIONS OF THE PGI

The validity, reliability, responsiveness and acceptability of the PGI have been assessed by administering it through a postal questionnaire to patients with one of four common conditions — low back pain, menorrhagia, suspected peptic ulcer and varicose veins — identified in general practices and hospital outpatient departments in North East Scotland (Ruta et al., 1994a; Garratt et al., 1995). The questionnaire was sent out to patients in general practice within two weeks of their initial consultation and to newly referred outpatients before their first appointment. The questionnaire contained, in addition to the PGI, the SF-36 health survey (Ware and Sherbourne 1992), a condition-specific instrument (Garratt, MacDonald, Ruta and Russell, 1993; Ruta et al., 1994; Ruta et al., 1995) and a series of socio-demographic questions.

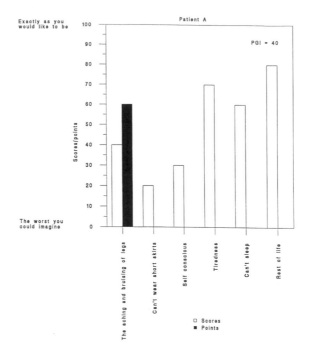

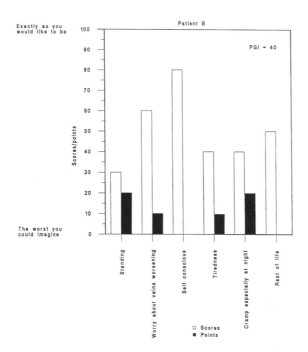

Figure 9.1 Quality of life for two varicose vein patients.

Evidence for the validity and reliability of the SF-36 has been found in United States (McHorney et al., 1992; McHorney et al., 1993) and United Kingdom patient populations (Garratt, Ruta and Abdalla, 1993; Ruta et al., 1994b). The condition-specific instruments were devised from questions commonly used in the clinical assessment of patients. Specific instruments have been developed in response to the need for measures that are responsive to clinically important changes in health-related quality of life. Their restricted focus means that specific instruments have greater potential to detect such changes.

ACCEPTABILITY OF THE PGI

The acceptability of the PGI has been assessed by looking at response rates, assessing response bias and following up patients who had difficulty completing the PGI through a series of interviews. In total, 1746 patients were recruited to the study of whom 1317 returned the questionnaire giving a response rate of 75.5%. These patients all provided responses to the SF-36 or specific instruments, 672 (51%) completed the PGI and 106 (8%) indicated that no areas of their lives were affected by their condition. Stepwise logistic regression (Armitage and Berry, 1987) was used to model the differences between patients who completed the PGI and those who failed to do so. Potential explanatory variables included the scores for the eight scales of the SF-36, patient source and socio-demographic variables. The resulting regression equation in Table 9.2 shows that, after adjusting for confounding variables, seven significant differences were found between patients who completed the PGI and those who failed to complete it.

Those failing to complete the PGI were more likely to: have left full-time education at a younger age; to have a lower score on the SF-36 scale of

Table 9.2 Response analysis: Logistic regression analysis of differences between those completing the PGI correctly and those failing to complete or not attempting the PGI

Variable	Regression coefficient	Standard error	Wald Statistic	Significance	Odds Ratio
Age on leaving full-time education	0.123	0.035	13.969	.001	1.15
Physical functioning	0.014	0.003	17.052	.001	1.01
Role-physical	−0.009	0.002	17.763	.001	0.99
Energy and fatigue	−0.007	0.004	3.957	.047	1.99
Patient divorced	−0.544	0.234	5.378	.020	0.58
Home rented from the council	−0.502	0.158	10.023	.002	0.61
Patient retired	−0.517	0.247	4.393	.036	0.60
(Constant)	−1.328	0.605	4.816	.028	

physical functioning; to have a higher score on the SF-36 scales of role-limitations due to physical problems, energy and fatigue; to be divorced or separated; to live in homes rented from the local authority; and to be retired.

RELIABILITY OF THE PGI

Reliability has been defined as the extent to which measurements on the same individual under different circumstances are similar (Streiner and Norman, 1989). Kirshner and Guyatt (1985) argue that the reliability of instruments intended for evaluative purposes should be assessed by the test-retest method. To this end, patients were sent an additional questionnaire two weeks after they returned the first. This included a question asking patients if their health had changed or stayed the same in the intervening period. For the PGI to be considered reliable there should be a high degree of concordance between the PGI scores for patients whose health remained the same over the two week period. Test-retest reliability was assessed by the intraclass correlation coefficient (Streiner and Norman, 1989) and the distribution of the differences for the two sets of scores (Bland and Altman, 1986). Correlating the two sets of scores for the 148 patients whose health stayed the same produced a reliability coefficient of 0.65 (p < 0.01). The differences between the two sets of scores was approximately normally distributed with a mean of − 0.6 and a standard error of 1.4 (standard deviation 16.6) which produces 95% confidence intervals of −3.3 to 2.1 and −33.2 to 31.9 for group and individual comparisons respectively. These results demonstrate that the PGI is sufficiently reliable for use in group comparisons but is of limited value for comparing individual patients.

VALIDITY OF THE PGI

In the search for evidence for the validity of the PGI, the following question must be asked: is the PGI measuring what it purports to measure: i.e., the gap between expectations and reality in those areas in which subjects most value an improvement? Without a "gold standard" measure of quality of life, this question can never be fully addressed. Validity testing has to be treated as an ongoing process that involves the accumulation of evidence relating the instrument under investigation to variables that might be expected to influence quality of life such as health, employment and marital status.

   In order to assess validity, patients' PGI scores were first correlated with their scores for the eight SF-36 scales and the condition-specific instruments. If the PGI is a valid measure of quality of life then a significant small to moderate correlation might be expected with the measures of HRQL. If the correlations were too high it could be construed that the PGI is simply measuring health and if they were too low it would follow that the PGI was measuring something unrelated to HRQL. In either case the validity of the PGI would be in doubt while in the former the measure would also be redundant.

Further tests of validity were undertaken. If it is hypothesised that patients referred to outpatient clinics are in poorer health than patients managed solely in general practice then lower PGI scores would be expected for referred patients than for those who are not referred. In the study of the four common conditions described above, general practitioners assessed symptom severity on a four point scale (none, mild, moderate and severe). Patients with severe symptoms as assessed by the general practitioner would be expected to have lower PGI scores than those with mild or moderate symptoms. Additional information collected from patients included the use of analgesic medication in the treatment of low back pain and a family history of ulcer disease in patients with suspected peptic ulcer. The occurence of either of these should be reflected in lower PGI scores. Finally, a number of hypothesis were tested in relation to socio-demographic variables: that PGI scores should be lower in female patients; higher in patients owning their own homes; higher in married patients; and lower in unemployed patients.

The correlations between the PGI scores and the measures of health-related quality of life are shown in Table 9.3. Across the four patient groups, the correlations were of a small to moderate magnitude, the largest being for low back pain followed by suspected peptic ulcer, varicose veins and menor-rhagia in descending order.

For the four patient groups highly significant, medium to low, correlations were found with the condition-specific scores, the largest being over 0.4 for

Table 9.3 Validity: Correlations between the PGI scores, the condition-specific scores and eight scales of the SF-36 condition-specific groups

Measure	Low back pain (n=359)	Menorrhagia (n=200)	Suspected peptic ulcer (n=120)	Varicose veins (n=158)
Condition-specific scores	0.42**	0.25**	0.39**	0.30**
SF-36 health profile scores:				
Physical functioning	0.26**	0.13	0.14	0.24*
Social functioning	0.38**	0.29**	0.24*	0.24*
Role-physical	0.27**	0.24**	0.18	0.15
Role-emotional	0.18**	0.20*	0.12	0.32**
Mental Health	0.23**	0.28**	0.24*	0.29**
Energy/fatigue	0.27**	0.23**	0.33**	0.28**
Pain	0.47**	0.29**	0.30**	0.29**
General health perception	0.13*	0.27**	0.39**	0.06

* $p < .01$; ** $p < .001$

low back pain patients. Significant correlations are also found between the PGI and most of the eight scales of the SF-36. For patients with low back pain and menorrhagia, the largest correlations were with the scales of pain and social functioning; for suspected peptic ulcer, with scales of general health perceptions and energy and fatigue; for varicose veins with the scales of role limitations due to emotional problems and pain.

Table 9.4 shows the results of the other tests of validity. In the majority of cases (19 out of 25) the results correspond to the construct, but most fail to achieve statistical significance.

For each of the four patient groups those referred to a specialist have lower PGI scores than those managed within general practice. For patients with low back pain and varicose veins, PGI scores appear to be related to general practitioner ratings of symptom severity for the categories: none, mild and moderate. For patients with low back pain, analgesic use and strength appear to be related to PGI scores. In patients with suspected peptic ulcer, PGI scores appear to be related to the presence of a family history of ulcer disease.

Male patients have higher PGI scores; patients who own their own homes have higher scores than those living in rented accommodation; patients who are single have lower scores than married; and unemployed patients have lower scores than those in work. Although the variables examined appear to be related to the PGI in accordance with certain postulated clinical and social theories or constructs, few of these associations reach statistical significance. These findings may simply reflect small sub-sample sizes, or they may indicate the weakness of the underlying hypothesis.

SENSITIVITY OF THE PGI

Instruments for assessing health outcomes must be responsive or sensitive to clinically important changes. The responsiveness of the PGI was assessed by mailing the four patients groups a follow-up questionnaire at one year. Standardised response means (SRMs), that is the mean change in scores divided by the standard deviation of the score change, allow comparisons of *responsiveness* to be made between instruments (Katz et al., 1992). Higher SRMs indicate greater responsiveness to clinical change, and as a rule of thumb, SRMs of 0.2, 0.5 and 0.8 or above represent small, moderate and large changes respectively (Katz et al., 1992). The sampling distribution of the SRMs was estimated using a jack-knife procedure (Liang et al., 1985). This allowed tests to be carried out for statistically significant differences between the SRMs for the PGI, SF-36 and condition-specific instruments.

Significant improvements in scores at one year for the PGI and the condition-specific instruments are seen for the groups of patients with low back pain, menorrhagia and suspected peptic ulcer (Table 9.5). For patients with low back pain, significant improvements occurred on the SF-36 scales of role-limitations attributed to physical and emotional problems, energy and

Table 9.4 Validity of the PGI: PGI scores for referral, symptom severity, gender, housing, marital status, employment and condition-specific variables

Variable	Low back pain n PGI Score (sd)			Menorrhagia n PGI score (sd)			Peptic ulcer n PGI score (sd)			Varicose veins n PGI score (sd)		
Patient referred:												
No	206	34.7**	(18.8)	47	33.6	(20.0)	62	43.8	(21.3)	29	41.5	(17.4)
Yes	153	29.2	(17.6)	153	30.4	(16.0)	58	38.3	(17.5)	129	39.9	(20.4)
GP severity rating:												
None	6	44.7	(28.8)	0			4	45.2	(34.6)	1	50.0	
Mild	81	37.0	(16.8)	14	33.3	(17.8)	23	43.6	(18.9)	13	46.1	(14.1)
Moderate	103	32.2	(19.1)	30	33.2	(20.6)	29	45.3	(22.7)	21	35.8	(20.9)
Severe	12	36.0	(22.9)	6	33.8	(22.0)	2	43.3	(21.2)	2	(50.4)	(11.2)
Gender:												
Male	191	32.6	(17.4)	—	—	—	75	43.8	(21.4)*	36	48.8	(20.2)**
Female	167	31.9	(19.6)	—	—	—	45	36.7	(15.6)	121	37.8	(19.0)
Housing tenure:												
Self ownership	255	33.4	(17.9)	145	31.9	(16.9)	82	40.9	(20.1)	107	41.3	(20.6)
Rented	104	29.7	(19.7)	55	29.2	(17.4)	34	39.8	(17.6)	48	38.1	(18.1)
Marital Status:												
Married	278	32.6	(18.6)	169	31.1	(31.1)	95	40.8	(19.7)	126	40.6	(19.2)
Single	78	31.4	(17.4)	31	31.9	(31.9)	23	40.8	(19.7)	29	37.6	(22.5)
Patient unemployed:												
No	350	32.4	(18.6)	194	31.3	(17.1)	118	40.8	(19.6)	152	40.5	(19.7)
Yes	8	28.0	(16.4)	6	27.6	(17.7)	0			4	28.0	(21.7)
Analgesic medication:												
Mild-moderate	64	35.9	(21.2)	—	—	—	—	—	—	—	—	—
Moderate-severe	295	31.6	(17.8)									
Analgesic strength[a]:												
Mild-moderate	58	33.1	(18.4)	—	—	—	—	—	—	—	—	—
Moderate-severe	172	30.2	(16.1)									
Family history of ulcer disease:												
No	—	—	—	—	—	—	62	43.8	(20.1)	—	—	—
Yes							55	38.8	(18.6)			

[a]: BNF classification of pain severity;
*p < 0.05; **p < 0.01.

fatigue, and pain. For patients with menorrhagia, significant improvements were seen on the SF-36 scales of social functioning and role limitations attributed to physical problems. For patients with suspected peptic ulcer and varicose veins there were no significant improvements on any of the SF-36 scales. For the three patient groups in which significant improvements occurred, the PGI and condition-specific instruments tended to be more responsive than the SF-36. Across these patient groups, the SRMs for the

Table 9.5 Mean changes in Patient Generated Index (PGI) Condition-specific and SF-36 Scores over Year and Standardised Response Means (SRMs) for Condition-specific Groups

Measure	Low back pain (n=124)			Menorrhagia (n=61)			Suspected peptic ulcer (n=27)			Varicose veins (n=27)		
	Mean	SD	SRM	Mean	SD	SRM	Mean	SD	SRM	Mean	SD	SRM
PGI	11.68**	22.53	0.52	8.67**	20.64	0.42	9.89**	21.35	0.47	-4.02	16.40	-0.17
Condition-specific instruments	8.13**	17.43	0.46	6.01**	13.12	0.45	11.86**	17.56	0.58	0.96	8.61	0.15
SF-36												
Physical functioning	2.11	21.39	0.09	-0.14	13.78	-0.01	1.99	12.13	0.08	2.96	14.63	0.19
Social functioning	4.55	29.98	0.12	3.90*	23.94	0.17	10.33	21.13	0.37	-2.74	21.66	-0.09
Role-physical	17.67**	41.08	0.43	14.75**	46.85	0.31	15.24	43.60	0.26	11.11	41.79	0.28
Role-emotional	8.74**	48.53	0.17	15.85	44.97	0.35	7.91	41.47	0.22	-1.23	52.69	-0.07
Mental Health	1.19	17.65	0.07	2.16	14.62	0.16	5.21	17.76	0.27	-1.04	12.43	-0.00
Energy/fatigue	4.34*	19.34	0.23	2.51	18.50	0.15	9.02	21.33	0.16	0.56	14.37	0.10
Pain	12.81**	24.75	0.52	2.37	21.86	0.12	18.53	28.29	0.39	3.70	23.47	0.16
General health perception	1.59	17.00	0.10	-1.40	13.07	-0.11*	-2.72	17.35	0.26	-0.96	12.17	-0.09

SD: standard deviation

Asterisks denote significant differences between baseline and follow-up scores: * P < 0.05; ** p < 0.01

Underlined values represent significantly lower SRMs relative to PGI: single underline p < 0.05; double underline p < 0.01

PGI and condition-specific instruments represented a small to moderate changes of closely similar size. For patients with low back pain, the SF-36 pain scale of produced an SRM of similar magnitude.

CONCLUSIONS

The PGI was developed in response to the need for a measure of quality of life that has meaning and relevance in the context of patients' everyday lives. Instruments used in clinical and health services research have tended to focus on something that is narrower than quality of life such as health status and health-related quality of life. Moreover, the domains and implicit values associated with such instruments rarely coincide exactly with the views of an individual patient. In taking a patient-centred approach to measurement, Calman's (1984) definition of quality of life — the gap between a patient's reality and expectations — has been used as the conceptual basis of an instrument designed for practical evaluative use across a wide variety of patients.

Given the limited evidence reviewed here, the PGI goes a good way to meeting the considerable demands placed upon it. Evidence for it validity was demonstrated by the small to moderate correlations with generic and specific measures of health and the relationship with condition-specific and socio-demographic variables. The reliability of the PGI, as measured by the test-retest method, is not as high as that demanded by some authors but is close to the level of 0.7, the generally accepted standard. Problems with the test-retest approach to reliability assessment have been well documented and include the possibility that change in perceived quality of life could have occurred between administrations of instruments (see also chapter 7 for discussion of discriminative versus evaluative instruments). It is also possible that patients may have changed nominated areas of life affected by their condition between administrations. In a study of low back pain patients it was found that patients reporting no change in health made an average of 1.7 changes in their nominated areas (Ruta et al., 1994b). Guyatt, Berman, Townsend and Taylor (1985) have shown that the reliability of health-related quality of life instruments can be improved by allowing subjects to see their previous responses at subsequent administrations, with no apparent adverse effects on the validity and responsiveness. Further work is required to examine whether similar methods are appropriate for the PGI, although it could be argued that to remind patients of their previous responses would be to deny the dynamic nature of quality of life.

The responsiveness of the PGI to changes in quality of life was assessed at one year with the standardised response mean (SRM) that also allows comparisons to be made between instruments. For the three conditions in which patients demonstrated significant improvements in health and quality of life the SRMs for the PGI were of a similar magnitude to those for condition-specific measures of health. It has been argued that the restricted focus of specific instruments makes them more responsive than generic measures to clinically important changes in health. The evidence reviewed here supports this proposition but it is encouraging that the PGI was as responsive as the specific instruments. The PGI is generic in nature but its inherent focus on patient and condition-specific aspects of quality of life, through the inclusion of the five areas listed by the patient is potentially more responsivene than generic measures of health and quality of life.

The PGI can be administered by interview or as a self-completed question-naire. Completion rates for interview approach 100% but if the instrument is to be used in the routine monitoring of health care interventions, the interview format is simply not practicable. Using the self-administered form of the PGI results in the completion rates that are substantially lower. In the study reported here, the PGI was completed by 59% of patients who re-sponded to more widely used instruments including the SF-36 health survey. A series of interviews has been conducted with a sample of the patients who failed to complete the PGI. The result is the simplified version of the instrument (Appendix). The main changes are more 'user friendly' presenta-tion and instructions, and a simplified scoring and points system. It is hoped that this version of the PGI will retain the attributes of validity, reliability and responsiveness of the parent instrument.

In conclusion, the PGI offers a new exciting approach to the measurement of quality of life and may have a valuable role to play in assessing the outcomes of care for different patient groups. Continued research and fresh applications will assist in the evaluation of the instrument in relation to the extent to which if fulfils the desired properties of an outcome measure for assessing changes in quality of life.

ACKNOWLEDGEMENTS

We thank the staff at Inverurie, Portlethen, Rubislaw Place and Westhill practices for recruiting patients; Jeremy Grimshaw, Jenny Duncan and Alison De Ville for help with data collection; and John Ware and his colleagues at the Health Institute of the New England Medical Centre for permission to use the SF-36. This research and the Health Services Research Unit are funded by the Chief Scientist's Office of the Scottish Office Home and Health Department; however, the opinions are those of the authors and not necessarily the SOHHD.

REFERENCES

Armitage, P. and Berry, G. (1987) *Statistical Methods in Medical Research*. Oxford, Blackwell Scientific Publications, 2nd edition.

Bergner, M., Bobbit, R., Carter, W. et al. (1981) Sickness impact profile. *Medical Care* **19**, 787–805.

Bergner, M. (1989) Quality of life, health status, and clinical research. *Medical Care* (suppl) **27**, S148–S56.

Bland J. M. and Altman D.G. (1986) Statistical methods for assessing agreement between two methods of clinical measurement. *Lancet* **i**, 307–310.

Calman, K. C. (1984) Quality of life in cancer patients — a hypothesis. *Journal of Medical Ethics* **10**, 124–7.

Cohen, C. (1982) On the quality of life: some philosophical reflections. *Circulation* **66** (suppl 3), 29–33.

Dupuis, G. (1988) International perspectives on quality of life and cardiovascular disease: the quality of life systemic inventory. Presented at the workshop on quality of life in cardiovascular disease. Winston-Salem, NC.

Garratt, A. M., Macdonald L. M., Ruta, D. A. and Russell, I. T. (1993) Towards the measurement of outcome for patients with varicose veins. *Quality in Health Care* **2**, 5–10.

Garratt, A. M., Ruta, D. A., Abdalla, M. I. et al. (1993) The SF 36 health survey questionnaire: an outcome measure suitable for routine use within the NHS? *British Medical Journal* **306**,1440–4.

Guyatt, G. H., Berman, L. B., Townsend, M. and Taylor, D. W. (1985) Should subjects see their previous responses? *Journal of Chronic Diseases* **38**, 1003–7.

Guyatt, G. H., Berman, L. B., Townsend, M. et al. (1987) A measure of quality of life for clinical trials in chronic lung disease. *Thorax*, **427**, 773–8.

Hunt, S. M. McEwen, J. and McKenna, S. P. (1985) Measuring health status: a new tool for epidemiologists. *Journal of the Royal College of General Practitioners*, **34**, 281–6.

Katz, J. N., Larson, M. G., Phillips, C. B. et al. (1992) Comparative measurement sensitivity of short and longer form health status instruments. *Medical Care*, **30**, 917–25.

Kirshner, B. and Guyatt, G. (1985) A methodological framework for assessing health indices. *Journal of Chronic Diseases* **38**, 27–36.

Liang, M. H., Larson, M. G., Cullen, K. E. and Schwartz, J. A. (1985) Comparative measurement efficiency and sensitivity of five health status instruments for arthritic research. *Arthritis and Rheumatology* **28**, 542–47.

McHorney, C. A., Ware, J. E., Rogers, W. et al. (1992) The validity and relative precision of MOS short- and long-form health status measures and Dartmouth COOP charts: results from the medical outcomes study. *Medical Care* (suppl) **30**, MS253–65.

McHorney, C. A., Ware, J. E. and Raczek, A. E. (1993) The MOS 36-item short-form health survey: II. Psychometric and clinical tests of validity in measuring physical and mental health constructs. *Medical Care* **31**, 247–63.

Nordenfelt, L. (1989) Quality of life and happiness. In *Assessing quality of life*. Bjork, S. & Vang, J. (eds). Linkoping: Samhall Klinland.

Presant, C. A. (1984) Quality of life in cancer patients. Who measures what? *American Journal of Clinical Oncology* **7**, 571–3.

Ruta, D. A., Garratt, A. M., Leng, M. et al. (1994a) A new approach to the measurement of quality of life: the patient generated index (PGI). *Medical Care* **32**, 1109–26.

Ruta, D. A., Garratt, A. M., Wardlaw, D. and Russell, I. T. (1994b) Developing a valid and reliable measure of health outcome for patients with low back pain. *Spine* **17**, 1887–96.

Ruta, D. A., Garratt, A. M., Chadha, Y. C. et al. (1995) Assessment of patients with menorrhagia: how valid is a structured clinical history as a measure of health status? *Quality of Life Research* **4**, 33–40.

Ruta, D. A., Garratt, A. M. and Russell, I. T. (1997) Patient centred assessment of quality of life for patients with four common conditions. *Quality in Health Care* (in review).

Siegrist, J. and Junge, A. (1989) Conceptual and methodological problems in research on the quality of life in clinical medicine. *Social Science and Medicine* **29**, 463–68.

Streiner, D. L. and Norman, G. R. (1989) *Health measurement scales: a practical guide to their development and use*. Oxford: Oxford University Press.

Van Dam, F. S. A. M., Somers, R. and van Beck-Couzijn, A. L. (1981) Quality of life: some theoretical issues. *Journal of Clinical Pharmacology* **21** (suppl 8–9), 166.

Ware, J. E. and Sherbourne, C. D. (1992) The MOS 36-item short-form health survey (SF-36): I. Conceptual framework and item selection. *Medical Care* **30**, 473–83.

10. THE SCHEDULE FOR THE EVALUATION OF INDIVIDUAL QUALITY OF LIFE

ANNE HICKEY, CIARÁN A. O'BOYLE, HANNAH M. McGEE
and C. R. B. JOYCE

Quality of life has become one of the key measurements in studies of health and medical outcomes. This chapter describes the development and application of the Schedule for the Evaluation of Individual Quality of Life (SEIQoL) which was specifically designed to assess quality of life from the perspective of the individual. Recent advances in the methodology are described. The SEIQoL permits collection of data implicit to the individual's understanding of quality of life which were thought previously to be beyond scientific enquiry.

INTRODUCTION

> *"The whole of science is nothing more than a refinement of everyday thinking"*
>
> Albert Einstein, 1950

The fundamental goal of medicine is to enhance the quality of life of the individual being treated. Medical research focuses largely on the clinical outcomes of treatment, such as reduction in blood pressure or gastric secretion. While such information is undoubtedly important, people do not consult their doctors because they are offended by sphygmomanometer readings or pH values, but because they are concerned about the implications of these medically important variables for the quality of their lives (Levine, 1990).

In drawing up its constitution in 1947, the World Health Organisation defined health as "complete physical, social and emotional wellbeing, and not simply the absence of disease or infirmity". Thus, for the first time, health was formally defined as extending beyond a purely physical dimension and seen to be completely involved with the individual's social life, wellbeing and emotional status. This definition underlies many of the outcome measures subsequently devised for use in health care settings (see, e.g., Bergner, Bobbitt, Carter and Gilson, 1981; Chambers, McDonald, Tugwell, Buchanan and Kraag, 1982; Hunt, McEwen and McKenna, 1986). In many instances, these measures have been incorporated into clinical outcome studies as measures of patient quality of life (e.g., Davis, Balart, Schiff, Lindsay, Bodenheimer, Perrillo et al., 1994; Colles, Burroughs, Rolles and Lloyd, 1995).

However, the use of such measures as indicators of patient quality of life has been found to be problematic. Problems with health-related quality of life measurement can be described under two major headings. Both relate to the fixed nature of instrument design. First, what is measured is predetermined and therefore may not represent the free choice of the individual whose quality of life is assessed. Implicit in measurements of health-related quality of life is the view that a specific subset of life domains accounts for most of the variance. Identifying these domains upon which respondents then rate themselves is thought to measure health-related quality of life. Typically, the people who identify these domains are health professionals, while the people assessed by these instruments most often are not. Thus, attempts to identify the particular domains most intimately related to health-related quality of life may well be misguided because they create an artificial, normative definition that may be of no relevance for a majority of the individuals to whom it is applied (O'Boyle, McGee and Joyce, 1994). Indeed, such an approach to quality of life measurement may unfairly favour one group of individuals over another simply because the questions posed are more relevant for that particular group. In sum, the use of such measures implies that quality of life means the same thing to everyone and can thus be defined in general terms by fixed questions that do not reflect the personal input of any individual.

The second major difficulty centres on the way in which health-related quality of life measures are scored. Again the scoring techniques assume a commonality of importance for different life areas for all individuals. Frequently, the answers to each question are equally weighted. But whether this is so or not, the weights will have been predetermined and may therefore be meaningless in regard to the particular individual. Methods and their scoring keys have usally been standardised on study samples other than the one currently being assessed. Disease-specific quality of life measures have been developed partly in order to lessen the importance of this problem, but disease-specific instruments are clearly of limited applicability. The fact that the attempt to develop a quality of life measure for every disease or condition is a costly and never-ending activity has not put an end to it. But the items and scoring key of a specific method are no nearer to reflecting the choices of the individual patient than are those of a general method. The life domains assessed and the weights associated with them will reflect the group upon whom the instrument was developed and not individuals within it.

If the individual's perspective on quality of life is to be validly captured, he must be permitted to influence each step of the assessment. The issues addressed should be those the individual holds to be important to the quality of his life, and he should then be able to assess the level of functioning or satisfaction in each of these self-nominated areas. (Level of functioning is the only aspect of measurement determined by the individual in typical health-related quality of life assessments.) Finally, he should indicate the relative personal importance of each area named. In this way, assumptions or generalisations based on faulty premises are avoided and the individual assesses his own quality of life based in terms of life issues that are personally relevant.

The genesis of an attempt to implement this approach is described in Chapter 1. The Schedule for the Evaluation of Individual Quality of Life

(SEIQoL) was the first practical consequence (McGee, O'Boyle, Hickey, O'Malley and Joyce, 1991; O'Boyle, McGee, Hickey, O'Malley and Joyce, 1992; O'Boyle, McGee, Hickey, Joyce, Browne, O'Malley and Hiltbrunner, 1993).

THE SCHEDULE FOR THE EVALUATION OF INDIVIDUAL QUALITY OF LIFE

The broad working definition that underlay development of the SEIQoL focussed on the individual's personal view of life and its quality. Quality of life was thus defined as "what the individual determines it to be" (Joyce, 1988; O'Boyle, 1992; O'Boyle et al., 1993). A number of propositions derive from this definition. First, quality of life is individual in nature. Aspects of life which may be important to one person may have little or no relevance for another. The only valid means of quality of life assessment, therefore, are by self-report. Second, the dynamic nature of quality of life is central to understanding of the concept. Thus, while an individual's judgment of their overall quality of life results in part from an assessment of level of functioning in each domain considered important, the relative importance of each may change. Change may occur, for example, as a result of a person growing older, or be due to an illness or other change in life circumstances, or due to a change in the perception of their own life circumstances. Third, in judging quality of life, an individual evaluates each important aspect in terms of its relationship to worst and best possible states. This yardstick will also be specific to each individual, resulting from the influences of a variety of factors, including experience and expectations. Finally, only the individual can validly judge his quality of life. Thus, evaluation that relies on third party assessments should not be taken as equivalent to the individual's own. Many studies have demonstrated low levels of concordance between individual's own ratings and those made by others, including physicians (Jachuck, Bierley, Jachuck and Willcox, 1982; Magaziner, Hebel and Warren, 1987; Pearlman and Uhlmann, 1988; Slevin, Stubbs, Plant, Wilson, Gregory, Armes and Downes, 1990).

JUDGMENT ANALYSIS

The SEIQoL was based upon a method derived from Social Judgment Theory (Hammond, Stewart, Brehmer and Steinmann, 1975; Stewart, 1988) called Judgment Analysis (JA). This makes use of a multiple regression analysis to model the structure of a given individual's judgment "policy" by quantifying the extent to which the individual utilises certain items of information to make a judgment. It has been used extensively to examine expert decision making in areas as diverse as selection of an optimal bullet for the

Denver, Colorado police force (Hammond and Adelman, 1986) and the treatment of marital conflict (Dhir and Markman, 1986). In the medical arena, JA has been used to examine the decision making of consultant physicians and general practitioners (e.g., Kirwan, Chaput de Saintonge, Joyce and Currey, 1983; Fisch, Hammond, Joyce and O'Reilly, 1981). Quality of life was a new application. Before describing this, it is necessary to understand a number of commonly used technical terms.

Cue: A factor or item of information used as a basis for judgment;
Case/cue profile: A set of cue values presented for judgment;
Judge: An individual making a judgment;
Judgment task: A set of cases presented to a judge in order to obtain a sample of his/her judgments;
Judgment policy: a quantitative representation of the basis for an individual's judgment derived from calculating the relative weight attributed to each cue.

The SEIQoL is administered in a standardised semi-structured interview format:

1. *Cue elicitation*: In the first step the individual is asked to name the 5 areas of life (cues) considered to be central to the quality of his life. Most respondents appear to have difficulty making judgments on combinations of more than 5 cues. This is reflected in diminished validity and reliability figures (cf. Stewart, 1988), but the use of fewer than 5 cues may be too limiting and yield too little information. The cues nominated by the individual are referred to as "elicited" cues. The investigator may sometimes provide cues from areas of special interest to the study in question. Such cues are referred to as "provided" cues. Much research indicates greater sensitivity when cues are elicited (O'Boyle et al., 1992). The meaning of each cue elicited from each individual is recorded together with the label he uses to naming it. Thus, for example, "religion" as a cue label may be nominated as a spiritual activity by one individual, as a social activity (meeting friends at religious services) by another or as an activity reflecting physical mobility (being able to walk to church) by a third. Defining what is meant by each cue label is essential in order to understand exactly what aspect of life the individual is addressing and for examining the incidence of cue use (O'Boyle et al., 1993).

2. *Determining current status on each cue*: The second step is to determine the individual's current status, or level of functioning, on each cue. Here respondents rate current status against a vertical visual analogue scale labelled at its extremities "as good as could possibly be" and "as bad as could possibly be", respectively. These ratings are recorded by the interviewer in the form of a bar chart (Fig. 1), each bar representing current status on a single cue. The score range for each bar is 0.0 – 100.0. A horizontal visual analogue scale, labelled in the same way as the vertical, is presented beneath the bar chart for the individual to make a rating of current overall quality of life.

3. *Relative weighting of each cue*: By examining its importance, this step quantifies the relative contribution of each cue to the judgment of the individual's overall quality of life. For this purpose, a series of "cases" are presented for judgment that may either have been selected in advance or randomly generated. The set of cases is identical for all participants in a given study, although each case is of course labelled with one of the 5 cues previously nominated by the individual. For each case, the respondent indicates on a horizontal visual analogue scale (labelled as above) his rating of the overall quality of life of that particular "case". A total of 30 cases is usually presented as the minimum requirement for 5 cues (Policy PC, 1986; Stewart, 1988; O'Boyle et al., 1993), 10 of these being repeats to allow the estimation of internal reliability.

The relative weight assigned by the individual to each cue is calculated using a multiple regression analysis programme developed for the purpose

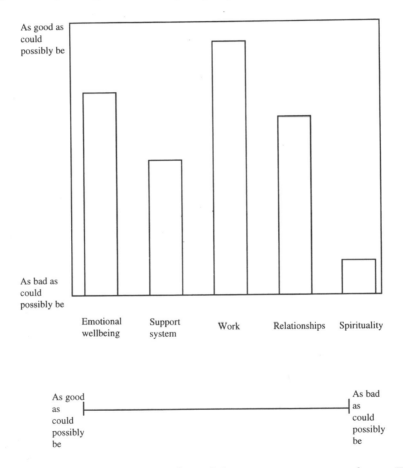

Figure 10.1 Step 2 of the SEIQoL: determining current status on each cue. This chart shows an example of a single individual's current cue profile.

(Policy PC, 1986). This package also computes an R^2 statistic which indicates the amount of variance in the overall judgment policy explained by the 5 cues used. R^2 values of 0.7 or greater are considered acceptable (Stewart, 1988). The R^2 statistic provides an estimate of the internal validity of the JA task. Internal reliability is calculated by correlating repeat case judgments. Thus, it is possible to assess how well the particular judgment policy models the individual's assessment of overall quality of life (R^2) and how reliably the individual uses this policy (r).

The SEIQoL allows measurement of quality of life to be completely individualised. The individual determines the life areas for consideration, indicates current status on each of these nominated areas and determines the relative weighting attributed to each area. There are situations, however, when it is considered necessary to present information as grouped data, particularly if it is desired to make comparisons between groups. A single index derived from the SEIQoL data, referred to as the SEIQoL index score, is calculated by multiplying each cue weight by the corresponding current self-rating and summing the products across the 5 cues:

$$\text{SEIQoL index score} = \sum (\text{levels} \times \text{weights})$$

This score can range from 0 to 100. As it is a continuous measure, it can be analysed using parametric statistical analyses.

APPLICATIONS

To date, the SEIQoL has been used with respondents ranging in age from eight to the early nineties. Given the cognitive requirements of the task, the SEIQoL, in its full form, is unlikely to be suitable for very young children, although the lower age limit is unknown.

The following sections provide examples of SEIQoL applications.

Individual Quality of Life in a Healthy Adult Population

The first study carried out comprised 42 healthy adults (20 male; 22 female) attending an immunisation clinic for appropriate vaccination and/or innoculation prior to travelling abroad (McGee et al., 1991). The mean age of the sample was 29 years (range 19–51). Cues were both elicited and provided. Provided cues were derived from those frequently contained in standard quality of life questionnaires, from the physical, emotional and social functioning, living conditions and general health domains. A number of these life areas, such as health, finances and social activities, were similar to those typically addressed in standard questionnaire assessments. However, many were unique and not typically assessed by standardised instruments, such as education and religion. Rather surprisingly, aesthetics, politics and the environment were each elicited once only.

There was considerable variation in the weightings assigned to the elicited and provided cues, but no significant difference in mean quality of life scores derived from them. Mean reliability was satisfactory for both the elicited and provided cues and the judgment policies accounted for a high percentage of the variability for both elicited and provided cues. The SEIQoL proved to be acceptable and feasible to this healthy adult population. The reliability and validity of the measure was acceptable.

The SEIQoL in Clinical Populations

The SEIQoL was used to examine the quality of life of patients with peptic ulcer disease (PUD) and irritable bowel syndrome (IBS), and also to compare the SEIQoL with some frequently used health and functional status measures. This was a cross-sectional study, involving a single interview with a consecutive series of attenders to an out-patient gastroenterology clinic. The sample consisted of 28 patients with IBS (16 female, 12 male; mean age: 33.2 (range 17–64)) and 28 patients with PUD (12 female, 16 male; mean age: 35.9 (range 19–72)). All patients were able to complete the SEIQoL using elicited cues only. Patients also completed the Gastrointestinal Symptom Rating Scale (GSRS; Svedlund, Sjodin and Dotevall, 1988), the Psychosocial Adjustment to Illness Scale (PAIS; Derogatis, 1986) and the Nottingham Health Profile (NHP; Hunt, McEwen and McKenna, 1986).

Both groups nominated family as the most important life area, followed by health for the IBS group and social and leisure pursuits for the PUD group. Social and leisure pursuits and work were the next most frequently nominated cues for the IBS group; health and work for the PUD group. Health was nominated significantly less frequently by the PUD than the IBS group (p < 0.05), despite the fact that both groups were attending hospital for management of their condition. The assumption that health is automatically the most important component of patients' perceived quality of life may thus not be warranted. It may be that health is viewed by patients as facilitating other important aspects of their lives rather than as something to be valued in isolation.

The SEIQoL, GSRS, PAIS and NHP (part 2) scores were compared. Patients with IBS suffered significantly higher levels of symptomatology than did the PUD group (GSRS scale) (p < 0.05). SEIQoL but not PAIS or NHP scores significantly distinguished the two groups (p < 0.01), indicating that IBS patients as a group had a significantly lower quality of life than the PUD patient group. This finding is supported by previous research findings and by clinical perceptions that IBS disrupts quality of life to a greater degree than does PUD (Whitehead, Winget, Fedoravicius, Wolley and Blackwell, 1982; Guthrie, Creed and Whopwell, 1987). Of most present interest were the observations that the SEIQoL was discriminative whereas the other instruments were not, and the absence of significant correlations between the SEIQoL scores and the GSRS, NHP (total) or PAIS (total and sub-scales).

However, the SEIQoL index score was significantly related to two subscales of part 1 of the NHP, sleep ($r = 0.38$, $p < 0.01$) and social isolation ($r = -0.29$, $p < 0.05$).

Use of the SEIQoL was found to be acceptable to and feasible in clinical populations, and yielded results that discriminated between two groups with different gastro-intestinal conditions than did health status or functional measurements. The low correlations between medically rated symptom severity on the GSRS and patient-related measures of quality of life indicated that quality of life is not directly proportional to clinically judged severity: further evidence that clinical assumptions about patient quality of life may not relate to patients' own perceptions.

Individual Quality of Life in a Surgical Population

The SEIQoL was administered pre- and post-operatively to assess the effect of surgical intervention on the individual quality of life of a cohort of 20 patients undergoing total hip replacement (O'Boyle et al., 1992). Consecutive attenders to a Dublin orthopaedic hospital with unilateral osteoarthritis of the hip were matched by age, sex and socioeconomic status to healthy community residents, identified through general practice registers. Both elicited and provided cues were employed. A general health status measure (McMaster Health Index Questionnaire), a disease specific health status questionnaire (Arthritis Impact Measurement Scales), and an objective measure of functional capacity (Harris Hip Rating) were also used, first during routine inpatient preoperative assessment 6 weeks prior to surgery and again 26 weeks after surgery in their own homes. The matched healthy community group were interviewed in their homes on two occasions 32 weeks apart.

The proportions of patients and controls nominating 'happiness' as an important life area differed significantly (25% of the patient group but none of the control group). SEIQoL index scores derived from elicited cues improved significantly for the patient group from the pre- to the post-operative assessment ($p < 0.02$), while SEIQoL scores did not change significantly for the control group. Patient and control scores differed significantly at 32 weeks but had not done so at baseline. SEIQoL index scores from provided cues yielded no significant differences either between groups or within groups over time. Individual quality of life scores based on elicited, but not provided cues are sensitive to changes following surgical intervention.

Individual Quality of Life in Older Persons

1. *Quality of life in healthy older persons*: was assessed over a 12 month period in 56 healthy adults (36 female, 22 male) recruited through general practice registers of those aged 65 or more (Browne, O'Boyle, McGee, Joyce, McDonald, O'Malley and Hiltbrunner, 1994).

Over the 12 month period, the number of respondents nominating 'social and leisure activities' as an important life area reduced significantly (p<0.05), whereas the number nominating 'finances' as important increased significantly (p < 0.05). Other changes were slight. Mean overall SEIQoL scores declined slightly but insignificantly over time. The quality of life of this healthy older group was at first significantly better than that of the (obviously, not strictly comparable) young healthy group described earlier, but although continuing to be slightly better at time 2, the difference was no longer significant. Internal reliability and validity coefficients were satisfactory. Acceptability by these healthy older subjects was also high.

2. *The quality of life in older individuals with dementia*: was assessed in 20 patients (15 female, 5 male) meeting DSM-IIIR criteria for mild dementia (Coen, O'Mahony, O'Boyle, Joyce, Hiltbrunner, Walsh and Coakley, 1993) to evaluate the feasibility, validity and reliability of the SEIQoL in dementia. All patients were able to nominate 5 important life areas although prompting was necessary in some cases. However, in 14 cases the interview had to be discontinued due to an inability or unwillingness of the patient to proceed. The 6 remaining participants were found to have significantly milder dementia. For these 6, internal reliability and validity were satisfactory. It is possible that in cases of mild cognitive impairment, the SEIQoL can be feasible, reliable and valid. As cognitive impairment increases, patients may be less able or willing to complete it. Proxy assessment may then become necessary, but these will not estimate individual quality of life in the sense used here.

Individual Quality of Life in Palliative Care Settings

Quality of life issues in terminal illness, especially in relation to end of life decisions are of increasing interest. They are discussed in Chapter 15 by Waldron.

PSYCHOMETRIC PROPERTIES OF THE SEIQoL

Reliability and validity data from the studies described above are summarized in the following table.

In general, individuals used judgment policies about their quality of life consistently (r) and that the combination of cues nominated by each individual explained much of the variance in terms of the judgment policy (R^2). Many studies in professional decision making suggest that experts may be largely unaware of how they make decisions. In medicine, for example, experts may find it difficult to make accurate predictions of the relative weights that they have assigned to different clinical parameters. Not surprisingly, their judgment

Population	Mean r	Mean R^2
Healthy adult s (n=42)	0.74	0.75
Irritable Bowel Syndrome (n=28)	0.62	0.73
Peptic Ulcer Disease (n=28)	0.70	0.79
Total hip replacement (THR: n=20)	0.64 (pre-op)	0.62 (pre-op)
	0.49 (7.5 months post-op)	0.65 (7.5 months)
	0.62 (24 months post-op)	0.64 (24 months)
Healthy controls for THR (n=20)	0.71 (baseline)	0.76 (baseline)
	0.62 (7.5 months)	0.72 (7.5 months)
	0.66 (24 months)	0.71 (24 months)
Healthy older persons (n=56)	0.66 (baseline)	0.72 (baseline)
	0.73 (12 months)	0.78 (12 months)
Dementia (N=6)	0.74	0.70
Palliative care (N=30)	0.84	0.84

policies also differ significantly from each other (Kirwan et al., 1983), and some may be very unreliable (Fisch et al., 1981). The data summarized here suggests that judgment about personal quality of life may be more accurate than judgment about third-parties.

SEIQoL'S COMPONENT PARTS: QUALITY OF LIFE DYNAMICS

Data presented so far have focused on comparisons of global SEIQoL index scores from different groups. However, the real strength of the SEIQoL is its individual nature: at any point in time it is possible to identify currently important life areas, their relative weights and satisfaction with their function. The qualitative information can be lost by focusing on the global index (Fig. 2). Two healthy adults attending an immunisation clinic (McGee et al., 1991) had similar cue profiles and global SEIQoL scores derived from provided cues. However, their relative weight is differed considerably. One attached great importance to health and physical functioning; the other, considerably less interested in these, attached greater importance to emotional functioning and living conditions. Similar overall quality of life scores may arise from very different cue profiles.

Prospective quality of life assessments emphasize the dynamic nature of quality of life. Over time, an individual may change the important issues that s/he considers to be important, the levels assigned to them, or their relative weights assigned to life areas. In time-series studies, respondents have been asked at each assessment to nominate their five most important cues and quality of life is determined in the usual way. Only are the same cases judged on cues from the previous assessment, so that judgments of quality of life from the first and subsequent assessments may be directly compared.

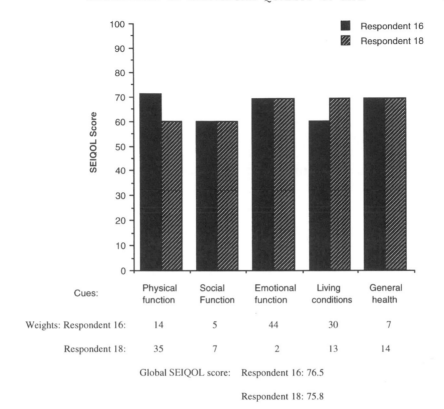

Figure 10.2 Two individuals with similar cue profiles and global quality of life scores but relative cue weights.

APPROPRIATE RESPONDENTS AND APPLICATIONS

The potential applications of the SEIQoL are not limited to health and illness. (Hickey, O'Boyle, Mcbee and McDonald, 1997) It seems clear that the method is culture-free and presents far few problems of the kind encountered when an instrument must be translated from one language to another, although this has not yet been investigated empirically. To date, the SEIQoL has been used successfully with respondents ranging from age eight to the early nineties, and in several different European languages.

The SEIQoL has been administered successfully to healthy adults and in a variety of clinical contexts, but its ability to assess individual quality of life is limited by conditions which impair cognitive functioning or motivational state. Successful completion of the SEIQoL requires respondents to identify and reflect upon issues of importance to them, to be able to think abstractly in considering hypothetical cases, to make judgments based on information presented in diagrammatic form, and to comprehend and make ratings on vertical and horizontal visual analogue scales. If any of these abilities is impaired, the use of the SEIQoL may be problematic. But it is not yet clear what other instrument, if any, can replace it. (We recommend that interviewers assess the respondent's comprehension of the task and motivation to complete in order to formally consider such aspects.)

The SEIQoL, as an individual measure of quality of life, is ideally suited for use in single subject and within-subject study designs in which respondents act as their own controls. However, the SEIQoL index score can also be used in between subject (group) studies. Reducing SEIQoL information to summary scores and grouped data compromises the individual nature of the measure. A middle path is to use the number of crude qualitative changes over time (positive, negative, no change) as the variable to be analysed.

A SHORT DIRECT WEIGHTING SEIQoL PROCEDURE (SEIQoL-DW)

If time available for the study of quality of life is limited by the fiat of a clinical investigator or for a more valid reason such as its incorporated into an investigation with other priorities and instruments, a simpler method of determining cue weights has been developed. Its reliability and validation against the full version of the SEIQoL have been found to be satisfactory (Browne, O'Boyle, McGee, McDonald and Joyce, 1997). The Direct Weighting (DW) procedure consists of a pie-chart containing five independently movable overlapping circles, each of which represents one quality of life factor chosen by the individual. The degree of overlap segments is adjusted and re-adjusted by the individual concerned until he is satisfied that the proportions of the pie chart given to each sector reflect the relative weights he desires to accord them. The five coloured laminated circular disks are mounted on a larger backing disk, which displays markings from 0 to 100. From this the relative size of each cue can be read off. The procedure is short, colourful, tactile and easy to understand.

The first clinical application of the SEIQoL-DW was with 52 people with a known HIV seropositive status recruited primarily through two Dublin inner city general practices, and a comparison group of age/sex matched healthy adults drawn from the same neighbourhood (Hickey, Bury, O'Boyle, Bradley, Kelly and Shannon, 1996). The expected individual differences were apparent, as were interesting differences in the cue choices of drug users and those whose infection was associated with sexual practices.

The SEIQoL-DW maintains each of the steps of the longer methodology, but replaces the JA method of deriving relative weights by a briefer and more explicit form of assigning weights. Developmental studies indicate that the measure is reproducible and has high criterion validity. The individual r and R^2 of the full method, however, are of course not calculable. Detailed psychometric information on the SEIQoL-DW is reported by Browne et al. (1997).

CONCLUSIONS

Apart from its research application, the semi-structured, individual format of the SEIQoL, in its full and short forms, may facilitate clinical consultations by heightening patient self-awareness and increasing physician insight into the patient's problems, leading to improvements in communication, joint decision making and patient satisfaction, thereby increasing levels of commitment and adherence to therapy.

The SEIQoL has also been used for other applications, such as symptom perception and quality of care. Some of these are discussed by Waldron (see Chapter 15).

In brief, the SEIQoL provides a method that permits the scientific study of an area that is often considered to be beyond the scope of such enquiry.

REFERENCES

Bergner, M., Bobbitt, R. A., Carter, W. and Gilson, B. (1981) The Sickness Impact Profile: development and final revision of a health status measure. *Medical Care* **19**, 787–805.

Browne, J. P., O'Boyle, C. A., McGee, H. M., Joyce, C. R. B., McDonald, N. J., O'Malley, K. M. and Hiltbrunner, B. (1994) Individual quality of life in the healthy elderly. *Quality of Life Research* **3**, 235–244.

Browne, J. P., O'Boyle, C. A., McGee, H. M., McDonald, N. J. and Joyce, C. R. B. (1997) Development of a direct weighting procedure for quality of life domains. *Quality of Life Research* **6** (in press).

Chambers, L. W., McDonald, L. A., Tugwell, P., Buchanan, W. W. and Kraag, G. (1982) The McMaster Health Index Questionnaire as a measure of quality of life for patients with rheumatoid disease. *Journal of Rheumatology* **9**, 780–784.

Coen, R., O'Mahony, D., O'Boyle, C., Joyce, C. R. B., Hiltbrunner, B., Walsh, J. B. and Coakley, D. (1993) Measuring the quality of life of dementia patients using the Schedule for the Evaluation of Individual Quality of Life. *Irish Journal of Psychology* **14**, 154–163.

Collis, I., Burroughs, A., Rolles, K. and Lloyd, G. (1995) Psychiatric and social outcome of liver transplantation. *British Journal of Psychiatry* **166**, 521–524.

Davis, G. L., Balart, L. A., Schiff, E. R., Lindsay, K., Bodenheimer, H. C., Perrillo, R. P. et al. (1994) Assessing health-related quality of life in chronic hepatitis C using the Sickness Impact Profile. *Clinical Therapeutics* **16**, 334–343.

Derogatis, L. R. (1986) The Psychosocial Adjustment to Illness Scale (PAIS). *Journal of Psychosomatic Research* **30**, 77–91.

Dhir, K. S. and Markman, H. J. (1986) Application of social judgment theory to understanding and treating marital conflict. In: Arkes, H. R. and Hammond K. R. (Eds.). *Judgment and Decision Making: an interdisciplinary reader*. USA: Cambridge University Press.

Fisch, H. -U., Hammond, K. R., Joyce, C. R. B., O'Reilly, M. (1981) An experimental study of the clinical judgment of general physicians in evaluating and prescribing for depression. *British Journal of Psychiatry* **138**, 100–109.

Guthrie, E., Creed, F. H. and Whopwell, P. J. (1987) Severe sexual dysfunction in women with irritable bowel syndrome: comparison with inflammatory bowel disease and duodenal ulceration. *British Medical Journal* **295**, 557–558.

Hammond, K. R. and Adelman, L. (1986) Science, values and human judgment. In: Arkes, H. R. and Hammond, K. R. (Eds.) *Judgment and Decision Making: an interdisciplinary reader*. USA: Cambridge University Press.

Hammond, K. R., Stewart, T. R., Brehmer, B. and Steinmann, D. (1975) Social Judgment theory. In: Kaplan, M. F. and Schwartz, S. (Eds.) *Human Judgment and Decision Processes: formal and mathematical approaches*. New York: Academic Press.

Hickey, A. M., Bury, G., O'Boyle, C. A., Bradley, F., O'Kelly, F. D. and Shannon, W. (1996) A new short-form individual quality of life measure (SEIQoL-DW). Application in a cohort of individuals with HIV/AIDS. *British Medical Journal* **313**, 29–33.

Hickey, A. M., O'Boyle, C. A., McGee, H. M. and McDonald N. J. (1997) The Relationship between post-trauma problem reporting and career quality of life after severe head injury. *Psychology and Health* **12**, 827–838.

Hunt, S. M., McEwen, J. and McKenna, S. P. (1986) *Measuring health status*. Kent: Croom Helm.

Jachuck, S. J., Bierley, H., Jachuck, S., and Willcox, P. M. (1982) The effect of hypotensive drugs on the quality of life. *Journal of the Royal College of General Practitioners* **32**, 103–105.

Joyce, C. R. B. (1988) Quality of life: the state of the art in clinical assessment. In: Walker, S. W. and Rosser, R. M. (eds.) *Quality of life assessment and application*. Lancaster: MTP Press, 169–179.

Kirwan, J. R., Chaput de Saintonge, D. M., Joyce, C. R. B. and Currey, H. F. L. (1983) Clinical judgment in rheumatoid arthritis II. Judging "current disease activity" in clinical practice. *Annals of the Rheumatic Diseases* **42**, 645–651.

Magaziner, J., Hebel, R. and Warren, J. W. (1987) The use of proxy responses for aged patients in long-term settings. *Comprehensive Gerontology* **Section B**, 118–121.

McGee, H. M., O'Boyle, C. A., Hickey, A. M., O'Malley, K. and Joyce, C. R. B. (1991) Assessing the quality of life of the individual: the SEIQoL with a healthy and a gastroenterology unit population. *Psychological Medicine* **21**, 749–759.

O'Boyle, C. A., McGee, H., Hickey, A., O'Malley, K. and Joyce, C. R. B. (1992) Individual quality of life in patients undergoing hip replacement. *Lancet* **339**, 1088–1091.

O'Boyle, C. A., McGee, H. and Joyce, C. R. B. (1994) Quality of life: assessing the individual. *Advances In Medical Sociology* **5**, 159–180.

O'Boyle, C. A., McGee, H. M., Hickey, A., Joyce, C. R. B., Browne, J., O'Malley, K. and Hiltbrunner, B. (1993) *The Schedule for the Evaluation of Individual Quality of Life. User manual*. Department of Psychology, Royal College of Surgeons in Ireland, St. Stephen's Green, Dublin 2.

O'Boyle, C. A. (1992) Assessment of quality of life in surgery. *British Journal of Surgery* **79**, 395–398.

Pearlmann, R. A. and Uhlmann, R. F. (1988) Quality of life in chronic diseases: perceptions of elderly patients. *Journal of Gerontology* **43**, M25-30.

Policy, P. C. (1986) *Software for judgment analysis*: version 2.0. Reference manual, 1st edition. Available from Executive Decision Services, PO Box 9102, Albany, New York.

Slevin, M. L., Stubbs, L., Plant, H. J., Wilson, P., Gregory, W. M., Armes, P. J. and Downes, S. M. (1990) Attitudes to chemotherapy: comparing views of patients with cancer with those of doctors, nurses and the general practitioner. *British Medical Journal* **300**, 1458–1460.

Stewart, T. R. Judgment analysis: procedures. In: Brehmer, B. & Joyce C. R. B. (eds.) (1988) *Human judgment. The social judgment theory view*. Amsterdam: North Holland, 41–74.

Svedlund, J., Sjodin, I. and Dotevall, G. (1988) GSRS — a clinical rating scale for gastrointestinal symptoms in patients with irritable bowel syndrome and peptic ulcer disease. *Digestive Diseases and Sciences* **33**, 129–134.

Whitehead, W. E., Winget, C., Fedoravicius, A. S., Wolley, S. and Blackwell, B. (1982) Learned illness behaviour in patients with irritable bowel syndrome and peptic ulcer disease. *Digestive Diseases and Sciences* **27**, 202–208.

World Health Organisation: The constitution of the World Health Organisation. (1947) *WHO Chronicle* **1**, 29.

11. METHODS FOR ASSESSING RELATIVE IMPORTANCE IN PREFERENCE BASED OUTCOME MEASURES*

ROBERT M. KAPLAN, DAVID FEENY and DENNIS A. REVICKI

This paper reviews issues relevant to preference assessment for utility based measures of health related quality of life. Cost/utility studies require a common measurement of health outcome, such as the quality adjusted life year (QALY). A key element in the QALY methodology is the measure of preference that estimates subjective health quality. Economists and psychologists differ on their preferred approach to preference measurement. Economists rely on utility assessment methods that formally consider economic trades. These methods include the standard gamble, time-trade off and person trade-off. However, some evidence suggests that many of the assumptions that underlie economic measurements of choice are open to challenge because human information processors do poorly at integrating complex probablility information when making decisions that involve risk. Further, economic analysis assumes that choices accurately correspond to the way rational humans use information. Psychology experiments suggest that methods commonly used for economic analysis do not represent the underlying true preference continuum and some evidence supports the use of simple ratlng scales. More recent research by economists attempts integrated cognitive models, while contemporary research by psychologists considers economic models of choice. The review also suggests that difference in preference between different social groups tends to be small.

INTRODUCTION

Health related quality of life (HRQL) data can be used to evaluate the cost/utility or cost/effectiveness of health care programmes. In cost/utility analysis, the outcomes of health care are expressed in terms of quality-adjusted life years or QALYs.[1,2] QALYs integrate mortality and morbidity to express health status in terms of equivalents of well-years of life. For example, if a man dies of heart disease at age 50 and we would have expected him to live to age 75, it might be concluded that the disease was associated with 25 lost life years. If 100 men died at age 50 (and also had a life expectancy of 75 years) we might conclude that 2500 (100 men × 25 years) life years had been lost.

In addition to death, heart disease may also cause impaired HRQL. Quality adjusted life years take into consideration the HRQL consequences of these illnesses. For example, a disease that reduces HRQL by one-half will take away 0.50 QALYs over the course of 1 year. If it effects two people, it will take away 1.0 year (2 × 0.50) over a 1 year period. A medical treatment that improves quality of life by 0.20 for each of five individuals will result in the equivalent of one QALY if the benefit is maintained over a 1 year period. QALYs consider both benefits and side-effects of programmes in common units. QALYs value a year of complete wellness as 1.0 and assign weights above 0.00 and less than 1.00 to years in which life quality is reduced. The

---

* This article is reprinted with permission from Quality of Life Research 1993, **2**, 467–495.

method for assigning these values and the source of this information are addressed in this paper.

DIMENSIONS OF HEALTH RELATED QUALITY OF LIFE

Nearly all HRQL measures have multiple dimensions. The exact dimensions vary from measure to measure.[3] There is considerable debate about which dimensions need to be included. For example, the most commonly included dimensions are physical functioning, role functioning, and mental health. The Medical Outcomes Study (MOS) includes eight health concepts.[4] Many measures of HRQL simply tabulate frequencies for different symptoms or represent health status using profiles of outcomes. Figure 11.1 is a representation of a series of two profiles from the SF-36. The first profile is for patients with depression (from Ref. 5) while the second profile is from unpublished data on patients on renal dialysis. Depressed patients are higher on measures of pain, physical and role functioning while dialysis patients score higher on measures of social and emotional functioning. The two groups are about equivalent on measures of energy and distress. Are depressed patients sicker than those on dialysis? Should we devote more resources to help them? Now suppose that a treatment for depression may improve scores on social and mental functioning, but will cause scores on energy and physical functioning to decline. Has the treatment worked? We must recognize that judgement about the relative importance of dimensions is common. Physicians may ignore a particular test result or a particular symptom because another one is more important to them. Typically, however, it is done implicitly, arbitrarily, and in an idiosyncratic way. We suggest that the process by which relative importance is evaluated can be studied explicitly and can be part of the overall model. Utility weighted models consider these preferences explicitly. There are a variety of methodological issues in preference assessment.[6–9] For example, differences in preference assessment yield different results. These differences might be expected because the various approaches are not derived from the same underlying conceptual models. The following sections attempt to resolve some of these conflicts.

THE CONCEPT OF UTILITY

The concept of quality-adjusted life years has been in the literature for nearly 25 years. Perhaps the first application was suggested by Fanshel and Bush.[10] Approximately at the same time, Torrance[11] introduced a conceptually similar model. Since then, a variety of applications have appeared. Although most of these models are conceptually alike, variations between the approaches have led to some inconsistent findings. We will highlight some of these inconsistencies in later sections.

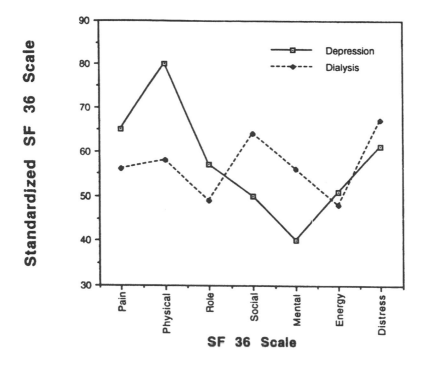

Figure 11.1 Comparison of SF-36 profiles for patients with depression and those on renal dialysis.

Despite the differences in approach, some important assumptions are similar. For example, all of these approaches assume that 1 full healthy year of life is scored 1.0. Years of life that are less than optimal health are scored as less than 1.0. The basic assumption is that 2 years scored as 0.50 add up to the equivalent of 1 year of complete wellness. Similarly, 4 years scored as 0.25 add up to the equivalent of 1 completely well year of life. A treatment that boosts a patient from 0.50 to 0.75 produces the equivalent of 0.25 QALYs. If applied to four individuals, and the duration of the treatment effect is 1 year, the effect of the treatment would be equivalent to 1 completely well year of life. There is disagreement over how the weights for cases between 0.00 and 1.00 are obtained.

THEORETICAL FOUNDATIONS OF UTILITY-BASED MEASURES

The history of the utility theory and its applications to health outcomes assessment has been reviewed by Torrance and Feeny.[12,13] Health utility assessment has its roots in the mathematical decision theory of Von Neumann and Morgenstern,[14] who characterized how a rational individual should make decisions when faced with uncertain outcomes. Von Neumann and

Morgenstern outlined axioms of choice that have been formally evaluated and have become basic foundations of decision analysis in busines, government and health care. This work has been expanded upon by Raiffa[15] and several others.[16, 17] Torrance and Feeny[12] emphasized that the use of the term 'utility theory' by Von Neumann and Morgenstern was unfortunate. Their reference to utility differs from the more common uses by economists which emphasize consumer satisfaction with commodities that are received *with certainty*. Nineteenth century philosophers and economists assumed the existence of a different form of a cardinal utility. A characteristic of this cardinal utility was that it could be averaged across individuals and ultimately used in aggregates as the basis of utilitarian social policy.

By the turn of the century, Bator[18] challenged the usefulness of cardinal utilities and demonstrated that ordinal utilities could represent consumer choice. This work was extended by Arrow and Debreu.[19] Arrow[20] further argued that there are inconsistencies in individual preferences under certainty and that meaningful cardinal preferences cannot be measured and cannot even exist. These arguments are presented to most introductory students of economics. As a result, most micro economists have come to doubt the value of preference ratings.

Perhaps the most important statement against the aggregation of individual preferences was Arrow's Impossibility Theorem.[20] In this classic work, Arrow considered the expected group decision based on the individual preferences of the group members. After laying out a set of very reasonable assumptions about how an aggregate decision should not contradict the apparent preferences of group members, Arrow demonstrated how aggregate decisions can violate the apparent will of the individual decision-makers.

There are several reasons why Arrow's Impossibility Theorem may not be applicable to the aggregation of utilities in the assessment of QALYs. First, utility expressions for QALYs are expressions of consumer preference *uncertainty*. Von Neumann and Morgenstern emphasized decisions under certainty and these two approaches are theoretically distinct. The traditional criticisms of micro-economists are directed toward decisions under certainty rather than uncertainty.[12]

A second issue is that Arrow assumed that the metric underlying utility was not meaningful and not standardized across individuals. Substantial psychometric evidence now suggests that preferences can be measured using scales that have meaningful interval or ratio properties. It should be noted, however, that in constructing an index of outcomes in the form of quality-adjusted life years, the analyst typically imposes the assumption that a year in perfect health is equally preferred by, or of the same value to, everyone and similarly, that death also has the same value to everyone. When cardinal (interval) utilities are used instead of rankings, many of the potential problems in the Impossibility Theorem are avoided.[21] It is also important to recognize that different approaches to the calculations of QALYs are based on very different underlying assumptions. One approach considers the duration of time someone is in a particular health state as conceptually independent from the utility for the state.[1,22] The other approach merges duration of the state and utility.[12] This distinction is central to the understanding of the difference in approaches and the required evidence for the validity of the utility assessment procedure.

In the approach advocated by Kaplan and Anderson[22] and Weinstein and Stason,[1] sources for health states are obtained at a single point in time. A person in a particular health state, for example, confined to a wheelchair but performing major social roles, is rated by peers. Suppose that this state is assigned a weight of 0.50. Then patients in this state are observed over the course of time to empirically determine their transitions to other states of wellness. If they remain in the state for 1 year, then they would lose the equivalent of 0.50 well years of life. The preferences only concern a single point in time and the transition is determined through observation or expert judgement. The alternative approach emphasized by Torrance and Feeny[12] and others,[23] obtains preference for both health state and for duration. These approaches also consider the more complex problems of uncertainty. Thus, they are consistent with the Von Neumann and Morgenstern notion of decision under uncertainty in which probabilities and trade-offs are considered explicitly by the judge.

METHODS FOR ASSESSING PREFERENCE

Cost/utility analysis requires an assessment of preferences for health states. A variety of different techniques have been used to assess these preferences. These techniques will be summarized briefly. Then, comparisons between the techniques will be considered.

Some analysts do not measure utilities directly. Instead, they evaluate health outcome by simply assigning reasonable preferences.[1] However, most current approaches have respondents assign weights to different health states on a scale ranging from 0 (for dead) to 1.0 (for wellness). The most common techniques include rating scales, magnitude estimations, the standard gamble, the time trade-off, and the equivalence person trade off. Each of these methods will be described briefly.

Rating Scales

Rating scales provide simple techniques for assigning a numerical value to health status. There are several methods for obtaining rating scale information. One is the category scale. This is a simple partition method in which participants are asked to assign each case a number selected from a set of numbered categories representing equal intervals. This method, exemplified by the familiar 10-point rating scale, is efficient, easy to use, and applicable in a large number of settings. Typically, the participants read the description of a case and rate it on a 10-point scale ranging from 0 for dead to 10 for optimum function without symptoms. Thus, the end-points of the scale are typically well defined. Another common rating scale method is the visual analogue scale. The visual analogue method shows a participant a line, typically 100 cm in length, with the endpoints well-defined. The participant's task is to mark the line to indicate where his or her preference rests in relation to the two poles.

Magnitude Estimation

Magnitude estimation is a common psychometric method that is believed by psychophysicists to yield ratio scale scores. In magnitude estimation, a specific case is selected as a standard and assigned a particular number. Then, other cases are rated in relation to the standard. Suppose, for example, the standard is assigned the number 10. If a case is regarded as half as desirable as the standard, it is given the number 5. If it is regarded as twice as desirable, it is given the number 20. Ratings across participants are standardized to a common measurement and aggregated using the geometric mean. Advocates for magnitude estimation argue that the method is meaningful because it provides a direct estimate of the subjective ratio. Thus, they believe, the magnitude estimate has the properties of a ratio scale. However, magnitude estimation has been challenged on several grounds. The method is not based on any specific theory of measurement and gains credibility only through face validity.[24] Further, the meaning of the scores has been challenged. For example, the values are not linked directly to any decision process. What does it mean if one case is rated as half as desirable as another? Does it mean that the respondent would be indifferent between a 50–50 chance of the higher valued outcome and a certainty of the alternative valued as half as desirable? These issues have not been systematically addressed in the quality of life measurement literature.

Standard Gamble

Category rating and magnitude estimation are methods commonly used by psychometricians. Typically, the tasks emphasize wellness at a particular point in time and do not ask participants to make trades or to consider aspects of uncertainty. Several methods more explicitly consider decisions under uncertainty. The standard gamble offers a choice between two alternatives: living in health state B with certainty or taking a gamble on treatment A for which the outcome is uncertain. Figure 11.2 shows this trade. The respondent is told that treatment A will lead to perfect health with a probability of p or immediate death with a probability of $1-p$. The health state described in B is intermediate between wellness and death. The probability (p) is varied until the participant is indifferent between choices A and B.

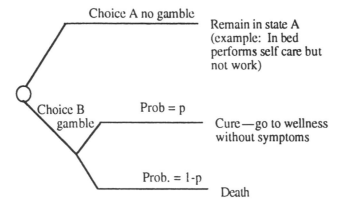

Figure 11.2 Example of standard gamble, adapted from Torrance and Feeny.[12]

The standard gamble is attractive because it is based on axions of utility theory. The choice between a certain outcome and a gamble conforms to the exercises originally proposed by Von Neumann and Morgenstern. Although the interval properties of the data obtained using the gamble have been assumed, they have not been empirically demonstrated.[7] A variety of other problems with the gamble have also become apparent. Although some believe that the standard gamble approximates choices made by medical patients[25] treatments of most chronic diseases do not approximate the gamble. Treatments for arthritis, for example, neither completely cure nor kill patients. In other words, the standard gamble task is not likely to include an option that has a realistic choice. Further, the cognitive demands of the task are high. The standard gamble method, however, does not require that the patient consider a gamble between perfect health and death. It requires only that the state in choice B be intermediately ranked relative to the probabilistic outcomes in choice A. For a presentation of alternative approaches using the standard gamble see Furlong et al.,[26] the underlying theory is discussed in Feeny and Torrance[13] and Torrance and Feeny.[12]

Time Trade-off

The concept of probability is difficult for some respondents and requires the use of visual aids or props to assist in the interview. An alternative to the standard gamble, (but one which is not fully consistent with the Von Neumann and Morgenstern axioms of choice), uses a trade-off in time. The participant is offered a choice of living for a defined amount of time in perfect health or a variable amount of time in an alternative state that is less desirable. Presumably, all participants would choose a year of wellness versus a year with some health problem. However, by reducing the time of wellness and leaving the time in the sub-optimal health state fixed (such as 1 year), an indifference point can be determined. For example, a participant may rate being in a wheelchair for 2 years as equivalent to perfect wellness for 1 year.

The time trade-off is theoretically appealing because it is conceptually similar to a QALY.

Person Trade-off

Finally, a person trade-off technique allows comparisons of the numbers of people helped in different states. For example, respondents might be asked to evaluate the equivalencies between the number of persons helped by different programmes. They might be asked how many persons in State B must be helped to provide a benefit equivalent to helping one person in State A. From a policy perspective, the person trade-off also directly seeks information similar to that required as the basis for policy decisions.

Several papers in the literature have compared utilities for health states as captured by different methods. These differences have been reviewed by Nord.[23] Although studies are inconsistent, standard gamble and time trade-off methods typically give higher values than rating scales. In about half of the studies reported, time trade-off yields lower utilities than standard gamble. In one of the earlier studies, Patrick and colleagues[27] found that person trade-off methods gave the same results as rating scales. However, these findings were not confirmed in more recent studies.[28] Magnitude estimation has produced results that are highly variable across studies.[23]

The variability of results across studies is hardly surprising. The methods differ substantially in the questions posed to respondents. In the next sections, we will address some of these differences and highlight some of the theoretical issues that new research must address.

PSYCHOLOGICAL VERSUS ECONOMIC MODEL

Psychometric models divide the decision process into component parts. Health states are observed and categorized. Scores are obtained as weights for these health states and the ratings apply to a particular point in time. They are analogous to consumer preferences under certainty. Probabilities are a separate dimension and are determined empirically. The model combines the empirically determined probabilities and the utilities. Psychologists and economists differ in their views about the appropriate model. Economists have challenged the psychometric approaches on several grounds.[23,29] First, they emphasize that data obtained using rating scales cannot be aggregated. They acknowledge that rating scales may provide ordinal data, but contend that they do not provide interval level information necessary for aggregation. These judgements under certainty are victims of all of the difficulties outlined by Arrow.[20]

Psychologists have also challenged the use of rating scales. For example, Stevens[30] questioned the assumption that subjective impressions can be discriminated equally at each level of a scale. He claimed that the rating scale method is biased because participants will attempt to use categories equally often, thus spreading their responses when the cases are actually close together and pushing them together when the true values are actually far apart. These biases would suggest that numbers obtained on rating scales are not meaningful.

Armed with these arguments, economists have proposed standard gamble or time trade-off methods as validity criteria for rating scales. The basic assumption is that methods which conform with the Von Neumann and Morgenstern axioms assess true utility. If rating scales produce results inconsistent with these utilities, they must assess an incorrect representation of preference. As compelling as these arguments are, they disregard a substantial literature which attempts to assess the process of human judgement.

COGNITIVE LIMITATIONS

Because the standard gamble technique meets the axiomatic requirements of the Von Neumann and Morgenstern theory of decision under uncertainty, some authors believe that the gamble should serve as a gold standard for evaluating other methods. However, there are concerns about the standard gamble and related techniques.[31]

Several studies have documented unexpected preferences using standard gamble or time trade off methodologies. For example, MacKeigan[32] found that patients preferred immediate death to being in a state of mild to moderate dysfunction for 3 months. Apparently, some patients misunderstood the nature of the trade-off or felt that any impaired quality of life was not worth enduring. McNeil, Weischselbaum and Pauker[33] obtained similar results. They found that if survival was less than 5 years, participants were unwilling to trade any years of life to avoid losing their normal speech. These results suggest that either patients have unexpected preferences or that they have difficulty using the trade-off methodologies. Cognitive psychologists have suggested explanations for these problems. Some methods, such as the standard gamble require only trade-offs. They may not require complex processing of probability information. However, other information processing biases may distort judgement. For instance, there is an anchoring and adjustment heuristic. Typically information is processed in a serial fashion. Participants begin with one piece of information and adjust their judgement as more information is added. However, experiments have suggested that the adjustments are often inadequate or biased.[34] Use of the standard gamble and trade-off methods could evoke bias due to the anchoring and adjustment heuristic.

There are other explanations for the inconsistent results in studies using trade-off methods. Some studies have been poorly designed or conducted. For example, there have been problems in studies that request a choice between a mild disability and a very severe disability. Often patients will not make this trade. However, a careful application of the methodology would identify a smaller trade off that the patient would take. Thus, some of the problems may be avoided with careful application of the methodology.[12]

Evidence for Rating Scales

Several lines of evidence argue against the use of rating scales. As noted above, rating scales are theoretically inconsistent with the uncertainty provisions of the Von Neumann-Morgenstern theory. According to microeconomic theory, rating scales should not produce data that can be aggregated. When compared against the theoretically more appealing standard gamble and time trade-off methods, rating scales produce different results. In addition, the use of rating scales has been challenged by psychophysicists, who argue that these methods produce, at best, ordinal level data.

Recent psychological research challenges these criticisms of rating scales. Although rating methods are subject to serious biases, most of these biases can be controlled. For example, it has been argued that participants have a tendency to use each category in a 10-point rating scale equally often. Thus, for stimuli that are close together, participants will use all categories from 0 through 10 on a 10-point rating scale. Similarly, for cases that represent broader variability in true wellness, participants will also use the entire range. As a result, it has been argued that any numbers obtained from rating scales are meaningless. However, systematic studies of health case descriptions do not confirm this property. Kaplan and Ernst,[35] for example, were unable to document these context effects for health case descriptions. Although there are known biases associated with the use of rating scales, these can typically be controlled. The real issue is whether or not rating scales can produce meaningful data. Most studies evaluating utilities have sought to demonstrate convergent validity which is achieved when different methods produce the same result.

Until recently, empirical tests evaluating the various approaches had not been conducted. Within the past few years, an empirical test of scale property has been introduced. The model takes into consideration the psychological process used in evaluating cases. Typically, preference assessment involves a global judgement of a case. The case is usually made up of multiple attributes. When the attributes of the case are systematically varied, parameters of the judgement process can be estimated. Substantial evidence suggests that human judges most often integrate multi-attribute information using an averaging rule.[24] The averaging rule yields an additive model of human judgement. This averaging process has been validated in specific experimental tests (see Anderson,[24] for a three-volume review of evidence). Once the averaging process has been established, an analysis of variance model can be used to evaluate the scale properties. Typically, this is done by systematically varying components of case descriptions as rows and columns in an experimental design.

Global judgements are obtained for each cell within the resulting matrix. The analysis of variance model allows parameter estimation for scale values and weights.

According to the functional measurement model, the absence of a significant interaction effect in the analysis of variance establishes the interval property, assuming that the participants are combining information using an averaging rule. Differences between utilities for two items which differ on only one attribute should be equal to the difference between two other items which differ only by that one attribute. These data confirm a large number of other studies that have also shown the interval property for rating scales.[24] However, studies have failed to confirm the interval property for magnitude estimation[36] or for trade-off methodologies.[37] The axioms underlying the functional measurement model have been published.[33] It should be noted, however, that the evidence for additive multi-attribute preferences is mixed. Within the context of multi-attribute preference functions for health applications a number of investigators have found that the data reject the additive form and support more complicated formulations of preferences such as the multiplicative function.[39–42]

In summary, there is substantial debate about which technique should be used to acquire utility information. Results obtained from different methods do not correspond although they typically have a high degree of similarity in the ranks they assign to outcomes. However, the differences in preferences yielded by alternative methods can result in discrepancies in allocation of resources if the preferences are not obtained on a linear or interval response scale. For example, suppose that the difference between the effect of a drug and a placebo is 0.05 units of well-being as assessed by rating scales and 0.02 as measured by magnitude estimation. The outcome would have to last 20 years to produce 1 QALY if rating scale utilities were used, and 50 years if magnitude estimation utilities were used. Aggregation of benefits necessarily requires an underlying linear response scale in which equal differences at different points along the response scale are equally meaningful. For example, the differences between 0.2 and 0.3 (0.1 QALY if the duration is 1 year) must have the same meaning as the difference between 0.7 and 0.8. A treatment that boosts patients from 0.2 to 0.3 must be considered of equal benefit to a treatment that brings patients from 0.7 to 0.8. Confirmation of this scale property has been presented for rating scales but not for the other methods.

Another difference among methods is the inclusion of information about uncertainty in the judgement process. Time trade-off, standard gamble, or person trade-off all theoretically include some judgement about duration of the health state. Magnitude estimation and rating scales typically separate preference at a point in time from probability. Considerably more theoretical and empirical work will be necessary to resolve these different approaches.

WHOSE PREFERENCES SHOULD BE USED IN THE MODEL?

Choices among alternatives in health care necessarily involve preference judgements. For example, the inclusion of some services in a basic benefits package and the exclusion of others is an exercise in value, choice, or preference. Some critics of cost/utility analysis begin with the assumption that preferences differ. For example, in most areas of preference assessment, it is easy to identify differences between different groups or different individuals. It might be argued that judgements about net health benefits for white Anglo men, should not be applied to Hispanic men who may give different weights to some symptoms. We all have different preferences for movies, clothing or political candidates. It is often assumed that these same differences must extend to health states and that the entire analysis will be highly dependent upon the particular group that provided the preference data. Allocation of resources to Medicaid recipients, for example, would be considered inappropriate when the preferences came from both Medicaid recipients and non recipients.[43] Other analysts have suggested that preference weights from the general population cannot be applied to any particular patient group. Rather, patient preferences from every individual group must be obtained.

Although critics commonly assume substantial variability in preferences, the evidence for differential preference is weak, at best. An early population study demonstrated some significant, but very small differences, between social and ethnic groups on preferences.[44] Studies have found little evidence for preference differences between patients and the general population. For example, Balaban and colleagues[45] compared preference weights obtained from arthritis patients with those obtained from the general population in San Diego. They found remarkable correspondence for ratings of cases involving arthritis patients. Nerenz and colleagues[46] reported similar results for cancer patients. Wisconsin cancer patients had preferences that were very similar to those of the San Diego general population.

There are very few differences by geographic location. Patrick and his colleagues[27] found essentially no differences between the preference for another health status measure among those who live in the UK and those who live in Seattle. A series of studies in European communities by the EuroQoL group suggest that differences in preference among the European community are small and non-significant.[47] We do recognize that there is considerable variability in estimating preferences for a particular case.[25] However, averaged across individuals, the mean preference for different cases in different groups may be quite similar. Although observed differences are sometimes statistically significant, these differences are typically a very small.[45] Further research is needed in order to determine whether these small differences affect the conclusions of various analyses. In addition, the importance of potential cross-cultural and cross-national differences warrants further attention.

SUMMARY

In summary, review of the literature on utility assessment suggests that preferences can be explicitly considered in a cost/utility analysis.[49] A variety of studies have evaluated the generalizability, the validity, and the reliability of the preference measures.[8,40,50] Methodological studies have tested some of the specific concerns about rating scale methods.[35,51] We have little evidence that preferences differ across groups or that the small observed differences reported by others have much influence upon decisions in policy analysis. We encourage continuing evaluations of these problems because they are expected to be important in the development of newer approaches to policy analysis.

REFERENCES

1. Weinstein, M. C. and Stason, W. B. (1976) *Hypertension: A Policy Perspective*. Cambridge, MA: Harvard University Press.
2. Kamlet, M. (1992) *The Comparative Benefits Modeling Project. A Framework for Cost-Utility Analysis of Government Health Care Programs*. Public Health Service, US Department of Health and Human Services.
3. Guyatt, G. H., Feeny, D. and Patick D. L. (1993) Measuring health related quality of life. *Ann Intern Med* **118**, 622–629.
4. Ware, J. E., and Sherbourne, C. D. (1992) The MOS 36-item short form health survey (SF-36): conceptual framework and items selection. *Med Care* **30**, 473–483.
5. Wu, A. W., Rubin, H. R., Mathews, W. C. et al. (1991) A health status questionnaire using 30 items from the medical outcome study: preliminary validation in persons with early HIV disease. *Med Care* **29**, 786–798.
6. Froberg, D. G. and Kane, R. L. (1989) Methodology for measuring health state preferences I: Measurement strategies. *J Clin Epidemiol* **42**, 345–352.
7. Froberg, D. G. and Kane, R. L. (1989) Methodology for measuring health state preferences II: Scaling methods. *J Clin Epidemiol* **42**, 459–471.
8. Froberg, D. G. and Kane R. L. (1989) Methodology for measuring health state preferences III: Population and context effects. *J Clin Epidemiol* **42**, 585–592.
9. Froberg, D. G. and Kane R. L. (1989) Methodology for measuring health state preferences IV: Progress and a research agenda. *J Clin Epidemiol* **42**, 675–685.
10. Fanshel, S. and Bush, J. W. (1970) A health-status index and its applications to health services outcomes. *Operations Res* **18**, 1021–1066.
11. Torrance, G. W. (1976) Social preferences for health states. An empirical evaluation of three measurement techniques. *Socio-Economic Plan Sci* **10**, 129–136.
12. Torrance, G. W. and Feeny, D. (1989) Utilities in quality-adjusted life years. *Int J Technol Assess Health Care* **5**, 559–575.
13. Feeny, D. and Torrance, G. W. (1989) Incorporating utility-based quality of life assessments in clinical trials: two examples. *Med Care* **27**, S190–S204.
14. Von Neumann, J. and Morgenstern, O. (1944) *Theory of Games and Economic Behavior*. Princeton, NJ: Princeton University Press.
15. Raiffa, H. (1968) Decision Analysis: *Introductory Lectures on Choices Under Uncertainty*. Reading, MA: Addison Wesley.

16. Bell, D. E. and Farquhar, P. H. (1986) Perspectives on utility theory. *Operations Res* **34**, 179–183.
17. Howard, R. A. (1988) Decision analysis: practice and promise. *Manage Sci* **34**, 679–695.
18. Bator, F. M. (1957) The simple analytics of welfare maximization. *Am Econ Rev* **47**, 22–59.
19. Arrow, K. J. and Debreu, G. (1954) Existence of equilibrium for a competitive economy. *Econometrica* **22,** 265–290.
20. Arrow, K. J. (1951) *Social Choice and Individual Values*. New York: Wiley.
21. Keeney, R. L. (1976) A group preference axiomatization with cardinal utility. *Manage Sci* **23**, 140–145.
22. Kaplan, R. M. and Anderson, J. P. (1990) The general health policy model: an integrated approach. In: Spilker, B, ed. Quality of Life Assessments in Clinical Trials. New York: Raven Press, 131–149.
23. Nord, E. (1992) Methods for quality adjustment of life years. *Soc Sci Med* **34**, 559–569.
24. Anderson, N. H. (1991) *Contributions to Information Integration Theory*, Vols 1–3. Hillsdale: Erlbaum Publishers.
25. Mulley, A. J. (1989) Assessing patient's utilities: can the ends justify the means? *Med Care* **27**, S269–S281.
26. Furlong, W., Feeny, D. Torrance, G. W., et al. Guide to design and development of health-state utility instrumentation. McMaster University Centre for Health Economics and Policy Analysis Working Paper No 90–9, June 1990.
27. Patrick, D. L., Bush, J. W. and Chen, M. M. (1973) Methods for measuring levels of well-being for a health status index. *Health Serv Res,* 228–245.
28. Nord, E. (1991) The validity of a visual analogue scale in determining social utility weights for health states. *Int J Health Plan Management*.
29. Richardson, l. (1991) *Economic Assessment in Health Care:Theory and Practice*. National Centre for Health Program Evaluation. Monash University.
30. Stevens, S. S. (1966) A metric for the social consensus. *Science* **151**, 530.
31. Tversky, A., Slovic, P. and Kahneman, D. (1990) The causes of preference reversals. *Am Econ Rev* **80,** 205–217.
32. MacKeigan, L. D. (1990) Context effects in health state utility assessment: etiology, framing and delay of health outcomes. Unpublished doctoral dissertation. Tucson: University of Arizona.
33. McNeil, B. J., Weischselbaum, R. and Pauker, S. G. (1981) Speech and survival: trade-offs between quality and quantity of life in laryngeal cancer. *New Engl J Med* **305**, 982–987.
34. Kahneman, D. and Tversky, A. (1983) Choices, values, and frames. *Am Psychol* **39**, 341–350.
35. Kaplan, R. M. and Ernst, J. A. (1983) Do category rating scales produce biased preference weights for a health index? *Med Care* **21**, 193–207.
36. Kaplan, R. M., Bush, J. W. and Berry, C. C. (1979) Health Status Index: category rating versus magnitude estimation for measuring levels of well-being. *Med Care* **17**, 501–525.
37. Zhu, S. H. and Anderson, N. H. (1991) Self-estimation of weight parameter in multiattribute analysis. *Organ Behav Hum Decis Processes* **48**, 36–54.
38. Luce, R. D. (1981) Axioms for the averaging and addition representations of functional measurement. *Math Soc Sci* **1**, 139–144.
39. Torrance, G. W., Boyle, M. H. and Horwood, S. P. (1982) Application of multi-attribute utility theory to measure social preferences for health states. *Operations Res* **30**, 1042–1069.

40. Krischer, J. P. (1976) The utility structure of a medical decision-making problem. *Operations Res* **24**, 951–972.
41. Torrance, G. W., Yueming, Z. and Feeny, D., et al. (1992) Multi-attribute preference functions for a comprehensive health status classification system. McMaster University Centre for Health Economics and Policy Analysis Working Paper No 92–18.
42. Feeny, D., Furlong, W. and Barr, R. D., et al. (1992) A comprehensive multi-attribute system for classifying the health status of survivors of childhood cancer. *J Clin Oncol* **10**, 923–928.
43. Daniels, N. (1991) Is the Oregon rationing plan fair? *J Am Med Assoc* **265**, 2232–2235.
44. Kaplan, R. M., Bush, J. W. and Berry, C. C. (1978) The reliability, stability, and generalizability of a health status index. *American Statistical Association, Proceedings of the Social Status Section*, 704–709.
45. Balaban, D. J., Fagi, P. C. and Goldfarb, N. l. et al. (1986) Weights for scoring the quality of well-being instrument among rheumatoid arthritics. *Med Care* **24**, 973–980.
46. Nerenz, D. R., Golob, K. and Trump, D. L. (1990) Preference weights for the quality of well-being scale as obtained from oncology patients. Unpublished paper; Henry Ford Hospital, Detroit, Ml.
47. EuroQOL Group. EuroQOL — a new facility for the measurement of health-related quality of life. *Health Policy* 1990, 16 December, 199–208.
48. Kaplan, R. M. (1993) *The Hippocratic Predicament: Affordibility, Access and Accountability in American Health Care*. San Diego, CA: Academic Press.
49. Torrance, G. W. (1986) Measurement of health state utilities for economic appraisal: a review *J Health Econ* **5**, 1.
50. Kaplan, R. M., Bush, J. W. and Berry, C. C. (1976) Health status: types of validity and the index of well being. *Health Serv Res* **11**, 478–507.
51. Kaplan, R. M. (1982) Human preference measurement for health decisions and the evaluation of long-term care. In Kane, R. L., Kane, R. A., eds. *Values and Long-term Care*. Lexington Books, 157–188.

Portions of this paper were adapted from a chapter by Robert, M. Kaplan, entitled, 'Utility assessment for estimating quality adjusted life years' to appear in Cost/effectiveness of Pharmaceuticals, edited by Frank Sloan, Cambridge Press, 1994.

12. SELECTED METHODS FOR ASSESSING INDIVIDUAL QUALITY OF LIFE

JOHN BROWNE

This chapter reviews a number of measures not covered in previous chapters but which incorporate some elements of the individual approach to quality of life measurement. The basic elements of quality of life measurement are (i) choice of domains to be covered, (ii) assessment of those domains according to particular criteria and (iii) weighting of the relative importance of these domains. The measures described below adopt an individually based approach to one or more of these elements. Information on the reliability and validity of these measures is included, where available. The chapter also includes a brief discussion of some questionnaires that measure concepts related to individual quality of life such as life satisfaction and subjective well-being.

AUDIT-DIABETES DEPENDENT QUALITY OF LIFE (ADDQoL)

Authors: Bradley, C.[1], Todd, C. J.[2], Gorton, T.[1], Plowright, R.E.A.[1] and Symonds, E.[1]
1: Royal Holloway, University of London, Egham, Surrey TW20 OEX, England.
2: Institute of Public Health, Cambridge CB2 2SR, England.

Overview

The ADDQoL is based upon the conceptual and methodological approach to quality of life measurement taken by the Schedule for the Evaluation of Individual Quality of Life (SEIQoL; O'Boyle, McGee, Hickey et al., 1993 — see chapter 9) and, like the SEIQoL, assesses individually generated life domains (Bradley, Todd, Gorton, Plowright, and Symonds, 1995; Bradley, 1996). It is a disease specific measure which focuses on the impact of diabetes, using a questionnaire format rather than a semi-structured interview as in the case of the SEIQoL.

Domains

The thirteen domains used in the ADDQoL were identified in pilot work as commonly affected by diabetes and its treatment. These include, *inter alia*, working life, social life, worries about the future and enjoyment of food.

Assessment

The questionnaire contains 15 items. The first elicits patient ratings of overall quality of life on a visual analogue scale adapted from the SEIQoL. The second assesses the impact of diabetes on overall quality of life. The remaining items require the respondent to rate the impact of diabetes on thirteen life domains specified in the questionnaire on a scale from −3 to +3 with 0 representing no impact. Respondents may indicate where domains are not applicable to them and such domains are ignored for scoring purposes.

Weights

Each applicable domain is rated for its importance to quality of life on a 0–3 scale with 0 representing no importance. These weights are multiplied by the impact assessments and the product divided by the number of applicable domains to provide an overall score which may range from −9 to +9.

Domains which are rated as having no importance to quality of life do not impact on the overall score.

Reliability

Cronbach's alpha, a measure of internal consistency, is reported to range from 0.86 to 0.90 in two samples of people with diabetes (n = 102 and 52 respectively).

Validity

As expected, people with complications of diabetes indicate greater impairment to diabetes dependent quality of life measured by the ADDQoL than those without complications. Patients with comorbid conditions in addition to non-insulin dependent diabetes tended to have poorer scores on generic measures such as the SF-36 but not on the diabetes specific ADDQoL. This finding suggests that the ADDQoL may detect changes caused by diabetes and its treatments, which can be masked in generic questionnaires by the impact of comorbid conditions (Woodcock, Bradley, Kinmoth and Julious, 1996).

Modifications to the ADDQoL

The ADDQoL has recently been modified and extended to be appropriate for people with end stage renal failure (Bradley, 1997).

CONTENT ANALYSIS METHODS

Overview

A growing number of researchers are using content analysis to measure quality of life. Gottschalk and Lolas (1992) underline the phenomenological nature of these measures in the following summation of content analysis methods:

"Most questionnaires beg the question of who decides what is valuable and what is not, taking for granted that the professional definition of quality of life is the one that should be used. Content analysis of spontaneous verbal communications (written or oral) is a natural, undistorted probing of biopsychosocial quality of life from the standpoint of people experiencing it.... (p. 76)"

The aim of content analysis is to examine the internal psychological life of the individual by analysing what they say or write and how they say or write it. At its core, the method attempts to identify recurring themes in verbal behaviour. These themes are then interpreted according to the theoretical standpoint of the interviewer be it psychoanalytic, behavioural or linguistic. The elicitation of themes usually involves recording a response to a general question about quality of life such as: "what is your life like at the moment?" The response is then broken down into clauses, and the theme of each clause noted. The exercise usually focuses on specific themes so that only these themes will be noted and their relative magnitude summed. The scales also usually take account of details such as the agent and/or recipient within a clause and non-verbal cues such as the emotion associated with a clause.

Content analysis is well established within psychology and has developed an elaborate methodology over the years. It is beyond the scope of this chapter to review the field. Instead the focus will be on a small number of scales that have been used to measure quality of life in the past. Gottschalk and Gleser (1969) have provided guidelines for the construction of new content analysis scales.

Domains

Content analysis scales usually focus on particular domains rather than quality of life as a whole. Therefore, a researcher must use a number of scales to ensure that all relevant domains are measured. Some scales, such as the Health-Sickness Scale (Gottschalk and Gleser, 1969) or the Human Relations Scale (Gottschalk, 1968) focus on traditional quality of life domains. However, most scales focus on psychological constructs with the aim of measuring directly the phenomenology of quality of life. Example of these measures include the Hope Scale (Gottschalk, 1974), the Positive Affect Scale (Westbrook, 1976) and the Pawn and Origin Scales (measures feelings of helplessness and incompetence; Westbrook and Viney, 1980).

Assessments

Content analysis measures adopt a unique approach to quality of life assessment. The respondent is not directly asked to evaluate their quality of life. Rather they reveal their true attitudes to aspects of life quality through their verbal behaviour. Often they will be informed that they are taking part in a linguistic experiment where they are required to provide a speech sample.

For example, in a study using scales such as the Health-Sickness Scale, Gottschalk and Lolas (1992) used the following instructions:

> "This is a study of speaking and conversational habits. I would like you to talk for 5 minutes about any interesting or dramatic personal life experiences you have ever had. While you are talking I would prefer not to answer any questions you might have. However, I will be happy to answer any questions you might have at the moment. (p. 71)".

In order to derive a score for the Health-Sickness Scale, references (in self or others) to feelings of well-being, health, being symptom-free are scored positively and references (again to self or others) to feelings of poor health, having symptoms, pain and suffering are scored negatively. These scores may be presented separately, or combined for an overall health score. Scores are usually calculated per 100 words.

Weights

By applying a number of scales to a verbal sample it is possible to derive a measure of the relative importance of various domains to quality of life. For example, frequently mentioned themes may be assumed to be of greater importance. This assumption obviously depends on the ability and willingness of the respondent to relate the true nature of their internal states and traits. Recognising the limitations with this approach, many scales attempt to measure the influence of such psychoanalytic constructs as defence mechanisms, particularly denial (Gottschalk and Lolas, 1992).

If domain-specific scales are not used, a completely individual definition of life domains and their relative importance may be derived from a verbal sample. This, it may be argued, is the essence of the individual approach, as the respondent is spontaneously describing the architecture of their internal quality of life experience.

Reliability

Gottschalk and Lolas (1992) report that inter-rater reliabilities of 0.80 and above are sought when analysing and scoring a verbal sample.

Validity

The validity of content analysis scales is a complex issue beyond the scope of this chapter. As mentioned above, the validity of the approach depends on the degree to which people are able and willing spontaneously to reveal their inner states and traits through verbal responses. This unresolved question is at the heart not only of projective testing, but also of the psychotherapeutic tradition.

GOAL ATTAINMENT MEASURES

Overview

Implicit in most quality of life measures is the assumption that striving towards a goal or goals is essential to personal well-being. Most researchers in the field would agree that quality of life assessment involves an appraisal of ones current state against some ideal (Cella and Tulsky, 1990) and that a good quality of life depends upon the degree to which an individual succeeds in attaining his desires (Calman, 1984). However, very few measures attempt to analyse the goals which people are trying to achieve, or use goal attainment as a proxy for quality of life.

The small number of measures which have used goal attainment to measure quality of life have all the attributes of the individual-centred approach. The personal nature of life goals requires the investigator to depend on the perceptions of the respondent and makes the imposition of pre-determined content impossible. At a practical level, the challenge for these measures has been to allow inter-individual comparison of the narratives elicited. At a conceptual level, the challenge has been to demonstrate that goal attainment is the most ecologically valid way of measuring the individuals experience of life quality and to explore the relationship between goal evaluation and higher order evaluations.

Little (1983) has described a personal project as an interrelated sequence of actions intended to achieve some personal goal. Palys and Little (1983) outlined what they saw as the major advantages of this approach. First, it focuses on the personal projects as construed by the individual concerned. Second, it allows access to the behavioural as well cognitive and affective realms: behaviour is generally ignored by standard quality of life measures. Third, it is allows an evaluation of the person in their temporal context, and not simply at one moment in their life.

The key to the goal attainment approach is the assumption that quality of life is something that is experienced at an everyday level and cannot be separated from everyday activities. Subjective well-being, on the other hand, is a higher order cognitive/affective concept, influenced by goal attainment activities but also influenced by factors such as disposition and cognitive strategies aimed at reducing distress. A chronically ill patient, for example, may be forced to abandon important life goals, which may reduce the sense of well-being. In order to reduce distress, the individual might then re-calibrate his/her perspective on the goal, perhaps choosing a more realistic project. These interactive processes are essential to any understanding of the individual's reaction to illness over time and quality of life measures which simply aggregate satisfaction with various life domains at one point in time are missing the dynamic essence of the concept.

Two goal attainment measures using an individual-centred approach will be reviewed here. The first is the Personal Strivings approach described by Emmons (1986). The second is the Idiographic Functional Status Assessment (IFSA) developed by Rapkin, Smith, Dumont, Correa, Palmer and Cohen (1994) for use with people suffering from AIDS. A further goal attainment measure, the Quality of Life Systemic Inventory (Duquette, Dupuis and Perrault, 1994) is also geared towards quality of life measurement. It is not reviewed here however, as the goals to be rated are pre-determined rather than generated by the individual respondent.

Domains

In goal attainment theory, personal strivings are the nearest equivalent to life domains. Emmons (1986) described personal strivings as what individuals are characteristically aiming to accomplish through their behaviour. The striving is not a particular goal but is the superordinate construct or theme around which a number of goals may cluster. Thus a person striving to be healthy may have subordinate goals for exercise, diet and smoking.

In both the Personal Strivings approach and the IFSA, personal strivings/goals are elicited from the individual in a semi-structured interview. The Personal Strivings approach allows respondents to nominate up to 15 personal strivings. To facilitate elicitation, the respondent is told that strivings are an objective that they are typically trying to accomplish or attain. Respondents are told that strivings may be positive (trying to be physically attractive) or negative (trying to avoid being noticed by others).

The IFSA also uses a semi-structured interview technique to elicit personal goals and goal attainment activities. Five types of goal are recorded: the main things the respondent wants to accomplish; the problems facing the respondent which they want to solve; the things the respondent wants to prevent or avoid; the things the respondent wants to keep the same; the commitments the respondent wants to relinquish. The goals elicited are then grouped into eight categories to facilitate inter-individual comparison: health; altruism and societal contributions; family; friends and interpersonal relations; psychological and spiritual well-being; personal attainment and self-expression; practical lifestyle and daily functioning; utilising systems and coping with society at large; and death and dying. Finally, the respondent describes the activities they have been pursuing in the past month to achieve the goals they want to achieve, and lists any goals they have been unable to pursue over the past month due to health problems.

Rapkin et al. (1994) report that in a sample of 224 people with AIDS, the average number of goals mentioned was 8.14. The number of goals mentioned varied by type with an average of 2.40 for achievement goals, 1.73 for prevention/avoidance goals, 1.65 for problem-solving goals, 1.61 for maintenance goals and 0.75 for disengagement goals.

Assessments

In the Personal Strivings approach respondents rate their strivings along a number of dimensions, using a mixture of rating scales and qualitative responses. The following dimensions are measured:

- Value (the joy/sorrow derived when the striving is achieved or is not achieved)
- Ambivalence (the unhappiness that will be felt when the striving is achieved)
- Commitment to the striving
- Importance attached to the striving
- Effort (the energy expended when trying to be successful in the striving)
- Difficulty associated with the striving
- Causal attribution (does success in the striving depend on internal or external factors?)
- Social desirability (the perceived social desirability of the striving)
- Clarity (the respondent's understanding of what is required to achieve the striving)
- Instrumentality (does success in one striving change the chances of success in other strivings?)
- Probability of success (likelihood of future success in the striving, rated from 0 to at least 90% chance of success)
- Confidence the respondent feels about the above probability estimation
- Probability if no action (likelihood of future success in striving if no effort is made, rated from 0 to at least 90% chance of success)
- Impact (how many other strivings require success in the striving being evaluated)
- Past attainment (recent success in the striving)
- Satisfaction with progress towards the striving
- Indicative outcomes (which concrete outcomes would indicate the striving had been successful?)
- Past attainment of indicative outcomes (percentage of time that indicative outcomes had occurred in the past, relative to how often they desired the outcome to occur)
- Goals (qualitative description of ways in which respondents attempt to achieve the striving)

An additional section assesses the cross-impact of each project. This requires the respondent to juxtapose the projects against each other and to identify where projects facilitate or are in conflict with other projects. A total conflict score may then be aggregated.

The IFSA limits the number of goals assessed to 15 (a maximum of three for each of the five types of goal elicited). Each goal is assessed in terms of (a) difficulty level, (b) amount of assistance received and (c) requirement for help in achieving the goal. The activities associated with each goal are then assessed to see if (i) they became harder to do over the last month (ii) they became easier to do over the past month (iii) they cause pain (iv) they cause fatigue (v) they take too long to finish.

Goal attainment measures produce two types of index. The first are indices which may be compared across individuals, such as the mean value attached to the strivings, or the mean ratings of difficulty for the goals. The second type are ipsative indexes which express relationships among variables within each individual. The correlation between the value and the importance attached to a personal striving is a particularly useful index.

Weights

The Personal Strivings approach elicits a rating of the importance of each striving in absolute terms on a 5-point scale. This does not allow for an assessment of the relative importance of each striving. The IFSA does not include an assessment of the importance of each goal.

Reliability

It should be noted that goals or personal strivings are inherently unstable, as it is inevitable that certain goals will be achieved or others abandoned over time. The stability of personal strivings derived from the Personal Projects approach was assessed by interviewing a sample of 40 college students over a 1-year period. Eighty-two percent of the strivings listed at baseline were also listed a year later (Emmons, 1986). The stability of the various assessments made on the strivings was measured with the same sample. The mean stability coefficient for all assessments over 1 month was 0.73, and over 3 months 0.60. Social desirability ($r = 0.70$) and importance ($r = 0.69$) were the most stable assessments over 3 months. The least stable assessments were impact ($r = 0.47$) and effort ($r = 0.46$).

The temporal stability of the IFSA was assessed in 26 patients with AIDS over a 2–6 week period. The mean test-retest interval was 24 days. The coefficient of stability of the goals elicited was 0.40. 31% of goals and 21% of activities were mentioned at both interviews. The stability of the various assessments was higher with a coefficient of 0.43 for the number of activities that got harder, 0.70 for those that got easier, 0.56 for those that caused pain, 0.26 for those that caused fatigue and 0.65 for those that took too long.

Validity

The construct validity of the assessments made in the Personal Strivings approach was examined through a principal-axes factor analysis on the responses of 40 college students (Emmons, 1986). Five underlying factors emerged, accounting for 73% of the variance in assessments. These were:

degree of striving, success, ease, instrumentality and a final factor which was difficult to interpret.

The concurrent validity of assessments made in the Personal Strivings approach was measured by correlating the assessments with measures of positive affect, negative affect and life satisfaction. Significant correlations ($p < 0.05$) with positive affect were recorded for value (0.39), importance (0.29), past fulfilment (0.36) and effort (0.26). With negative affect, significant correlations were noted for ambivalence (0.52), probability of success (−0.34) and conflict (0.33). Life satisfaction was significantly correlated with value (0.34), importance (0.52), lack of action (0.32), past fulfilment (0.26) and conflict (−0.34).

In order to assess the concurrent validity of the various IFSA measures in a sample of 224 people with AIDS, correlations were calculated with the Medical Outcomes Study Short-Form Twenty Item General Health Survey (MOS-SF20) a health-related quality of life measure with six subscales (Stewart, Hays and Ware, 1988). The sections of the IFSA that were most highly correlated ($p < 0.001$) with the MOS-SF20 were: number of goals not pursued; number of activities that had become harder; number of painful activities (all significantly correlated with physical functioning, role functioning, social functioning, pain and overall health); overall difficulty associated with activities (significantly correlated with physical functioning, role functioning and mental health) and the number of activities that took too long to achieve (significantly correlated with physical functioning and role functioning).

QUALITY OF LIFE INDEX (QLI)

Authors
Ferrans, C. E. and Powers, M.
Department of Medical-Surgical Nursing, College of Nursing, 845 South Damen Avenue, 7th Floor. Chicago, Illinois 60612-7350, USA.

Overview

The Quality of Life Index (QLI) is a generic quality of life questionnaire that may be self-administered by healthy and ill individuals. The measure, like many others in the field, is based on the assumption that quality of life is the sum of satisfactions derived from important life domains (see Andrews and Withey, 1976 and Flanagan, 1978 for classic examples of this approach). Unlike these measures however, the QLI accepts that importance, as much as satisfaction, determines the overall impact of a domain on quality of life. Thus, respondents rate the importance of each domain for their overall quality of life as well as their satisfaction with that domain. The following description relates to the generic version of the QLI but versions for use with cancer patients (Ferrans, 1990) and cardiac patients (Bliley and Ferrans, 1993) are also available.

Domains

The QLI has four main domains for which corresponding sub-scale scores may be calculated: health and functioning (twelve items); social and economic aspects (nine items); psychological and spiritual aspects (seven items); and family (four items). The scale covers sixteen sub-domains as follows: health care; physical health and functioning; marriage; family; friends; stress; standard of living; occupation; education; leisure; future retirement; peace of mind; personal faith; life goals; personal appearance; self-acceptance. General happiness and general satisfaction are also assessed. Ferrans and Powers (1985) in the original paper on the measure, explain how the above domains and sub-domains were chosen following an extensive review of the existing literature on quality of life measurement.

Assessments

The QLI is divided into two sections each containing thirty-four items. In part I, respondents rate their satisfaction with various aspects of their life on a six-point Likert scale ranging from very dissatisfied to very satisfied. For scoring purposes, the scale is centred on zero as follows: very dissatisfied = –2.5; moderately dissatisfied = –1.5; slightly dissatisfied = –0.5; slightly satisfied = +0.5; moderately satisfied = +1.5; very satisfied = +2.5.

Weights

In part II of the QLI, respondents rate the importance of the thirty-four items rated in part I. Again the rating scale is Likert-type with 6 points: very unimportant = 1; moderately unimportant = 2; slightly unimportant = 3; slightly important = 4; moderately important = 5; very important = 6. To derive an overall score, paired satisfaction and importance scores are multiplied and the products summed. The resulting score is divided by the number of items used to eliminate the effect of missing values. Finally, fifteen is added to eliminate negative values. The possible range of scores for both the QLI as a whole and the four sub-scales is 0–30.

Reliability

Ferrans and Powers (1985) reported a two-week test-retest reliability coefficient of 0.87 with a group of graduate students (n = 69) and a one-month coefficient of 0.81 with a group of dialysis patients (n = 20). In the same study the internal consistency of the QLI was high with Cronbach's alphas of 0.93 (graduate students) and 0.90 (dialysis patients) recorded. Ferrans and

Powers (1992) measured the internal consistency of the overall scale and of the four sub-scales in a study of 349 dialysis patients. High levels of internal consistency for the overall scale (*alpha* = 0.93) and for the four sub-scales (*alpha* = 0.87, 0.82, 0.90 and 0.77) were recorded.

Validity

Ferrans and Powers (1985) measured concurrent validity by correlating the overall QLI score with overall life satisfaction. Correlations of 0.76 (graduate students) and 0.65 (dialysis patients) were observed. In a study of the construct validity of the QLI, 349 dialysis patients completed the QLI (Ferrans and Powers, 1992). Factor analysis revealed that the four factor structure described above best fitted the data. In the same study, the correlation between overall QLI scores and the life satisfaction item was again high (r = 0.77).

Further support for the construct validity of the QLI was found in studies using the cancer and cardiac versions of the instrument. In a study of 111 patients with breast cancer, patients with less pain and depression and who were coping better with stress had significantly higher scores as a group on the cancer version of the QLI (Ferrans, 1990). The cardiac version of the QLI was also found to be sensitive to health status. Forty patients were interviewed the evening before, and four to six weeks after undergoing percutaneous transluminal coronary angioplasty. The overall quality of life scale and the health and functioning scales showed significant improvement following the operation (Bliley and Ferrans, 1993).

REPERTORY GRID TECHNIQUES

Overview

The Repertory Grid is a well established approach to the measurement of personality. The technique was developed by Kelly (1955) to complement his theory of personal constructs. The theory proposes that, in order to successfully adapt to and change their environment, individuals develop an internal model of the world, based on a hierarchical system of constructs about the elements of the world they contact. Elements may be concrete (e.g., father) or abstract (e.g., liberty). Constructs are the qualities which may be used to describe elements, such as softness, healthiness or sociability. Constructs and their place in the overall model develop constantly and are tested against experiences for their efficiency in predicting how elements work (e.g., testing whether ones construction of healthiness is successful in predicting ones own health state). Their function is to serve as ideal benchmarks against which real states may be measured.

The Repertory Grid technique is designed to create a representation of personal constructs and to apply these to particular elements of interest. The main advantage of the technique is that it directly taps the value structure of the individual. The challenge is to present the information gained in a useful way for researchers and clinicians. In recent years a number of researchers have attempted to use the Repertory Grid technique to describe the quality of life of the individual. Two approaches will be described here. The first is the SmithKline Beecham Quality of Scale (SBQoL) developed by Dunbar, Stoker, Hodges and Beaumont (1992). The second is a technique developed by Thunedborg, Allerup, Bech and Joyce (1993).

Domains

The closest equivalent to life domains within the Repertory Grid technique are personal constructs. It is possible to allow the respondent to describe their own elements and constructs but these are generally pre-defined by the researchers. In the SBQoL, ten pre-defined domains are assessed: psychic well-being; physical well-being; social relationships; activities/hobbies/interests; mood; locus of control; sexual function; work/employment; religion; and finances. These were selected from a review of other quality of life measures (Dunbar, Stoker, Hodges and Beaumont, 1992). The ten pre-selected domains are further divided into 28 sub-domains. These were selected by a factor analysis and a cluster analysis on 74 sub-domains originally chosen by the authors. Each sub-domain corresponds to a distinct construct and each construct falls within one of the ten domains. The constructs used are not evenly distributed among the domains: psychic well-being, for example is covered by six domains while sexual function has only one construct.

In the technique described by Thunedborg et al. (1993), pre-defined elements and constructs were used, but nominations by respondents were also included. Seventeen fixed elements were provided covering a broad range of self (e.g., you as you are now), other (e.g., your closest friend) and projective perspectives (e.g., the person who lives a life which seems to you to be almost ideal). For five of the pre-defined elements, the respondent was asked to name a specific person from a fixed list of significant others (e.g., close friends, family, role models). The respondent was allowed to nominate up to three additional elements. Twelve fixed constructs were provided covering the physical, cognitive, affective, social and economic life domains. The respondent was allowed to nominate up to 13 additional constructs. These were elicited using the triad technique (Beail, 1985). This requires the respondent to describe ways in which three elements are similar or differ from each other on quality of life domains. The make-up of the triads, and the total number to be compared is at the discretion of the interviewer. The goal of the technique is to probe the respondent's conception of the most important aspects of quality of life: these are then translated into additional constructs by the interviewer. Thunedborg et al. (1993) reported that in interviews with 33 patients in a clinical trial for a generalised anxiety disorder, an average of 10.4 free constructs and one free element were elicited.

Assessment

The SBQoL is computerised to increase user friendliness. Each of 28 constructs are rated on a ten-point scale anchored by the opposite extremes of that construct ("I feel useful" versus "I feel useless"). When rating constructs, respondents are asked to use two separate perspectives (elements): self-now and ideal-self. Using dedicated software (Flexigrid) it is then possible to generate a cognitive map based on the ratings for each individual. The cognitive map is literally a spatial representation of the distances between ideal-self and self-now, plotted against the construct dimensions rated. Over time, it is possible to observe changes in the distance between the two elements: this is then used as a proxy measure for changes in quality of life.

In the Thunedborg et al. technique, each construct was described only in positive terms (e.g., have a meaningful job). As in the case of the SBQoL, each construct was rated separately using the perspective of each element. Respondents were asked to judge the association between the construct description and each element, on a three-point scale (positive, negative or uncertain). Respondents could also indicate that a construct description for a particular element was meaningless (e.g., rating the health status of a dead person). By using a complex factor analysis on these assessments, it is possible to generate a cognitive map of the internal quality of life architecture of individual respondents. Again, the focus is on the distance between self-now, self before treatment and ideal-self. An overall improvement score, comparable across individuals, may be calculated by dividing the distance between self before treatment and self-now by the distance between self before treatment and ideal-self (measured using a path that intersects with self-now).

Weights

Neither of the Repertory Grid techniques described above address the issue of domain importance. Given that the domains covered are generally pre-defined, a standard set of weights would add little to the individual sensitivity of the measures.

Reliability

The test-retest reliability and internal consistency of the SBQoL over a 12 week period were reported as satisfactory in a study of 129 patients with major depression or generalised anxiety disorder (Stoker, Dunbar and Beaumont, 1992).

Validity

The original construct validity of the SBQoL was assessed with a sample of 1,000 off-the-street volunteers. The 28 constructs used in the measure were selected from an original list of 74 by cluster and factor analysis. Within the factor analysis, 24 constructs that accounted for 69% of self-now judgments, 76% of sick-self judgments and 84% of ideal-self judgments were recorded. Three constructs were discarded because less than 80% of respondents had rated self-now as either higher than ideal-self or lower than sick-self. A cluster analysis revealed an additional five constructs that had not been adequately covered. The concurrent validity of the SBQoL was established by Stoker, Dunbar and Beaumont (1992). SBQoL scores tracked scores on the Sickness Impact Profile and the General Health Questionnaire over a 12 week period to a high degree without becoming redundant.

A factor analysis on the judgments made using the Thunedborg et al. technique found that the total explained variance ranged from 40% to 83% (Thunedborg et al., 1993).

SUBJECTIVE QUALITY OF LIFE PROFILE (SQLP)

Authors
Dazord, A., Gerin, P. and Boissel, J. P.
SCRIPT (INSERM) Hôpital St. Jean de Dieu. 69373 Lyon, France.

Overview

The SQLP is based firmly upon the individual-centred approach to quality of life measurement. The authors explicitly state an individual's personal experience is the only realistic reference for use in the subjective quality of life assessment and consequently, it is the person himself who is best qualified to make this assessment (Gerin, Dazord, Boissel and Chifflet, 1992). While the authors state they are influenced by the goal attainment model, the SQLP does not directly measure goals or personal strivings and is therefore considered separately from such measures.

The SQLP is designed to assess the individual experience of striving towards various goals within different domains. Specifically, it assesses (i) the importance attributed to domains; (ii) tolerance of the distance between current position and goal position and (iii) ability to cope with this distance over time by, for example, changing the importance of goals. The authors reject the notion that the positive and negative aspects of quality of life can be represented in an aggregate or index form and prefer to present results as a profile of various domains (Dazord, Gerin and Boissel, 1994).

Domains

The SQLP assesses four pre-defined main domains of life through thirty-three items. The first domain is functional life which includes motor function, psychological life, sensory function, sexual life, sleep, digestion and pain. The second domain is social life and is divided into specific relationships, social roles and interest in the exterior world. The third domain is material life and includes income and housing. The fourth domain is spiritual life and includes religious beliefs, faith and inner life (reflections, reading, meditation).

The authors acknowledge that a taxonomy of domains for all individuals is impossible. They point in particular to the influence of culture in determining quality of life priorities. To make the questionnaire more sensitive to individual concerns therefore, the SQLP allows for a fifth, unspecified domain to be considered. This domain is elicited through the question: "What is the most important (or the most satisfying or the most worrying) thing in your current life?"

Assessments

The SQLP requires four assessments for each domain, with responses made on four or five point Likert scales. Firstly, the respondent's assessments of ability is measured for each domain item. Any change in ability is also measured. Secondly, the respondent's satisfaction with each domain item is measured. The change anticipated over the coming months for each item is then elicited. Finally the respondent's perceived ability to cope with difficulties encountered is assessed for each item. Outside of the four specified domains, a number of global measures of subjective quality of life are also assessed. These include overall happiness, sense of humour and overall satisfaction with treatment and treatment personnel.

Weights

The importance that respondents attribute to each domain is elicited by simply asking how important is this domain to you?. Responses are on a simple three-point Likert scale (unimportant, fairly important and very important). No attempt is made to integrate the weight attached to a domain with the various assessments taken. Results are presented as profiles throughout, with the aim being to build up a picture of the respondent's internal life (Dazord, Gerin and Boissel, 1994).

Reliability

Internal consistency by split-half correlation was reported as 0.93, and by Cronbach's alpha as 0.90. The test-retest of the item on the importance of domains was reported as being 0.5 (p < 0.0005) using the Spearman rho test for correlating ranks (Dazord, Gerin and Boissel, 1994).

Validity

As a measure of convergent validity the SQLP summary satisfaction scores were correlated with scores on the Montgomery Asberg Depression Rating

Scale (MADRS; Montgomery and Asberg, 1979) for a group of 65 depressed patients. Spearman rho correlations of 0.40 (p < 0.001) were reported (Dazord, Gerin and Boissel, 1994). In a further study with 50 patients suffering from sever lung cancer, satisfaction on the SQLP with activities of daily living was correlated with the Karnofsky index (Karnofsky and Burchenal, 1949). A Spearman rho of 0.61 (p = 0.05) was reported (Dazord, Gerin and Boissel, 1994).

The construct validity of the SQLP has been examined through a principal components analysis on the responses of a number of patient populations (overall n = 3,000). The analysis is performed on the satisfaction component of the SQLP. The authors report that in most studies three components emerge (health, relationships and a psychological factor). The health component is predominant (Dazord, Mercier, Manificat and Nicolas, in press).

WISCONSIN QUALITY OF LIFE QUESTIONNAIRE (W-QLI)

Authors
Becker, M., Diamond, R. and Sainfort, F.
University of Wisconsin Madison, Health and Human Issues, Division of Continuing Studies. 315 Lowell Hall, 610 Langdon Street, Madison, WI 53703-1195, USA.

Overview

The W-QLI is a self-administered questionnaire designed for persons with a mental disorder. Different versions of the questionnaire are available for the client, care professionals and for family members/friends and are intended to complement each other. The W-QLI has also appeared originally in press as the Quality of Life Index for Mental Health (QLI-MH; Becker, Diamond and Sainfort, 1993) but will be referred to here by its alternative name to avoid confusion with the QLI developed by Ferrans and Powers (see above). The WQL-I is a complicated instrument which is still in the early stage of validation. It is based, like the QLI, on the assumption that overall quality of life is a product of the satisfaction and importance of underlying domains. Unlike the QLI, the WQL-I uses a number of response formats, and produces an in-depth profile of the respondent as well as an overall index of quality of life. The diversity of response formats arises because the WQL-I includes a number of established measures.

Domains

The client version of the instrument contains nine domains: satisfaction with indicators such as housing and transport; occupational activities; psychological well-being; physical health; social relations; economics; activities of daily living; psychiatric symptoms; and goal attainment (Becker, Diamond and Sainfort, 1993). The domains chosen were based on a review of domains commonly used in quality of life measures. Information on alcohol and drug use and global quality of life is also recorded.

The family/friends version of the questionnaire is designed mainly to provide background information on the well-being of the client. The respondent provides information on the quality of care provided by both formal care providers and family/friends. The respondent also provides proxy information on goal attainment and the overall quality of life for the client. The care provider version of the questionnaire follows the format of the client questionnaire more closely with some equivalent information elicited for all domains apart from objective quality of life satisfaction.

Assessments

As noted above, only five of the nine domains follow a standard procedure within the client questionnaire (satisfaction with objective quality of life indicators, physical health, social relations, economics and goal attainment). For four of these domains, satisfaction with subsidiary items is rated on a seven-point Likert scale from "very dissatisfied" to "very satisfied". For the goal attainment domain, the assessment procedure changes slightly, with the respondent asked to nominate the goals they hope to accomplish as a result of their mental health treatment and then to rate the extent to which they feel they have achieved these goals. The response format used here is a 3-point Likert scale ("not at all", "somewhat" and "completely"). The remaining domains follow no standard response format and are not linked to ratings of importance.

Most of the items in the client version of the WQL-I are derived from established measures. The following measures were used to develop the questionnaire:

- *Satisfaction with objective quality of life indicators*: Indicators of life quality developed by Andrews and Withey (1976).
- *Occupational activities*: Factual information on the respondent's work, school or other day activities. Not derived from an established measure.
- *Psychological well-being*: The Bradburn Affect Scale (Bradburn, 1969).
- *Physical health*: Global evaluations of health are elicited. Not derived from an established measure.
- *Activities of daily living*: The Life Skills Profile (LSP; Rosen, Hadzi-Pavlovic and Parker (1989) and the QL-Index (Spitzer, Dobson, Hall et al., 1981).
- *Social relations*: Includes the entire outcome scale used in the International Pilot Study of Schizophrenia (IPSS; Strauss and Carpenter, 1974).
- *Psychiatric symptoms*: The Brief Psychiatric Rating Scale (BPRS; Overall and Gorham, 1962).

- *Goal attainment*: Open-ended items are used as described above.

The assessment of overall quality of life is made on a 10 point scale with value labels only at the anchors ("lowest quality" and "highest quality").

Weights

Ratings of importance within the client version of the WQL-I mirror the assessment procedures described above. For four domains the importance of items previously rated for satisfaction is assessed. The response format used is a five-point Likert scale from "not at all important" to "extremely important". The response format for the goal attainment domain uses a 3-point Likert scale ("not very important", "somewhat important" and "extremely important").

In order to derive scores for items where ratings of importance are taken, the importance weight is multiplied by the equivalent satisfaction rating. These weighted items scores are then summed to derive a domain score. Where established measures are used, the scoring methods used by the original developers are employed.

The nine sub-scale scores are obviously incomparable at this stage and a complex procedure is required to derive an overall WQL-I score. This involves (i) rescaling each item to a common scale through a linear transformation, (ii) aggregating items within a domains to produce new domain scores and (iii) averaging domain scores to produce an overall score.

Reliability

The authors note that most of the items in the questionnaire were derived from measures where reliability has already been established (Becker, Diamond and Sainfort, 1993). Nevertheless the test-retest reliability of the WQL-I was assessed by administering the measure to ten schizophrenic outpatients and their care professionals at baseline and 3–10 day later. Reliability was measured by examining the number of responses that were exactly the same at each administration. The percentage matches were as follows: satisfaction level, 0.83; occupational activities, 0.87; psychological well-being, 0.82; physical health, 0.86; social relations, 0.82; economics, 0.85; activities of daily living, 0.82; symptoms, 0.86; goal attainment, 0.85; and total score 0.84.

Validity

There has been little substantial validation of the WQL-I. The questionnaire contains many previously validated measures, but this sheds no light on the validity of the overall score. The authors report a correlation of 0.58 between overall WQL-I patient scores and Spitzer QL-Index scores provided by care professionals indicating some level of criterion-related validity (Becker, Diamond and Sainfort, 1993).

Standard Measures of Well-being

One approach to quality of life measurement deals specifically with the psychological concomitants of life quality. This approach attempts to directly assess subjective well-being and to then to identify the external influences that predict it. Flanagan (1978), for example, identified 15 factors as predictors of well-being, which he grouped into five domains: physical and material well-being; relations with other people; social, community and civic activities; personal development and fulfilment; and recreation. From this perspective, quality of life is synonymous with well-being rather than a dynamic between life circumstances and well-being (Andrews and Withey, 1976; Blair, 1977; Campbell, Converse and Rodgers, 1976; Heal and Chadsey-Rusch, 1985).

Well-being measures do not generally work within the value structure of the individual. The measures attempt to tap universally experienced states, which, it is argued, are recognised by all humans. Subjective well-being involves a host of related variables, and many measures have been developed to separately represent these. Life satisfaction is generally thought to be the cognitive aspect of well-being, and may be measured using the Life Satisfaction Index (Neugarten, Havighurst and Tobin, 1961) or the Satisfaction with Life Scale (Diener, Emmons, Larsen and Griffin, 1985). Positive and negative affect represent the emotional dimension of well-being and are commonly measured using the Affect Balance Scale (Bradburn, 1969). Finally, some measures focus directly on subjective well-being. The Spiritual Well-Being Scale (Ellison, 1983) focuses on one form of well-being spirituality. The Views of Life Scale (Williams, Eyring, Gaynor and Long, 1991) measures well-being in three broad areas: inherent value of life, effective life management and a sense of physical and psychological health. The Anamnestic Comparative Self-Assessment scale (Bernheim and Buyse, 1983) is a global one-item measure of well-being where respondents rate their current status in relation to the best and worst periods of their life.

REFERENCES

Andrews, R. M. and Withey, S. B. (1976) Social Indicators of Well-Being: America's Perception of Life Quality. New York: Plenum Press.

Beail, N. (ed.) (1985) Repertory Grid Technique and Personal Constructs: Applications in Clinical and Educational Settings. Beckenham: Croom Helm.

Becker, M., Diamond, R. and Sainfort, F. (1993) A new patient focused index for measuring quality of life in persons with severe and persistent mental illness. Quality of Life Research 2, 239–251.

Bernheim, J. L. and Buyse, M. (1983) The Anamnestic Comparative Self-Assessment for measuring the subjective quality of life of cancer patients. Journal of Psychosocial Oncology 1, 25–38.

Blair, T. H. (1977) Quality of life, social indicators and criteria of change. *Professional Psychology* **8**, 464–473.

Bliley, A. V. and Ferrans, C. E. (1993) Quality of life after coronary angioplasty. *Heart and Lung* **22**, 193–199.

Bradburn, N. M. (1969) *The Structure of Psychological Well-Being*. Chicago: Aldine.

Bradley, C., Todd, C. J., Gorton, T., Plowright, R. E. A. and Symonds, E. A patient-centred measure of the impact of a chronic disorder on quality of life: design and development of the ADDQOL. Presented at conference on Scientific Basis of Health Services, London, 1995.

Bradley, C. (1996) Measuring quality of life in diabetes. *The Diabetes Annual* **10**, 207–224.

Bradley, C. (1997) Design of a renal-specific individualised quality of life questionnaire: RDQOL. Paper presented at the 17th International Conference on Peritoneal Dialysis, Feb 16–18, Denver, Colorado.

Calman, K. C. (1984) The quality of life in cancer patients — an hypothesis. *Journal of Medical Ethics* **10**, 124–129.

Campbell, A., Converse, P. E. and Rodgers, W. L. (1976) *The Quality of American Life: Perceptions, Evaluations and Satisfactions*. New York: Russell Sage Foundation.

Cella, D. F. and Tulsky, D. S. (1990) Measuring quality of life today: Methodological aspects. *Oncology* **4**, 29–39.

Dazord, A., Gerin, P. and Boissel, J. P. (1994) Subjective Quality of Life Assessment in Therapeutic Trials: Presentation of a New Instrument in France (SQLP: Subjective Quality of Life Profile) and First Results. In: *Quality of Life Assessment: International Perspectives.* J. Orley and W. Kuyken (eds) pp. 185–195. Berlin: Heidelberg.

Dazord, A., Mercier, C., Manificat, S. and Nicolas, J. (in press) French subjective quality of life questionnaire: main results. Revue Européenne de Psychologie Appliquée (in press)

Diener, E., Emmons, R. A., Larsen, R. J. and Griffin, S. (1985) The satisfaction with life scale. *Journal of Personality Assessment* **49**, 71–75.

Duquette, R. L., Dupuis, G. and Perrault, J. (1994) A new approach for quality of life assessment in cardiac patients: rationale and validation of the Quality of Life Systemic Inventory. *Canadian Journal of Cardiology* **10**, 106–112.

Dunbar, G. C., Stoker, M. J., Hodges, T. C. P. and Beaumont, G. (1992) The development of SBQOL — a unique scale for measuring quality of life. *British Journal of Medical Economics* **2**, 65–74.

Ellison, C. W. (1983) Spiritual well-being: conceptualisation and measurement. *Journal of Psychology and Theology* **11**, 330–340.

Emmons, R. A. (1986) Personal strivings: an approach to personality and subjective well-being. *Journal of Personality and Social Psychology* **51**, 1058–1068.

Ferrans, C. E. and Powers, M. (1985) Quality of Life Index: development and psychometric properties. *Advances in Nursing Science* **8**, 15–24.

Ferrans, C. E. (1990) Development of a Quality of Life Index for patients with cancer. *Oncology Nursing Forum* **17**, 15–21.

Ferrans, C. E. and Powers, M. J. (1992) Psychometric assessment of the quality of life index. *Research in Nursing and Health* **15**, 29–38.

Flanagan, J. C. (1978) A research approach to improving our quality of life. *American Psychologist* **33**, 138–147.

Gerin, P., Dazord, A., Boissel, J. P. and Chifflet, R. (1992) Quality of life assessment in therapeutic trials: rationale for and presentation of a more appropriate instrument. *Fundamentals of Clinical Pharmacology* **6**, 263–276.

Gottschalk, L. A. (1968) Some applications of the psychoanalytic concept of object-relatedness: Preliminary studies on a human relations scale applicable to verbal samples. *Comprehensive Psychiatry* **9**, 608–620.

Gottschalk, L. A. and Gleser, G. C. (1969) *The Measurement of Psychological States through the Content Analysis of Verbal Behaviour*. Los Angeles: University of California Press.

Gottschalk, L. A. (1974) A hope scale applicable to verbal samples. *Archives of General Psychiatry* **30**, 779–785.

Gottschalk, L. A. and Lolas, F. (1992) The measurement of quality of life through the content analysis of verbal behaviour. *Psychotherapy and Psychosomatics* **58**, 69–78.

Heal, L. W. and Chadsey-Rusch, J. (1985) The Lifestyle Satisfaction Scale (LSS): Assessing individuals' satisfaction with residence, community setting and associated services. *Applied Research in Mental Retardation* **6**, 475–490.

Karnofsky, D. A. and Burchenal, J. H. (1949) The clinical evaluation of chemotherapeutic agents against cancer. In: *Evaluation of Chemotherapeutic Agents*. C. M. McLeod (ed). New York: Columbia University Press.

Kelly, G. A. (1955) *The Psychology of Personal Constructs*. New York: Norton.

Little, B. R. (1983) Personal projects: a rationale and method for investigation. *Environment and Behaviour* **15**, 273–309.

Montgomery, S. A. and Asberg, M. (1979) A new depression scale designed to be sensitive to change. *British Journal of Psychiatry* **134**, 382–389.

Neugarten, B. L., Havighurst, R. J. and Tobin, S. S. (1961) The measurement of life satisfaction. *Journal of Gerontology* **16**, 134–143.

O'Boyle, C. A., McGee, H. M., Hickey, A., Joyce, C. R. B., Browne, J. P., O'Malley, K. and Hiltbrunner, B. (1993) *The Schedule for the Evaluation of Individual Quality of Life (SEIQoL): Administration manual*. Royal College of Surgeons in Ireland.

Overall, J. E. and Gorham, D. R. (1962) The brief psychiatric rating scale. *Psychological Reports* **10**, 799–812.

Palys, T. S. and Little, B. R. (1983) Perceived life satisfaction and the organisation of personal project systems. *Journal of Personality and Social Psychology* **44**, 1221–1230.

Rapkin, B. D., Smith, M. Y., Dumont, K., Correa, A., Palmer, S. and Cohen, S. (1994) Development of the Idiographic Functional Status Assessment: a measure of the personal goals and goal attainment activities of people with AIDS. *Psychology and Health* **9**, 111–129.

Rosen, A., Hadzi-Pavlovic, D. and Parker, G. (1989) The life skills profile: a measure assessing function and disability in schizophrenia. *Schizophrenia Bulletin* **15**, 325–337.

Spitzer, W. O., Dobson, A. J., Hall, J., Chesterman, E., Levi, J., Shepherd, R., Battista, R. N. and Catchlove, B. R. (1981) Measuring the quality of life of cancer patients: a concise QL-index for use by physicians. *Journal of Chronic Disease* **34**, 585–597.

Stewart, A. L., Hays, R. D. and Ware, J. E. (1988) The MOS Short-form General Health Survey: reliability and validity in a patient population. *Medical Care* **26**, 724–732.

Stoker, M. J., Dunbar, G. C. and Beaumont, G. (1992) The SmithKline Beecham quality of life scale: a validation and reliability study in patients with affective disorder. *Quality of Life Research* **1**, 385–395.

Strauss, J. S. and Carpenter, W. T. (1974) The prediction of outcome in schizophrenia: II. Relationships between predictor and outcome variables: a report from the WHO international pilot study of schizophrenia. *Archives of General Psychiatry* **31**, 37–42.

Thunedborg, K., Allerup, P., Bech, P. and Joyce, C. R. B. (1993) Development of the repertory grid for measurement of individual quality of life in clinical trials. *International Journal of Methods in Psychiatric Research* **3**, 45–56.

Westbrook, M. T. (1976) Positive affect: a method of content analysis for verbal samples. *Journal of Consulting and Clinical Psychology* **44**, 715–719.

Westbrook, M. T. and Viney, L. L. (1980) Scales of origin and pawn perception using content analysis of speech. *Journal of Personality Assessment* **44**, 157–167.

Williams, R. L., Eyring, M., Gaynor, P. and Long, J. D. (1991) Development of Views of Life Scale. *Psychology and Health* **5**, 165–181.

Woodcock, A. J., Bradley, C., Kinmonth, A. L. and Julious, S. (1996) Quality of life in non-insulin-dependent diabetes: the effect of comorbidity. *Diabetic Medicine* **13** (Suppl. 7), S14.

III

APPLICATIONS OF INDIVIDUAL
QUALITY OF LIFE ASSESSMENT

13. INDIVIDUAL QUALITY OF LIFE AND POPULATION STUDIES

ANN BOWLING

INTRODUCTION

The methods that social scientists use to investigate the characteristics of populations depends upon their assumptions about society. The measurement of health and disease is based on quantitative methodology, which derives in part from positivism. This assumes that human behaviour is a reaction to external stimuli and that it is possible to observe and measure social phenomena, using the principles of the natural scientist, to establish a reliable and valid body of knowledge about its operation. Positivism holds that social life, like matter, is governed by underlying laws and principles that can therefore be measured and discovered through methods akin to the physical sciences. In other words, social behaviour is determined and can be explained in terms of cause and effect relationships. It is argued that sociology should concern itself only with what is observable and that theories should be built in a rigid, linear and methodical way on a base of verifiable fact. As such, sociology has traditionally developed alongside the physical sciences. The tools used are surveys and experimental methods, and statistical techniques of analysis.

A sociological perspective within the positivist tradition — functionalism — has also influenced the development of scales of health and functional status. Scales of physical functioning, and their sub-domains in generic health status and quality of life scales, focus on the performance of activities of daily living (e.g. personal care, domestic roles, mobility) and on role functioning (e.g. work, finance, family, friend, social). Functionalism studies the whole social system, and when focusing on illness will conceptualise this in relation to the impact on, and consequences for, the immediate (e.g. family, work, and personal finance) and the wider social systems (e.g. the wider socialisation and nurturing functions of families upon which law, order and stability in society are dependent), employment and the economy. Consequences that interfere with the system and its values are called dysfunctional, and those which contribute to its functioning are called functional.

However, among some contemporary social scientists positivism is viewed as often misleading as it encourages an emphasis on superfical facts without understanding the underlying mechanisms observed, or their meanings to individuals. Phenomenologists (along with ethnomethodologists, interpretive and interactionist social scientists) argue that the use of the research methods of the physical sciences is inappropriate for the study and understanding of social life and human behaviour. Phenomenology is based on the paradigm that 'reality' is socially constructed through the interaction of individuals who use symbols to interpret each other and assign meaning to perceptions and experience. The methods favoured are qualitative interviews and observation. Phenomenologists would argue that health related quality of life is dependent upon the interpretation and perceptions of the individual and that listing items in measurement scales is unsatisfactory because it is unknown whether all the domains pertinent to each respondent are included, and that this method does not capture the subjectivity of human beings.

Illustrations of these theoretical influences can be clearly seen in the conceptualisation and measurement of physical functioning and in the broader health status scales. All health status and health related quality of life scales assume that social phenomena in relation to health and illness can be measured (in the positivist tradition), and most have adopted a functionalist perspective. Traditionally, the measurement of health status, and health related quality of life among people with conditions affecting their mobility (eg. stroke, certain cancers, rheumatism and arthritis) has focused on their level of physical functioning (Karnofsky, Abelmann, Burchenal and Craver, 1948; Mahoney and Barthel, 1965; Fries, Spitz and Young, 1982; Meenan, Mason, Anderson, Guccione and Kazis, 1992). Typically, scales focus on role performance in relation to daily activities, including personal and domestic chores and, in the case of the more extreme and negative Barthel Index, the need for help from others. These approaches fit the functionalist model of ability to function in order to perform personal, social and economic roles (and contribute to the maintenance of society). Broader health status scales can also be seen to fit this model as they focus largely on physical functioning and mobility and ability to perform social, recreational, domestic and, in some cases, work roles (Bergner, Bobbitt, Carter and Gilson, 1981; Hunt, McEwan, and McKenna, 1986; Ware, Snow, Kosinski and Gandek, 1993).

Recently more sensitive approaches to measurement taking a hermeneutic perspective into account, in the spirit of, but not akin to phenomenology, have been attempted. Some scale developers have simply inserted an item in their list of activities which attempts to tap the individual's values, in the light of which results are analysed and interpreted — for example, the McMaster-Toronto Arthritis Patient Function Preference Questionnaire (MACTAR) adds: ' Which of these activities would you most like to be able to do without the pain or discomfort of your arthritis?' (Tugwell, Bombardier, Buchanan, Goldsmith, Grace and Hanna, 1987).

The disease specific quality of life scales of Guyatt et al. (1987; 1989a; 1989b) include patient-generated items as well as a structured list of items about the impact of the condition on life (Guyatt, Berman, Townsend, Pugsley and Chambers, 1987; Guyatt, Mitchell, Irvine et al., 1989a; Guyatt, Nogradi, Halcrow, Singer, Sullivan and Fallen, 1989b). Ruta, Garratt, Leng, Russell and MacDonald (1994) developed a Patient Generated Index in which respondents are asked about the five most important areas or activities of their life affected by their condition; then to rate each according to how badly affected they are (Ruta et al., 1994). The Schedule for the Evaluation of Individual Quality of life (SEIQoL), developed by O'Boyle, McGee, Hickey, O'Malley and Joyce (1992) asks individual respondents to nominate five areas of quality of life that are important to them personally (O'Boyle et al., 1992; O'Boyle, McGee, Hickey, O'Malley and Joyce, 1989; O'Boyle, McGee, Hickey, Joyce and O'Malley, 1993). Respondents are then asked to rate their current status on each area against vertical visual analogue scales (VAS). Although these are all highly quantified approaches to measurement in the positivist tradition, they are also attempting to adopt a hermeneutic approach.

The latter approaches would not satisfy phenomenologists who only value pure qualitative methodology, but they do attempt to recognise the importance of the phenomenological argument in relation to individual meaning. There is little point in measuring an individual's ability to walk up and down stairs if he rarely or never encounters stairs, or if that activity rates low on their scale of priorities in life or is irrelevant to their condition.

In terms of the intensity of personal contact and numbers of people investigated, the large scale survey and experiment are at one polar extreme (positivism and scientific methodology) and in-depth, qualitative interviews and observations are at the other (phenomenology and hermeneutics). In the past there was a great deal of hostile debate between the two schools on the merits of the different methodologies. Now there is more agreement that both methods can be valid if applied to appropriate research questions and they should complement each other. Qualitative techniques are essential for exploring new topics and obtaining insightful and rich data on complex issues. They are essential in the initial stages of questionnaire design and scale construction. Quantitative techniques are appropriate if the issue is defined, relatively simple and unambiguous. If these conditions are satisfied, there is always scope for using triangulated methods or supplementary quantitative techniques in order to check the accuracy, content, validity and relevance (meaning) to the respondents of the quantitative data collected.

That these new, more hermeneutic approaches are essential in measuring health related quality of life has been demonstrated in research based on a national population by this author (Bowling, 1995). Using a large scale survey approach, but with open-ended questions similar to those developed for the SEIQoL it was found that people mention different areas as important when asked about the five most important areas of life and the five most important areas of life affected by their medical conditions; open-ended questions enabled respondents to mention pertinent life areas affected by the condition other than those contained in pre-coded questions; and several life areas given priority by respondents were not included in the most popularly used scales of broader health status and health related quality of life. The results of the study have been published elsewhere, but are summarised below.

THE SURVEY

A national survey of a large random sample of the public in Great Britain, based on the Office of Population Censuses and Surveys (OPCS) Omnibus Survey, was intended to provide population norms on the dimensions of life that people perceive to be important, in relation to quality of life in general and health-related quality of life in particular.

METHODS

The study design was an interview survey of a random sample of 2,000 people in Great Britain taken by the OPCS for their Omnibus Survey. The OPCS Omnibus Survey is a monthly survey of 2,000 randomly selected people (using postcode sectors and addresses) in Great Britain. It offers the opportunity for other researchers to buy into the survey with their own questions.

The sampling frame for the OPCS Omnibus Survey is the Postcode Address File of 'small users', which includes all private household addresses. The proportion of ineligible addresses on the file (new and empty properties, some business addresses) is about 11–12%. They are eliminated from the sample before response rates are calculated. The sample was stratified by region, the proportion of households renting from local authorities and the proportion in which the head of household is in socio-economic groups 1–5 or 13 (i.e. professional, employer or manager). A new sample of 100 postal sectors is selected for each month's Omnibus Survey. The postal sectors are selected with probability proportionate to size and, within each sector, 30 addresses are selected randomly. If an address contains more than one household, the interviewer uses a standard OPCS procedure to select just one household randomly. Within households with more than one adult member, just one person aged 16 or over is selected with the use of random number tables. The interviewer endeavours to interview that person, and no proxies are sampled.

Because only one household member is interviewed, people in households containing few adults have a better chance of selection than those in households with many. A weighting factor is applied to correct for this unequal probability. Responses are first weighted by the number of adults in the household, to correct the proportions, and then adjusted to give a total sample size equal to the number of informants actually interviewed. This weighting is used for the OPCS analyses reported here, which then use the individual adult as the unit of analysis.

The method of sampling and the consequent weighting affect the sampling errors of the survey estimates. The effect can be shown by calculating the 'effective sample size' which gives the size of an equal probability sample which is equivalent in precision to the unequal probability sample actually used. An achieved sample of 2,000 individual adults in the Omnibus Survey is equivalent to an equal probability sample of about 1700. The response rate to the survey was 77%. The total number of adults interviewed was 2033, resulting in 2031 usable questionnaires.

All interviews were carried out face-to-face by OPCS trained interviewers. Advance letters were sent by OPCS to all addresses giving a brief account of the survey. Interviewing was completed within two weeks. The interviewer made at least three calls at an address at different times of the day before recording a non-response. A quality check on field work is made by OPCS through recall interviews to ensure that interviews actually took place, and to check the consistency of responses.

MEASUREMENTS

In consideration of the lack of agreement about definition of quality of life and its components, the approach taken in this research was hermeneutic, and the aim was to ask respondents themselves simply about what was important in their lives (positive and negative domains). This approach to measuring quality of life was based on the questions developed for the SEIQoL and the disease-specific quality of life questionnaires, developed by Guyatt and his colleagues.

Although this research aimed to ask people about the domains of life important to them as individuals, the investigator's own assumptions about quality of life should be made explicit. Quality of life was taken to encompass in a broad sense the social, psychological and physical domains of life, incorporating a subjective assessment of important life domains in relation to achieving satisfaction. While it was beyond the scope of this research to measure the circumstances of people's lives in these respects, and the extent to which aspirations have been achieved, an attempt was made to measure what people regard as important, and to rate their lives in relation to these things. In this sense, quality of life was operationalised as the things people regard as important in their lives (good and bad). The questionnaire was a mixture of semi-structured questions, in order to elicit people's free responses. Respondents could mention as many items as they wished, but only up to five were coded. Respondents selected the code from a showcard to represent the items mentioned, and both their free responses (which were compared with their coded responses by the researcher, to check consistency) and selected codes were recorded. The items on the showcard were chosen after analysis of the items mentioned by O'Boyle et al's. (1992, 1993) respondents, and responses to other surveys of quality of life. Items which did not fit the pre-codes were listed and coded by the interviewers under "other". An extension to the coding frame was designed to enable the latter to be re-coded later by OPCS coders. Respondents were then asked to place the items mentioned in rank order of importance. Both respondents' selected codes of life areas, and their free responses (which were coded later) were analysed and compared. Then respondents were asked to rate their current status for each item mentioned against a categorical scale, labelled at each extremity 'as good as could possibly be' and 'as bad as could possibly be'. Respondents were then asked to rate their overall life on a similarly labelled categorical scale. Respondents who reported any limiting longstanding illness, disability or infirmity were next asked to define and rate the most important effects of this on their lives using the same techniques. The method was adapted from the SEIQoL (O'Boyle et al., 1992) which was too complex to be used in a large national survey. The OPCS Omnibus survey uses 100 interviewers, who are briefed by post, necessitating the use of conventional, standardised questionnaire design.

Data were analysed by age sex, marital status, health status, longstanding illness, disability or infirmity (and type, where numbers permitted), housing tenure, socio-economic group, economic activity, income, social class, education, age left school and qualifications, and region. These were standard OPCS questions. Attention has been drawn to differences which were statistically significant at levels of $p < 0.05$.

RESULTS

Age and sex characteristics of the sample were similar to that of the adult population of Great Britain. Most respondents were married or cohabiting (68%), owned their own home or had a mortgage (75%), 52% were female, most left school before age 17 (66%), and 37% had no educational or other qualification. Most (93%) were white (which was expected, but precluded analyses of responses by ethnic group). Fifty one per cent of respondents were in paid employment, and 55% were in social classes I, II or III (non-manual). Full details of respondents, and the complete analyses of the study, have been reported elsewhere (Bowling, 1995).

Respondents were most likely to mention relationships with either family or relatives as the first most important thing in their lives (30%), followed by their own health (25%) and the health of a close or dependent other (19%), and finances/standard of living/housing (10%). In relation to the second, third and fourth most important things in their lives, respondents were most likely to select finances/standard of living/housing (selected by between 19–30%), and social life/leisure activities was most likely to be selected as the fifth most important item (22%). Analysis of the replies coded as 'other' showed that the largest categories were 'politics'/'government' and 'happiness/satisfaction/well-being', although the proportions mentioning these were small (<1–3%). The final 'other' category consisted largely of the importance of pets to respondents (e.g. cat, dog, horse). These analyses related to the open coded results of respondents' free responses.

Current Quality of Life Status

Respondents were then asked to rate their current status for each 'most important thing' they had mentioned against a categorical scale, labelled at each extremity 'as good as could possibly be' and 'as bad as could possibly be'. They were also asked to rate their overall life on a similarly labelled horizontal visual analogue scale. In relation to their feelings about life in all areas ranked 1–5, few respondents said that the important things in their lives were 'as good as can be'; between 46–53% said they were 'very good' or 'good'. The proportion who ranked their lives as 'bad', 'very bad', and 'as bad as can be' increased with the things which they had ranked in declining order of importance. In relation to their rating of life as a whole, 18% said it was 'as good as can be', 31% said it was 'very good', 31% said it was 'good', 18% said it was 'all right', 2% said it was 'bad' and less than 1% in each case said it was either 'very bad' or 'as bad as can be'.

Effects of Long-standing Illness or Condition on Lives

Respondents were asked the standard OPCS question: 'Do you have long-standing illness, disability or infirmity? By long-standing I mean anything that has troubled you over a period of time or that is likely to affect you over a period of time?' Respondents who said 'yes' were asked what the condition was (and later about the condition that had most affected their life as a whole, over the last 12 months, if more than one was reported), and whether it 'limits your activities in any way?' A relatively high proportion, 40% reported a long-standing illness, disability or infirmity, and 60% of these reported that it limited their activities in some way. The proportion who reported long-standing illness was similar to the proportions reported in the 1991 and 1992 OPCS Health Surveys.

Those who reported more than one long-standing illness or condition were asked to select the condition which had most affected their life as a whole over the last 12 months for the subsequent questions on how their lives had been affected. Respondents' free responses were recorded by the interviewer for later coding, and they were also asked to select codes themselves from a showcard to represent the things they had mentioned, and then list them in order of importance. Respondents' own coding of their free response choices and the office coding of their recorded responses were analysed and compared.

The analyses reported here are based on the office coding of respondents' verbatim replies. The table shows that the most common, freely mentioned, first important effects of the longstanding illness on their lives were (in order of frequency) ability to get out and about/stand/walk/go out shopping (25%), being able to work/find a job (14%) and effects on social life/leisure activities (13%). The full range of responses has been noted in Bowling (1995). When respondents selected their own codes from a showcard in relation to health

effects, however (prior to the office recoding), there were some discrepancies
with their (office coded) verbatim replies. The showcard apparently had the
effect of prompting them to code areas of life that they had not previously
mentioned to the interviewer. Consequently, the most commonly mentioned
FIRST most important effects of the longstanding illness on their lives (when
coded from the showcard by respondents) were (in order of frequency) pain
(20%), tiredness/lack of energy/lethargy (16%), social life/leisure activities
(14%), and availability of work/ability to work (10%).

The results showed that people with different conditions often prioritised
different areas of life as being most affected, as would be expected. For
example, people with neoplasms, mental health problems and disorders of
the nervous system were all most likely to rate availability of work/ability to
work as the first most important area affected, and the most frequently
mentioned area. People with eye conditions, cardiovascular disease, respiratory disease and disorders of the musculo-skeletal system were all most likely
to mention ability to get out and about as the first most important area and
it was the area most frequently mentioned by this group. Respondents with
hearing problems were most likely to mention their social life/leisure activities
as the first most important area affected. Respondents with digestive and
endocrine disorders were most likely to mention dietary restrictions as the
most important effect, and as the most frequently mentioned affect.
Respondents with disorders of the genito-urinary system were most likely to
mention ability to get out and about as the first most important area
affected, but depression was most frequently mentioned.

CONCLUSION

These national population norms for priority ranks, and frequencies, of the
important things in respondents' lives, and the important things affected by
longstanding illness, have implications for the content and weighting of both
generic and disease specific health related quality of life scales. While the full
SEIQoL instrument was too complex for use in a large population survey,
this research provides some empirical data against which generic scales can
be assessed. While disease-specific scales will continue to be tested on specific patient groups, and in greater depth than was possible in a global
national survey, the data on global disease conditions and areas of life
affected provides some useful data against which to validate scales. Health-
related quality of life questionnaires also need to be sensitive to the type of
respondents (e.g. in relation to age and sex and condition). The results
reported here support the need for hermeneutic approaches to measurement.

The relevant dimensions of health related quality of life which should be
included in measurement scales are still the subject of vigorous debate and
disagreement. The public, and specific groups of patients, are the best
judges of how medical conditions adversely affect the quality of their lives.

Few scales have been developed and rigorously tested using large enough samples.

In sum, health status and health related quality of life are usually assessed using nomothetic measurement instruments (i.e., they seek to measure traits based on pre-conceived assumptions of quality of life and their relevance to all individuals). In contrast, ideographic measures, which measure those things which are unique to individuals, are rarely used in health status and health related quality of life measurement, although there is a slow but increasing trend to encompass these within the structure of traditional measurement scales.

ACKNOWLEDGEMENTS

Material from the OPCS Omnibus Survey, made available through the Office of Population Censuses and Surveys, has been used with the permission of the Controller of HM Stationary Office. The dataset is held on the ESRC Data Archive at the University of Essex. The research was funded by the Economic and Social Science Research Countil.

REFERENCES

Bergner, M., Bobbit, R. A., Carter, W. B. and Gilson, B. S. (1981) The Sickness Impact Profile: Devlopment and final revision of a health status measure. *Medical Care* **19**, 787–805.

Bowling, A. (1995) What things are important in people's lives? A survey of the public's judgements to inform scales of health related quality of life. *Social Science and Medicine* **10**, 1447–62.

Fries, J. F., Spitz, P. W. and Young, D. Y. (1982) The dimensions of health outcomes: The Health Assessment Questionnaire, disability and pain scales. *Journal of Rheumatology* **9**, 787–93.

Guyatt, G. H., Berman, L. B., Townsend, M., Pugsley, S. O. and Chambers, L. W. (1987) A measure of quality of life for clinical trials in chronic lung disease. *Thorax* **42**, 773–8.

Guyatt, G. H., Mitchell, A., Irvine, E. J., Singer, J., Williams, N., Goodacre, R. and Tompkins, C. (1989a) A new measure of health status for clinical trials in inflammatory bowel disease. *Gastroenterology* **96**, 804–10.

Guyatt, G. H., Nogradi, S., Halcrow, S., Singer, J., Sullivan, M. J. and Fallen, E. L. (1989b) Development and testing of a new measure of health status for clinical trials in heart failure. *Journal of General and Internal Medicine* **4**, 101–7.

Hunt, S. M., McEwan, J. and McKenna, S. P. (1986) *Measuring Health Status.* Beckenham: Croom Helm.

Karnofsky, D. A., Abelmann, W. H., Burchenal, J. H. and Craver, L. F. (1948) The use of nitrogen mustards in the palliative treatment of cancer. *Cancer* **1**, 634–56.

Mahoney, F. I. and Barthel, D. W. (1965) Functional evaluation: the Bartel Index. *Maryland State Medical Journal* **14**, 61–5.

Meenan, R. F., Mason, J. H., Anderson, J. J., Guccione, A. A. and Kazis, L. E. (1992) AIMS2. The content and properties of a revised and expanded Arthritis Impact Measurement Scales Health status Questionnaire. *Arthritis and Rheumatism* **35**, 1–10.

O'Boyle, C. A., McGee, H., Hickey, A., O'Malley, K. and Joyce, C.R.B. (1992) Individual quality of life in patients undergoing hip replacement. *The Lancet* **339**, 1088–91.

O'Boyle, C. A., McGee, H., Hickey, A., O'Malley, K. and Joyce, C. R. B. (1989) Reliability and validity of judgement analysis as a method for assessing quality of life. *British Journal of Clinical Pharmacology* **27**, 155P.

O'Boyle, C. A., McGee, H., Hickey, A., Joyce, C. R. B. and O'Malley, K. (1993) *The schedule for the evaluation of individual quality of life (SEIQOL). Administration Manual (Draft)*. Dublin: Department of Psychology, Royal College of Surgeons in Ireland.

Ruta, D. A., Garrett, A. M., Leng, M., Russell, I. T. and MacDonald, L. M. (1994) A new approach to the measurement of quality of life. The Patient-Generated Index. *Medical Care* **32**, 1109–26.

Tugwell, P., Bombardier, C., Buchanan, W., Goldsmith, C. H., Grace, E. and Hanna, B. (1987) The MACTAR Patient Preference Disablity Questionnaire: an individual functional priority approach for assessing improvement in physical disability in clinical trials in rheumatoid arthritis. *Journal of Rheumatology* **14**, 446–51.

Ware, J. E., Snow, K. K., Kosinski, M. and Gandek, B. (1993) *SF-36 Health Survey: Manual and Interpretation guide*. Boston, MA: The Health Institute, New England Medical Centre.

14. INDIVIDUAL QUALITY OF LIFE AND ASSESSMENT BY CARERS OR 'PROXY' RESPONDENTS

ROBERT F. COEN

In reviewing key papers in the literature on proxy decision making this chapter addresses issues that arise in the proxy evaluation of the quality of life of cognitively incapacitated individuals by medical personnel and significant others. Issues include clarification of the quality of life concept, consideration of how successful or otherwise proxies have been in rating the quality of life of another, the problem of carers with interests of their own, and the impact of adaptation and shared experience on proxy-patient concordance. Some limited strategies to improve proxy quality of life evaluation are discussed.

INTRODUCTION

The heated controversy surrounding a recent case in Ireland (Maddock, McDonagh, McEneaney and McKenna, 1995) in which a Supreme Court ruling upheld the removal of a feeding tube by which a woman had been sustained in a near permanent vegetative state for 23 years served to highlight once again the moral, legal and medical dilemmas that arise when people are asked to make decisions on behalf of individuals who are no longer capable of doing so themselves ("proxy" or surrogate decision making). This is an increasing problem which has led over the past several years to the introduction in the USA, Australia and Europe of legislation in an attempt to provide guidelines for health care providers and significant others.

Two competing standards for judgement in such cases have emerged: substituted judgement and best interest judgement (Emanuel, 1993). Substituted judgement requires that the proxy make a decision based on what the patient would decide, were he or she capable. If it is not possible to determine what the patient would decide then it is recommended that proxy decisions be based instead on the best interests of the patient (Buchanan and Brock, 1989). The substituted judgement standard is intended to be based on the patient's own values and differs from the best interest standard, which is based on an objective standard of benefits and burden (Emanuel, 1988). While not explicitly stated, the patient's quality of life is likely to be an important factor considered by anyone trying to guage either the patient's preferences or that which is in the patient's best interest. Consistent with similar recent cases such as that of Nancy Cruzan (White, Siegler, Singer, and Iserson, 1991) and in view of the obvious difficulties in trying to establish a substituted judgement, the Irish ruling was based on the best interest standard. The medical intervention was deemed not to be in the best interests of the patient and was therefore rejected by the presiding magistrates (Maddock et al., 1995).

Such life or death cases represent extreme examples of a dilemma that is encountered much more widely whenever a proxy is asked to speak on behalf of a mentally incapacitated or incompent individual. Common cases include those incompetent due to mental retardation, mental illness, brain damage from trauma, stroke or alcoholism, and the growing numbers of those who develop dementing disorders such as Alzheimer's disease. Progressive and eventually global cognitive impairment is a hallmark of Alzheimer's disease, while survival time may be in excess of 15–20 years. With advancing illness, Alzheimer's disease patients lose the capacity to make evaluations and cease to introspect on, or at least do not report reliably on, interior states or phenomena (Lawton 1994). The central problem in dementia is that the very ability to assess one's own quality of life and communicate this assessment is affected by the disorder. (Whitehouse and Rabins, 1992). The evaluation of individual quality of life, which focuses on the perceptions of the individual and which requires complex judgemental skills, may not be feasible in those cases where global cognitive impairment has progressed beyond the mild stage (Coen, O'Mahony, O'Boyle et al., 1993). In fact, for patients with Alzheimer's disease beyond the relatively early stage, measurement of the subjective aspects of quality of life is usually foregone (Lawton, 1994).

PROXY RATINGS OF QUALITY OF LIFE

There is a growing concensus that quality of life is a multi-dimensional construct and that the patient should be the primary source of information regarding his/her quality of life (Sprangers and Aaronson, 1992; O'Boyle, McGee and Joyce, 1994; Joyce, 1994a). Where it is not possible to obtain such information directly from the patient the use of surrogates to rate patients' quality of life by proxy has been relied on as an alternative. It is important to draw here the distinction between proxy ratings of another's quality of life, where the rater attempts to rate the patient's quality of life from the *patient's* perspective, as opposed to ratings of the patient's quality of life by significant others where the rating is in fact based on the perspective of the rater. Proxy rating of quality of life is therefore an example of substituted judgement, which requires the proxy to "stand in the shoes" of the patient (Sanders, 1993). This can be particularly difficult in the case of cognitive impairment as we may in many instances reasonably ask "are there any shoes to stand in?". Yet this is exactly what is asked of proxy respondents when they are asked to make a substituted judgement of an individual's perception of his or her quality of life. Some have argued that in the absence of reliable evidence of the patient's views all the proxy can do is offer an unverifiable guess (Emanuel, 1988). The concept of the advance directive, or "living will", has recently been developed as one attempt to improve substituted judgement by providing information concerning the values and preferences of mentally incapacitated individuals (Annas, 1991; Emanuel, 1993). This is a document in which a mentally competent individual sets forth directions regarding medical treatment in the event of future incapacitation. Although advance directives represent an attempt to increase patient autonomy in relation to subsequent decisions, few people yet complete them (Hare and Nelson, 1991). Advance directives have a number of drawbacks, one of the most problematic being the effect of transforming experiences over time. It is possible, because of response shift, that the choices made at the time of completion of advance directives may not represent the view or wishes of the subsequently incompetent patient. That said, if the proxy can take into account the same mix of considerations used by the patient in making his or her advance directives, the accuracy with which proxy judgements reflect the views of the patient will probably be improved rather than diminished (Emanuel, 1993).

THE CONCEPT OF QUALITY OF LIFE IN PROXY JUDGMENTS

Several issues are important in considering the extent to which proxy respondents may be expected to provide accurate evaluations of another's quality of life. Quality of life has a cognitive and an affective aspect (Glatzer, 1991). In the words of Callahan (1992) "I feel, desire, observe, evaluate, and try to make sense of the world I am constantly perceiving and experiencing". Appreciation of both aspects is important because, while cognition is impaired in conditions such as Alzheimer's disease, there is little evidence to suggest that the same applies to the patient's emotional capability. While it may be almost impossible to discern the thoughts of another from observation alone, there is evidence that affective state can be inferred with reasonable accuracy by an observer (Sinha, Zelman, Nelson et al., 1992; Lawton, 1994). This, as discussed below, offers one limited line of approach in trying to guage the perceived quality of life of a mentally incapacitated individual.

Quality of life may also be construed as having both objective and subjective components and it may be that the objective component can be accurately appraised by others. Lawton's model of quality of life (Lawton, 1983), depicted in Figure14.1, provides a useful conceptual framework within which to view the task of the proxy attempting to rate the quality of life of a mentally incapacitated individual.

According to this model, quality of life encompasses four broad sectors termed behavioural competence, objective environment, psychological wellbeing, and perceived quality of life. Behavioural competence includes the five additional domains of health, functional ability, cognition, time use, and social behaviour. The sectors overlap and can be evaluated to a greater or lesser extent from an objective or subjective perspective. Therefore, objective environment and behavioural competence can be measured by physical and social-normative criteria, whereas perceived quality of self and

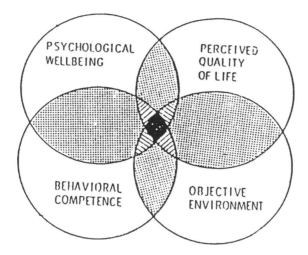

Figure 14.1 Four sectors of quality of life. (From Lawton, 1983, p. 351. Copyright Gerontological Society of America, reprinted with permission).

subjective environment can obviously be measured only by subjective criteria. For example, "number of people per room" is an objective environmental characteristic, whereas "crowding" is a subjectively experienced characteristic of perceived quality of life (Lawton, 1983).

Individual approaches to quality of life emphasise the central importance of the individual's perceptions and judgements. From this perspective quality of life has been defined as "what the patient tells him/herself it is" and the focus is on internal as opposed to external variables (Joyce, 1994a,b). However, the individual's perception of his/her quality of life may be distorted by mental illness, deprivation or lack of awareness. Anosognosia, the unawareness or denial of illness, is very common in dementia. Distorted or unrealistic thinking frequently occurs in serious psychiatric conditions such as schizophrenia and manic disorders. Therefore it has been argued that both objective and subjective evaluations are required to provide a comprehensive view of an individual's quality of life (Glatzer, 1991; Lawton, 1994). Proxies are likely to encounter particular difficulties in attempting to provide subjective evaluations from the perspective of mentally incapacitated individuals, and may revert instead to "own perspective" evaluations, which are indeed subjective but not necessarily representative of the views of the individual who's quality of life is being assessed.

VALIDITY OF PROXY QUALITY OF LIFE RATINGS

In a review of the proxy evaluation of the quality of life of patients with chronic disease (e.g. cancer, arthritis, chronic pain), Sprangers and Aaronson

(1992) evaluated the extent to which health care providers and significant others were able to assess accurately the patients' quality of life. Based on the findings of 37 studies they identified a number of clear trends. The most important conclusion was that both health care providers and significant others tended, in general, to underestimate patient quality of life. Nurses tended to overestimate patients' feelings of anxiety, depression, and distress. A similar lack of concordance was evident between physicians and patients. Consideration of a wider range of quality of life domains (e.g. perceptions of general health, self-care deficits, awareness of life problems) also revealed only moderate levels of agreement between ratings by physicians and/or nurses and those of the patients themselves. In an interview-based study comparing quality of life ratings of physicians and chronically ill elderly patients Pearlman and Uhlmann (1988) found that physicians placed more emphasis on medical criteria whereas patients emphasised non-medical factors such as psychological well-being and socio-economic factors, resulting in poor concordance. Slevin, Plant, Lynch, Drinkwater and Gregory, (1988) also found poor concordance between physician and cancer patient ratings on scales designed for rapid evaluation of patient "quality of life" by the doctor. With regard to significant others, the majority of studies reviewed by Sprangers and Aaronson (1992) suggested that, like health care providers, relatives tend to underrate patient performance status and quality of life. In general, health care providers and significant others appear equally inaccurate in assessing patient quality of life.

Perhaps it is too global a question to ask whether or not health care providers and significant others can provide valid and reliable proxy evaluations of patient quality of life. Sprangers and Aaronson (1992) rephrased the question to ask which dimensions of quality of life proxies can rate accurately, and under what conditions. They concluded that concordance between patient and observer ratings depends, in part, on the concreteness, visibility and salience of the quality of life domains under consideration. The lowest patient-proxy concordance was found for the most subjective domains, such as emotional health and satisfaction. In a typical study of 361 elderly hip fracture patients and their proxies, Magaziner, Simonsick, Kashner and Hebel, (1988) found that the less concrete, less observable, or more private the behaviour, activity or quality assessed, the poorer the agreement between patient and proxy. Epstein, Hall, Tognetti, Son and Conant, (1989) found generally similar ratings by proxies and patients for overall health, functional status and social activity, whereas proxy reports of emotional health and satisfaction were significantly lower. This may be due in part to the fact that evidence of functional health, overall health, and social activity is generally available to an external observer, whereas emotional status and satisfaction are more likely to be experienced as private feelings and opinions. Rothman, Hedrick, Bulcroft, Hickam and Rubenstein (1991) reported high levels of agreement between patients and proxies for physical scores on the Sickness Impact Profile, whereas concordance for psychosocial scores was poor. In terms of Lawton's quality of life model described above, it is the subjective as opposed to the objective aspects of the patient's quality of life which present the greatest difficulties for proxy respondents. Unfortunately, it is also the subjective aspects which are at the core of quality of life evaluation.

Agreement is not necessarily high even when more observable aspects of the patient's status are under consideration. A number of studies have reported a tendency for all types of proxies to over-report functional disability relative to the patient (Rubenstein, Schairer, Weiland, and Kane, 1984; Clipp and Elder, 1987; Magaziner et al., 1988), although others have reported good concordance (Epstein et al., 1989; Weinberger, Samsa, Schmader, Greenberg, Carr and Wildman, 1992). In understanding discrepancies between ratings, several authors have highlighted important characteristics of the proxy and the patient (Magaziner et al., 1988; Sprangers and Aaronson, 1992; Weinberger et al., 1992). Magaziner et al. (1988) found that, in general, the greater the proxy contact or involvement with the patient the better the agreement in ratings of health and functional status. While "partner" status does not necessarily increase the proxy's knowledge of the patient's quality of life, living in the same house appears to improve the accuracy of proxy quality of life ratings (McCusker and Stoddard, 1984; Spear Bassett, Magaziner and Hebel, 1990; Sprangers and Aaronson, 1992). Greater involvement with the patient can be expected to increase knowledge of the patient and therefore enhance the accuracy of observer ratings. However, involvement can also distort the proxy's perception of the patient. Caring for an incapacitated patient can be highly burdensome, and can lead to an exaggeration of patient impairment by the carer (Poulshock and Deimling, 1984). Rothman et al. (1991) found that the accuracy of proxy ratings of psychosocial function was negatively influenced by the perceived burden of caregiving. Similar findings were reported by Epstein et al. (1989). Magaziner et al. (1988) also reported that when proxies in close contact with the patient did disagree, they tended to err on the more disabled side. They speculated that a respondent less intimately involved in the patient's daily care, but who still maintained close contact with the patient, may be the preferred proxy.

With regard to patient characteristics, cognitive impairment is associated with poor patient-proxy concordance. Weinberger et al. (1992) found good concordance on functional ratings when patients were cognitively intact, whereas agreement was poor for cognitively impaired patients. Magaziner et al. (1988) found that even mild levels of patient cognitive impairment were associated with lower patient-proxy response comparability. Their discussion of this finding raised another important issue. It had been decided, a priori, that a cognitively impaired patient is not an appropriate judge of his or her health and functional status, and that the proxy provides the more valid response. However, Magaziner et al. (1988) fully acknowledged that without objective measures of functioning it is impossible to ascertain whether the patient or the proxy provided the more accurate assessment. The impact of burden on the proxy's perception of the impaired patient implies that the proxy's estimation is not always the more valid. Mangone, Sanguinetti, Baumann et al. (1993) partly addressed this issue by comparing ratings of the functional status of Alzheimer's disease patients by their carers against direct measures of the patients' actual functional competence. The patients showed better functional performance on the direct assessment than had been reported by carers. It was concluded that burden may foster growing intolerance, leading to an underestimation of the patient's actual functional competence.

CARERS WITH INTERESTS OF THEIR OWN

There is an element of "Catch-22" in asking a proxy to rate the individual quality of life of a mentally incapacitated person. Due to his/her incompetence the patient is assumed to be an inappropriate judge of their quality of life. The proxy is asked to speak on behalf of the patient, ideally applying the substituted judgement standard. However, it is not possible for the proxy to "stand in the patient's shoes". There is no way of knowing what the incompetent person would say if competent, or even if there is any relation between needs, desires and perceived quality of life in the two states. Some authors have argued that, at least with regard to decisions concerning medical treatment, "the very condition of incompetency makes the doctrine of substituted judgement a cruel charade" (Emanuel, 1988). The proxy may try instead to apply the best interest standard. Here again, in order to decide what is in the best interest of the patient with a view to improving the patient's quality of life, the proxy must try to guage some sense of the patient's individual quality of life, but without any means to verifying the accuracy of his/her judgements.

Hardwig (1993) has drawn attention to a further complication. To what extent can we be sure that the proxy's judgement of that which is best for the patient is not tainted by his/her own interests? Caring for an incapacitated person is highly burdensome. In a general population study Jones and Peters (1992) found that many carers were caring for elderly dependents at enormous cost to themselves in terms of lifestyle and quality of life. Based on reports from 256 carers (enrolled from a random sample of 1079 elderly individuals) the negative impact of caring for an elderly dependent on the carer's quality of life included deleteriosly affected health (27%), impaired social life (28%), impaired family life (16%), and a lot or unbearable stress (18%). 29% of the carers suffered from anxiety and 11% from depression, compared to 6% and 5% respectively in the general population. In addition, 24% reported not having had a holiday (a week or more away) for more than 5 years, and 20% had not had a two day break (e.g. weekend away) over the same period. 11% reported giving up work to care for their dependent, while the emergence of a caring role prevented a substantial number of

others from considering paid employment. In an overview of carer quality of
life in Alzheimer's disease Guerriero-Austrom and Hendrie (1992) found
that many carers were both physically and mentally exhausted. Important
factors having a negative impact on carer quality of life included marital
relationships which were either strained (children/relative carers) or
nonexistent (spouse carers), impaired social life, financial pressures, and
patient personality and behavioural changes. In our own research (Coen,
Swanwick, O'Boyle and Coakley, 1997) in a sample of 50 primary carers of
Alzheimer's disease patients attending a hospital memory clinic (Swanwick,
Coen, O'Mahony et al., 1996), patient behavioural disturbance in particular,
and informal social support to a lesser extent, were significant but independent
predictors of burden, which was very high in many carers.

Given the burdensome nature of caring, how can we know if a carer acting
as proxy is covertly requesting care and treatment options that the proxy
wants for the patient, rather than options the patient would want? These
questions are directly relevant to the clinical management and institutionali-
sation of incompetent individuals such as patients with dementia. Cognitive
abnormalities and behavioural disturbances frequently occur in Alzheimer's
disease. Decisions to administer sedating medications or even to institution-
alise the patient may be based as much on improving the quality of life of the
carer as that of the patient, though it may be felt by all concerned that it's all
in the patient's "best interest". The family's quality of life comes more to the
forefront of care as the patient deteriorates (Whitehouse and Rabins, 1992).
There is a very difficult balance here between the needs of the patient and
the needs of the family. Neuroleptic medication may well reduce agitation in
the patient and improve the carer's quality of life, as the patient is now more
docile and manageable. The reduced agitation and improved care
environment may be expected to positively benifit the patient, but at the cost
of deceased mobility, decreased engagement and further compromised
cognitive functioning.

ADAPTATION AND SHARED EXPERIENCE

The key assumption underlying the evaluation by a proxy of another's
quality of life is that the proxy is capable of assuming someone else's quality
of life values, priorities and preferences. However, values, priorities and
preferences can and do change over time, and adaptation to changing
circumstances may play an inportant role in altering perceived quality of life.
To what extent can a proxy reasonably be expected to have insight into
another's situation, perceptions and emotions if the proxy has never been in
the same situation? This is a question that lies at the core of the problem of
trying to rate in surrogate fashion the quality of life of a mentally incompetent
person. The main obstacle to establishing the accuracy of the proxy's
judgements is the absence of any yardstick by which it can be verified, as the

mentally incompetent patient is by definition unable to provide the requisite information for comparison. As a first step in tackling this difficult question we recently used the SEIQoL-DW (O'Boyle, Browne, Hickey, McGee and Joyce, 1996; Hickey, Bury, O'Boyle, Bradley, O'Kelly and Shannon, 1996) to evaluate the accuracy with which mentally competent elderly spouse couples (in whom neither, one, or both partners had a chronic disorder) could rate each other's quality of life (Browne, Coen and O'Boyle, submitted for publication). We found that concordance between individual and proxy ratings of quality of life was best in those cases where both partners were suffering from a chronic health disorder, lending support to the idea that shared experience may improve one's ability to "put oneself in another's shoes". In order to understand the ability to adapt to a disease it may be important to experience the adaptation process, or at least to be sensitive to the adaptation process in another.

STRATEGIES FOR IMPROVEMENT

This brings us to a consideration of strategies by which the evaluation of the individual quality of life of mentally incapacitated persons might be improved. Proxy decision making that is informed by prior discussion is likely to be considerably more accurate, less burdensome, and less conflicting than proxy decision making in the absence of prior discussion (Emanuel, 1993). In rating individual quality of life by proxy, consideration should be given to the quality of life values and preferences of the individual before cognitive impairment developed. At the very least these factors draw attention to the importance of prior communication and discussion between patient and proxy. The level of communication between proxy and patient is often poor. Luchins and Hanrahan (1993) found that while 92% of family members proffered themselves as proxies, only 42% said that they had discussed preferences with the relatives concerned. Greater communication, while still possible, between proxies and those in their care should therefore be actively encouraged.

A novel though admittedly limited approach to the evaluation of the quality of life of patients with moderate to severe Alzheimer's disease has been reported by Lawton, (1994). He argues that, in general, we must rely on externally evaluated behaviour as our window on the individual quality of life of the cognitively impaired person, particularly with regard to manifestations of positive and negative affect. Health-related quality of life assessment in particular is primarily concerned with decrements from average, and far too little attention is paid to uplifting, enriching, and engaging states. The same point has been made by Joyce, (1994b) in pointing out that many quality of life methods fail to allow for the positive aspect of "quality". In fact this ability to tap into both negative and positive experiences is one feature that distinguishes individual quality of life measures like the SEIQoL from more traditional health-related quality of life measures. In Lawton's view, observable affective responses are seen as the major key to learning about the preferences of dementia patients and their responses to interventions. Using a newly developed Affect Rating Scale, aspects of patient positive and negative affect are rated by observers on the basis of facial expression, body movement, and observed interaction. Generally adequate inter-rater reliability has been demonstrated between observers concerning which emotion is present at a given moment. The scale allows the identification of activities and situations that are accompanied by positive or negative emotions, and provides insights into the needs and preferences of cognitively impaired patients. Factors such as level of cognitive impairment, functional status and pathological behaviour provide additional indicators of quality of life, but the perceived or individual component is based on manifestations of positive and negative affect. The major limitation in this approach rests in the distinction between "state" and "trait" aspects of quality of life. Trait influences are relatively stable over time, whereas states are more limited in duration and less predictable in their effects. Quality of life is generally conceptualised in terms of its more enduring, or "trait" characteristics, whereas short-term variations in state may be indicators of health status rather than perceived quality of life (Joyce, 1994b). Despite its limitations, attention to manifestations of positive and negative affect in patients with moderate to severe dementia offers a window on the patient's subjective state that is generally not afforded by other measures and may therefore prove to be an important aid to proxy judgement and decision making.

REFERENCES

Annas, G. J. (1991) The health proxy and the living will. *New England Journal of Medicine* **324,** 1210–1213.

Browne, J. P., Coen, R. F. and O'Boyle, C. A. Proxy assessment of quality of life in healthy and chronically ill elderly couples. (submitted for publication)

Buchanan, A. E. and Brock, D. W. (1989) *Deciding for others: The ethics of surrogate decision making.* Cambridge: Cambridge University Press.

Callahan, S. (1992) Ethics and dementia: Current issues. Quality of life. *Alzheimer's disease and Associated Disorders* **6,** 138–144.

Clipp, E. C. and Elder, G. H. (1987) Elderly confidants in geriatric assessment. *Comparative Gerontology B* **1,** 35–40.

Coen, R. F., O'Mahony, D., O'Boyle, C. A., Joyce, C. R. B., Hiltbrunner, B., Walsh, J. B. and Coakley, D. (1993) Measuring the quality of life of dementia patients using the Schedule for the Evaluation of Individual Quality of Life. *Irish Journal of Psychology* **14,** 154–163.

Coen, R. F., Swanwick, G. R. J., O'Boyle, C. A. and Coakley, D. (1997) Behaviour disturbance and other predictors of carer burden in Alzheimer's disease. *International Journal of Geriatric Psychiatry* **12,** 331–336.

Emanuel, E. J. (1988) What criteria should guide decision makers for incompetent patients? *Lancet* **335,** 170–171.

Emanuel, L. L. (1993) Advance directives: what have we learned so far? *Journal of Clinical Ethics* **4**, 8–16.

Epstein, A. M., Hall, J. A., Tognetti, J., Son, L. H. and Conant, L. (1989) Using proxies to evaluate quality of life. *Medical Care* **27**(Suppl 3), S91–S98.

Glatzer, W. (1991) Quality of life in advanced industrialised countries: The case of West Germany. In: *Subjective well-being. An interdisciplinary perspective*. F. Strack, M. Argyle and N. Schwartz (eds) pp. 261–275. Oxford: Pergamon Press.

Guerriero-Austrom, M. and Hendrie, H. C. (1992) Quality of Life: The family and Alzheimer's disease. *Journal of Palliative Care* **8**, 56–60.

Hardwig, J. (1993) The problem of proxies with interests of their own: Towards a better theory of proxy decisions. *Journal of Clinical Ethics* **4**, 20–28.

Hare, J. and Nelson, C. (1991) Will outpatients complete living wills? *Journal of General Internal Medicine* **6**, 41–46.

Hickey, A. M., Bury, G., O'Boyle, C. A., Bradley, F., O'Kelly, F. D. and Shannon, W. (1996) A new short form individual quality of life measure (SEIQOL-DW): application in a cohort of individuals with HIV/AIDS. *British Medical Journal* **313**, 29–33.

Jones, D. A. and Peters, T. J. (1992) Caring for elderly dependants: Effects on the carer's quality of life. *Age and Ageing* **21**, 421–428.

Joyce, C. R. B. (1994a) Health status and quality of life: Which matters to the patient? *Journal of Cardiovascular Pharmacology* **23**(Suppl 3), S26–S33.

Joyce, C. R. B. (1994b) Requirements for the assessment of individual quality of life. In: *Quality of life following renal failure. Psychosocial challenges accompanying high technology medicine*. H. McGee and C. Bradley (eds) pp. 43–54. Reading: Harwood Academic Publishers.

Lawton, M. P. (1983) Environment and other determinants of well-being in older people. *The Gerontologist*, **23**, 349–357.

Lawton, M. P. (1994) Quality of life in Alzheimer's disease. *Alzheimer's disease and Associated Disorders* **8**(Suppl 3), 138–150.

Luchins, D. J. and Hanrahan, P. (1993) What is appropriate health care for end-stage dementia?. *Journal of the American Geriatrics Society* **41**, 25–30.

Maddock, J., McDonagh, M., McEneaney, A. and McKenna, G. (1995) Why we must now let this woman die. *Irish Independent* **104**(179), 1 and 11–15.

Magaziner, J., Simonsick, E. M., Kashner, T. M. and Hebel, J. R. (1988) Patient-proxy response comparability on measures of patient health and functional status. *Journal of Clinical Epidemiology* **41**, 1065–1074.

Mangone, C. A., Sanguinetti, R. M., Baumann, P. D., Gonzalez, R. C., Pereyra, S., Bozzola, F. G., Gorelick, P. B. and Sica, R.E.P. (1993) Influence of feelings of burden on the caregiver's perception of the patient's functional status. *Dementia* **4**, 287–293.

McCusker, J. and Stoddard, A. M. (1984) Use of a surrogate for the sickness impact profile. *Medical Care* **22**, 789–795.

O'Boyle, C. A., Browne, J., Hickey, A., McGee, H. and Joyce, C. R. B. (1996) *Schedule for the Evaluation of Individual Quality of Life (SEIQOL): a direct weighting procedure for quality of life domains*. Dublin: Department of Psychology, Royal College of Surgeons in Ireland.

O'Boyle, C. A., McGee, H. and Joyce, C. R. B. (1994) Quality of life: assessing the individual. *Advances in Medical Sociology* **5**, 159–180.

Pearlman, R. A. and Uhlmann, R. F. (1988) Quality of life in chronic diseases: perceptions of elderly patients. *Journal of Gerontology* **43**, M25–M30.

Poulshock, S. W. and Deimling, G. T. (1984) Families caring for elders in residence: Issues in the measurement of burden, *Journal of Gerontology* **39**, 230–239.

Rothman, M. L., Hedrick, S. C., Bulcroft, K. A., Hickam, D. H. and Rubenstein, L. Z. (1991) The validity of proxy-generated scores as measures of patient health status. *Medical Care* **29,** 115–124.

Rubenstein, L. Z., Schairer, C., Weiland, G. D. and Kane, R. (1984) Systematic biases in functional status assessment of elderly adults: effects of different data sources. *Journal of Gerontology* **39,** 686–691.

Sanders, K. (1993) Proxy law in New York State and Victoria, Australia: a social work perspective. *Social Work in Health Care* **18,** 67–77.

Sinha, D., Zelman, F. P., Nelson, S., Bienenfeld, D., Thienhaus, O., Ramaswamy, G. and Hamilton, S. (1992) A new scale for assessing behavioural agitation in dementia. *Psychiatry Research* **41,** 73–88.

Slevin, M. L., Plant, H., Lynch, D., Drinkwater, J. and Gregory, W. M. (1988) Who should measure quality of life, the doctor or the patient? *British Journal of Cancer* **57,** 109–112.

Spear Bassett, S., Magaziner, J. and Hebel, J. R. (1990) Reliability of proxy response on mental health indices for aged, community-dwelling women. *Psychology and Aging* **5,** 127–132.

Sprangers, M. A. G. and Aaronson, N. K. (1992) The role of health care providers and significant others in evaluating the quality of life of patients with chronic disease: a review. *Journal of Clinical Epidemiology* **45,** 743–760.

Swanwick, G. R. J., Coen, R. F., O'Mahony, D., Tully, M., Bruce, I., Buggy, F., Lawlor, B. A., Walsh, J. B. and Coakley, D. (1996) A memory clinic for the assessment of mild dementia. *Irish Medical Journal* **89,** 104–105.

Weinberger, M., Samsa, G. P., Schmader, K., Greenberg, S. M., Carr, D. B. and Wildman, D. S. (1992) Comparing proxy and patients' perceptions of patients' functional status: results from an outpatient geriatric clinic. *Journal of the American Geriatrics Society* **40,** 585–588.

White, B. D., Siegler, M., Singer, P. A. and Iserson, K. V. (1991) What does Cruzan mean to the practicing physician? *Archives of Internal Medicine* **151,** 925–928.

Whitehouse, P. J. and Rabins, P. V. (1992) Editorial. Quality of life and dementia. *Alzheimer's disease and Associated Disorders* **6,** 135–137.

15. INDIVIDUAL QUALITY OF LIFE IN PALLIATIVE CARE

DYMPNA WALDRON and CIARAN A O'BOYLE

In this chapter the scope of palliative medicine and the particular relevance of quality of life in this context is explored. The emphasis that palliative care places on assessing the quality of life of the individual patient and his or her family is highlighted. Particular attention is paid to the timing of such assessments, and the validity of assumptions that are based largely on studies of health related quality of life is examined.

INTRODUCTION

" What has become perfect, all that is ripe — wants to die. All that is unripe wants to live, that it may become ripe and joyous and longing — longing for what is further, higher, brighter."

Nietzsche 1959.

Nietzsche had a comforting message for health care professionals, especially those involved in palliative care: if one could help the patient experience an increased satisfaction in life it could help allay the fear of death. Is there any empirical evidence for such a concept?

Hinton (1975) studied sixty patients with terminal cancer, relating their attitudes to such matters as 'sense of satisfaction or fulfilment in life', with their feelings and reactions. He observed that: "When life had appeared satisfying, dying was less troublesome... lesser satisfaction with past life went with a more troubled view of the illness and its outcome". As Yalom (1980) put it: "The less the life satisfaction, the greater the death anxiety". Thus, the greater the depression, anger, and overall concern about the illness and the lower the degree of satisfaction with the medical care.

Palliative care was developed to shift the focus from unattainable cure to the concerns of individual patients, and to help patients address these concerns during the time perceived as remaining to them. The ultimate aim of palliative medicine is to allow patients deal with present reality, and to help them achieve the best life satisfaction possible. This objective is often described as emphasising "quality versus quantity" time (Twycross, 1987). It is, therefore, appropriate to explore not only patients' present experiences but also to uncover their own view of their previous life.

In this chapter the scope of palliative medicine is explored, especially its direct relationship to individual patients' quality of life. The definition and methods of assessing quality of life are discussed in detail in other chapters and, consequently, the present discussion is restricted to the connections between quality of life and palliative care. At its centre is the emphasis that palliative care places on assessing the quality of life of the individual patient and his or her family. Particular attention is paid to the timing of such assessments, and the validity of assumptions that are based largely on studies of health related quality of life is examined.

PALLIATIVE MEDICINE AS A SPECIALITY

A primary aim of palliative care is the elimination, or at lest the reduction, of pain. Pain control has improved beyond all expectations in the last two decades. Today, with appropriate specialist advice, most patients with cancer can expect full pain control and patients with difficult pain problems can expect up to 95% relief.

Western medicine has been developed on the medical model of disease, the health care professional acting as a 'problem solver' on the patient's behalf; the disease is the problem to be solved and restoration to the state before the onset of the disease its solution. Although such a model has been very successful, this 'cause and effect' approach sometimes resembles a battleground, unfortunately with many casualties. According to Kearney (1992): "the dying...increasingly discovered themselves to be unwanted anomalies in the system of high technology medicine which has evolved in the search of cure. In developing its competence, western medicine had lost its caring touch".

The modern hospice movement began when pioneers such as Mother Mary Aikenhead, Dame Cicely Saunders and Dr. Elizabeth Kubler-Ross initiated a distinct approach to the care of dying patients and their families. The goal was to meet their needs in a compassionate way, addressing areas not being attended to by contemporary western medicine. Palliative medicine was not developed to give 'tender loving care' but 'effective loving care' (Saunders, 1993). The speciality was therefore developed to use the most up-to-date and effective methods of symptom control, with constant awareness of the needs of each individual and of the family. It was accepted as a medical speciality in 1987. The definition adopted (Hillier, 1988) reads:

> "Palliative medicine is the study and management of patients with active, progressive, far advanced disease for whom prognosis is limited and the focus of care is quality of life."

The following definition of palliative care has been suggested by the World Health Organisation (WHO, 1990):

> "The active total care of patients whose disease is not responsive to curative treatment. Control of pain, of other symptoms, and of psychological, social and spiritual problems, is paramount. The goal of palliative care is achievement of the best quality of life for patients and their families. Many aspects of palliative care are applicable earlier in the course of the illness in conjunction with anti-cancer treatment."

Palliative care, therefore, is a multidisciplinary speciality in which measuring quality of life is of central importance (O'Boyle, 1996; O'Boyle and Waldron, 1997).

DEFINITION OF QUALITY OF LIFE IN PALLIATIVE CARE

Quality of life assessment in modern medicine is relevant at a number of levels which might be termed micro, meso and meta respectively. The 'micro' level is concerned with the personal psychosocial and spiritual interests of the patient in contrast to the 'meso' level which is concerned with groups rather than individuals (e.g. groups of patients with cancer, patients in general or those suffering from specific cancers, such as breast cancer). The 'meta' level refers to whole populations. Ahmedzai (1993) proposes that the meso level is the most fruitful for the assessment of quality of life in palliative care. He suggests that standardised data may be invaluable for comparing the effectiveness of different treatments, for evaluating the quality of care in specific settings, to support audit and as prognostic indicators. Such proposals fail to recognise the essentially individual nature of patient quality of life and underestimate the importance of assessment at the level of the individual (micro level) in palliative care.

QUALITY OF LIFE AND PALLIATIVE CARE: THE PRESENT SITUATION

Published studies on the measurement of quality of life in patients receiving palliative care are rare, although numerous articles discuss its importance in depth (Twycross, 1987; Roy, 1992; Dundgeon, 1992; Bullinger, 1992; Cohen and Mount, 1992; Cella, 1992; MacDonald, 1992; Dush, 1993; Ahmedzai, 1993; Finlay and Dunlop, 1994; Loew and Rapin, 1994). In contrast, there has been a vast increase in the number of studies using quality of life instruments to evaluate treatment outcomes in oncology (Lancet Editorial, 1995).

One reason frequently offered for the reluctance to assess quality of life in palliative care is that patients are too ill and too frail to withstand such testing. Very few health care professionals seem to have examined this assumption. Does it truly reflect a desire to protect patients, or does it conceal an arrogant belief that health care professionals can judge what is and what is not relevant to patients' quality of life without directly asking them?

Over a decade ago Cassel (1982), writing about a particular patient's suffering, made three observations: first, that her suffering was not confined to physical symptoms; second, that she suffered not only from her disease but also as a result of treatment; third, that one could not anticipate what she would describe as a source of suffering. To improve patient quality of life, the suffering must be confronted. Cassel wrote that his patient "had to be asked".

WHEN SHOULD PALLIATIVE CARE BEGIN?

Many aspects of palliative care apply to the earlier course of the illness, when for example anti-cancer treatment is begun. It can be argued that quality of life should also be evaluated from an early stage and not solely when the patient may be too ill to benefit from the outcome.

Palliative care is directed at symptoms of disease rather than at the disease itself. This applies particularly to the management of many solid tumours (breast cancer and in most carcinomas of the lung, alimentary tract, ovaries, endometrium, uterine cervix, head and neck, kidney, urinary bladder, brain, melanoma, soft tissue sarcoma and low grade non-Hodgkin's lymphoma) especially with chemotherapy (Rubens et al., 1992). With any of these tumours, consideration of chemotherapy means that the patient's disease has already entered the phase when only palliative treatment is realistic. The input of a palliative care team is often not initiated until the disease is considered "terminal" which generally means a three to six month prognosis (Dudgeon et al., 1995).

As appropriate services develop, it emerges that palliative care may be of benefit to a patient and the family from a much earlier stage. A recent report compared the spectrum and intensity of needs expressed by cancer patients at the time of first recurrence with those at the time of disease progression (Dudgeon et al., 1995). The 75 patients in each group rated from "none" to "very much" the severity of physical symptoms, emotional, psychological and social problems and difficulties of daily living. The group in which the disease was progressing reported significantly more problems on nearly half of the symptom scales. The same group also expressed greater needs in almost one in five of the questions related to function. There were no differences between the groups in reported psychological problems, responses to recurrence, or matters of greater concern. Such results underline the need for palliative care throughout the entire course of the illness, and reflect the WHO definition of palliative care outlined above.

Quality of life should be assessed before the "terminal" phase, if maximal improvement in a patient's situation is to be achieved. This would allow more satisfactory measurement, for patients would be less frail and better able to complete assessments. There would also be more time to intervene in the whole spectrum of patient concerns, providing better "quality time" for the patient and his or her carers. As Schipper (1992) put it in relation to cancer: "The various methodologies derived to measure quality of life offer the potential for a final common pathway for assessing the multidisciplinary inputs of basic scientists and clinicians to diagnostic and treatment processes".

METHODS OF ASSESSMENT USED IN PALLIATIVE CARE

As most patients receiving palliative care have a diagnosis of cancer, the literature was reviewed to identify the methods of assessing quality of life that have been used in oncology and palliative care. Selected instruments are shown in Table 15.1.

Whereas oncology was one of the first disciplines explicitly to consider quality of life as well as clinical criteria in evaluating therapy, the methods used for assessing quality of life are mainly restricted to health status or health-related quality of life which, as the term itself shows, places health at the centre. The few studies of quality of life in palliative care have used health-related quality of life questionnaires (Morris et al., 1986; MacAdam and Smith, 1987; Fowlie et al., 1989).

Most authors in the field have recommended that comprehensive evaluation should cover the key domains of physical symptoms, physical role and social functioning, psychological distress, cognitive function, body image and sexual functioning (Cella, 1992). Some have also recognised the importance of meaning and transcendence. Based on the work of Frankl, the Purpose in Life Test was developed by Crumbaugh (1968) and Cohen et al. (1995) have developed a questionnaire that specifically incorporates the 'meaning of life' as an important component. Salmon et al. (1996) describe the Life Evaluation Questionnaire which also incorporates an existential dimension.

Deciding on appropriate measures is difficult. On one hand, it is desired to cover all important areas in a single instrument and on the other hand the

Table 15.1 Selected quality of life scales for use in palliative care

Linear Analogue Self-Assessment (LASA) Scale: (Priestman and Baum, 1976)

Spitzer Quality of life (QL) Index: (Spitzer et al., 1981)

The Quality of Life Index-QLI (Ferrans and Power, 1985)

The Spitzer Uniscale (Morris et al., 1986)

The Functional Living Index-Cancer (FLIC): (Schipper et al., 1984; Schipper and Levitt, 1986)

The MacAdam Scale (MacAdam and Smith, 1987)

The European Organisation For Research and Treatment of Cancer (EORTC) Questionnaire: (Aaronson, 1990, Aaronson et al., 1991,1993)

The Support Team Assessment Schedule (STAS): (Higginson and McCarthy, 1993)

Hospice Quality of life Index (HQLI) (McMillan and Mahon, 1994)

McGill Quality of life Questionnaire (MQOL): (Cohen et al., 1996, 1997)

The Life Evaluation Questionnaire (LEQ): (Salmon et al., 1996)

McMaster Quality of life Scale (MQLS) (Sterkenburg, 1996)

The Life Satisfaction Questionnaire (LSQ-32) (Carlsson et al., 1996)

measure should be as short as possible, especially for those who are near death. As well as being acceptable to the patients, the instrument must also be sensitive to changes due to treatment, progression of the disease, and time itself. A single question, to be answered on a visual analogue scale, has been proposed for this purpose (Morris et al., 1986), as has a categorical scale (Donnelly and Walsh, 1996). These may be overly simplistic, however. It is disconcerting that scales which do not stand up to critical appraisal are often used; for example, some methods of measurement are inherently flawed because they lack a clear definition of the concept of quality of life.

All of the methods listed in Table 15.1 involve questions that have either been formulated by a pool of specialists or by a patient group whose members are inevitably not those under care of the current physician. They therefore impose an external value system that may omit issues relevant to an individual (O'Boyle, 1996).

The rigorous testing of many methods, and the demonstration that they possess good psychometric properties, important though this is, may now be tending to obscure actual patients and their needs. The demand that an instrument for the assessment of quality of life be easy to use and brief, and give statistically valid answers is in line with the tendency of western medicine as a whole to advance "in linear and concrete terms" (Kearney, 1992). But patients must be asked about their individual suffering and its influence upon their quality of life (Cassel, 1982). Otherwise, those who require palliative care may be left behind by conventional approaches that have 'cure' as their aim and regard death as a failure.

A PHENOMENOLOGICAL APPROACH TO QUALITY OF LIFE: THE SEIQoL

The Schedule for Evaluation of Individual Quality of Life (SEIQoL), a recent method developed specifically to capture individual concerns, has been discussed at length in other chapters and is described in detail elsewhere (O'Boyle et al., 1993). It appeared to be particularly suitable for the assessment of quality of life in palliative care, despite the concern that it is too lengthy and difficult for such patients to understand (Ahmedzai, 1994). Waldron, O'Boyle, Moriarty et al. (1995) have demonstrated the applicability of the SEIQoL in a palliative care population. The method was well accepted: all patients successfully completed the short form SEIQoL-DW (Hickey et al., 1996) and 75% the full SEIQoL. The results showed both very high internal reliability and validity, the validity being the highest of any patient population so far studied with the SEIQoL. Three typical patient profiles are presented and commented upon in Figures 15.1–15.3.

A phenomenological approach to assessment in palliative care is possible. Patients were able reliably and validly, to discuss what mattered to them despite suffering terminal illness. Individual patient profiles gave a detailed

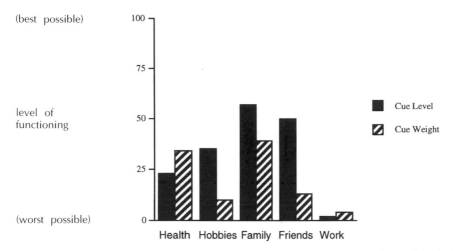

Figure 15.1 A 65 year old widow with advanced gastric carcinoma admitted to the hospice for terminal care. SEIQoL result = 40, R^2 = 0.88, Pearson's r = 0.88. Health and family are both important to this patient (high weights), but neither is very satisfactory (low levels), hence the low quality of life score. Care should therefore address the family dysfunction, as well as trying to improve physical condition as much as possible.

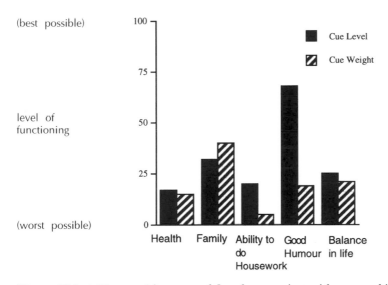

Figure 15.2 A 36 year old separated female outpatient with young children. Breast cancer diagnosed 18 months previously (hepatic metastases). Discontinuation of third line chemo-therapy possible because of side effects. Quality of life score = 35. R^2 = 0.91, Pearson's r = 0.91. Family issues are paramount, but the family is perceived as functioning very poorly, hence the very low total score. Health, though also functioning poorly, was fourth in order of magnitude. This may reflect this patient's realisation that her health is not going to improve. The profile gives a clear message that the resolution of difficult family issues is of major importance.

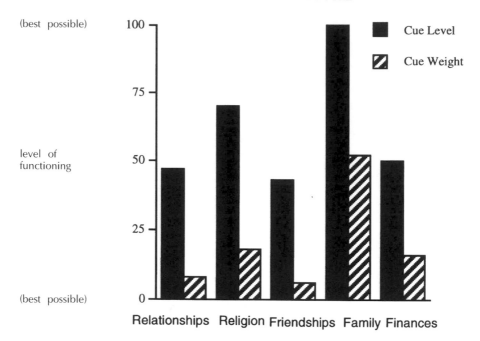

Figure 15.3 A 53 year old woman outpatient with advanced breast cancer who died two weeks later. Quality of life score = 76, R^2 = 0.85, Pearson's r = 0.97.

In spite of her very advanced disease and awareness of her poor prognosis this patient did not consider her health an important factor. Her quality of life was quite good because the area of greatest importance, her family, was functioning very well.

picture of the factors (cues) that mattered to the individual, and the function and relative weight of each cue. This represents a degree of genuine insight into the individual differences that prevail across patients.

The study is ongoing; further results confirm those from the pilot study. The SEIQoL is suitable for the assessment of quality of life in palliative care, but the SEIQoL-DW has the obvious advantage of brevity for use in a busy clinic. The information contained in an individual profile gives invaluable insight into those matters of concern to the patient and the total SEIQoL score allows within-individual comparisons over time and between patients in the same groups.

Palliative care patients appear particularly perceptive and insightful in regard to their own quality of life despite their serious illness and approaching death. This was beautifully expressed by the poet Ted Rosenthal when he was terminally ill:

"I am changed: I'll always be changed. I'll always be happier for what I have gone through, only because it has enabled me to have the courage to open myself up to anything that happens and I am no longer afraid of death. At least I am not afraid of death the way I might have been had I not become sick" (Rosenthal 1973).

CAN PATIENT CONCERNS BE ACCURATELY PREDICTED?

There are some tentative indications that quality of life may predict survival time. Maltori et al. (1995) and Ganz et al. (1991) examined the possibility of valid prediction. Although one should regard the conclusions from such studies with caution, it is encouraging that both groups found it possible to make predictions with a significant degree of accuracy, despite the fact that they examined patients with different kinds of cancer used different measuring instruments and employed different methods of analysis.

One of the major difficulties in considering quality of life as a predictor of survival time, is that the information is dependent on the method of measurement. Methods that focus heavily on physical functioning may be impressive prognosticators but do not really measure quality of life. If it is correct that "Quality of life is what the patient says it is" (see Chapter 1), studies to assess its accuracy as a prognostic indicator should be based upon this definition.

The ability of health care professionals accurately to predict a patient's concerns is limited (see Chapter 14). The paternalistic medical approach is now changing as the autonomy of the patient increases, and the history of methodological development reflects this change. At first, questionnaires were almost invariably intended to be completed by the doctor (Karnofsky and Burchenal, 1949; Spitzer et al., 1981). However, research suggests that the validity of doctors and nurses ratings is poor (Slevin et al., 1990; Presant, 1984). For example, Higginson and McCarthy (1993) compared a palliative care team's ratings with those of patients and members of their families, and found demonstrable differences in the perceptions of problems. Team members tended to record pain as slightly less severe than either the patient or family member, whereas patients rated their own anxiety as much less severe than did either the team member or the family member. Family members perceived more problems than either the team or the patient, and the team member's assessment usually lay between that of the patient and the family member. In another study, hospice patients were asked to identify and grade their perceptions of major problems (Rathbone et al., 1994). Three out of five identified problems not detected by the nursing and medical staff, of which half were psychosocial in origin.

QUALITY OF LIFE AND DECISION MAKING IN PALLIATIVE CARE

Health care professionals often presume to know which treatment option is best for maintaining or improving patient quality of life. Such presumptions are often based upon professional concepts of ill-health and quality of life, and may be inaccurate. Sugarbaker et al. (1982) compared, in a randomised controlled trial, the impact of amputation plus chemotherapy and limb-saving surgery plus radiation therapy and chemotherapy on the quality of life of 26 patients with soft tissue sarcoma, using a number of well-validated tests. The expectation that patients would prefer to avoid amputation was not supported. Certain sub-set analyses (for example, of sexual functioning) even suggested that patients receiving radiation therapy showed a greater disability. Slevin et al. (1990) compared attitudes to chemotherapy on the part of patients with cancer, doctors, nurses and members of the general public. Cancer patients were much more likely to opt for radical treatment with minimal chance of benefit than people without cancer, including medical and nursing professionals. Coates et al. (1987) compared attitudes to continuous and intermittent chemotherapy for advanced breast cancer. Contrary to physician's expectations, continuous chemotherapy was considered to be superior in improving quality of life. Earl et al. (1991) randomised patients with small cell carcinoma of the lung to receive either regular "planned" chemotherapy or chemotherapy given "as required". Again, contrary to expectations, the "as required" group scored themselves as having more severe symptoms than those receiving planned treatment.

While caution is necessary when interpreting such results, the findings do point to the need for patient generated ratings of quality of life. Not only do professionals' preconceptions influence their own beliefs about what is best for the patient, but they may also influence their presentation of the situation to the patient, possibly resulting in poor decisions about treatment options.

ARE HEALTH CARE PROFESSIONALS INFLUENCED BY QUALITY OF LIFE?

Gough et al. (1991) asked 542 health professionals (392 general practitioners, 20 specialist oncologists and 130 oncology nurses) about their views of the importance of quality of life assessment during palliative chemotherapy. The first part of the questionnaire described a hypothetical patient, defined the assessment criteria and asked whether chemotherapy should be continued or stopped, given various patterns of response. The second part assessed the extent of the respondents' experience of patients with advanced cancer. Finally, they were asked to rank the methods of assessment they considered most important to their decisions on future chemotherapy. In both sections of the questionnaire, all three groups rated quality of life higher than other standard methods of assessment (such as tumour response, treatment toxicity and the patient's physical activity level), with 60% of all respondents ranking it first (81% of nurses, 53% of general practitioners and 50% of oncologists).

Taylor et al. (1991) conducted an in-depth semi-structured interview with 60 oncologists in the USA and Canada. Most respondents perceived quality of life as important but reported a tendency to use this information informally and not in all situations. Eighty-eight percent felt that the concept could be defined and formally measured but their definitions differed. Only a third considered that the current instruments provided valid and reliable data. However, they noted that the use of quality of life assessment as an endpoint seemed to encourage both physician and patient participation in clinical trials. Somewhat paradoxically, they considered that the inclusion of such assessments might adversely affect the decision-making process. It would be interesting to discover whether the oncologists held this seemingly self-contradictory opinion because they felt that present instruments do not truly reflect quality of life, or if they feared that many patients with solid tumours and a consequently poor prognosis would refuse treatments with hazardous side effects if decisions took too great an account of information about quality of life.

SYMPTOMS AND QUALITY OF LIFE IN PALLIATIVE CARE

Symptom control is a major component of palliative care. Most health-related quality of life instruments include physical functioning scales and some ask specific questions about symptoms relevant to a specific illness. At present, the absence of instruments to assess the degree of "bother" caused the patient by symptoms and patient perception of the degree to which symptoms interfere with their quality of life represent important gaps in the literature (O'Boyle and Waldron, 1997).

QUALITY OF LIFE IN PALLIATIVE CARE: CHANGING DIRECTIONS AND THE FUTURE

There has been a great deal of progress in the last decade. A 1986 study of quality of life in a large number of hospice patients in Canada and the USA used only of third party judgements, mainly of functional aspects of patient status. At the time, this was considered to be quite appropriate (Morris et al., 1986). In a recent questionnaire, specifically developed for use in palliative care (Cohen et al., 1995), the predominance of the physical domain makes way for the existential or 'meaning of life'. Many authors now accept the importance of subjective measurement of quality of life in palliative care (Roy and Schipper, 1992; Dudgeon et al., 1992; Bullinger, 1992; Cella, 1992; MacDonald, 1992; Dush, 1993: Ahmedzai, 1993, 1994; Finlay and Dunlop, 1994; Loew and Rapin, 1994; O'Boyle 1996; O'Boyle and Waldron, 1997) and discourage the use of third-party assessments, unless the patient is unable to communicate. However, in order to capture the individual perspective on quality of life, one must go further. The patient must influence each step of the assessment. Each individual should identify the factors of personal significance, assess the level of functioning or satisfaction in regard

to each of these factors (typically the only aspect of measurement determined by the individual in conventional methods of assessment) and finally
indicate its relative personal importance.

Psychological models appropriate to palliative care are needed (O'Boyle,
1996). A phenomenological perspective acknowledges the dynamic nature of
quality of life and separates it from definitions of health furnished by other
people. As death approaches, symptoms and physical factors may become
relatively less important and intrapsychic factors more so. Individual quality
of life assessment in palliative care is likely to increase in importance over
the coming decade. As Harvey Schipper put it the challenges and benefits
are likely to be substantial.

*"We thread on new and unfamiliar ground. Quality of life studies will force us
to come out from under the comfort of technological medicine into a world that
isless concrete and less controllable but more human. The relevance and validity
of some of our most trusted measures will be reassessed. Out of it we will be better
physicians, more sensitive to the vigour, complexity and adaptability of the
human soul."*

Shipper, 1983.

REFERENCES

Aaronson, N. K., Ahmedzai, S., Bergman, B. et al. (1993) The European Organisation for
    Research and Treatment of Cancer QLQ-C30: A quality of life instrument for use in
    international clinical trials in oncology. *Journal of National Cancer Instititute* **85,** 5,
    365–376.
Aaronson, N. K., Ahmedzai, S., Bullinger, M. et al. (1991) The EORTC core quality of life
    questionnaire: interim results of an international field study. *In Effects of Cancer on Quality
    of Life.* D. Osoba D. (ed.) Bock Raton, CA: CRC Press.
Aaronson, N. K. (1990) Quality of life research in cancer clinical trials: a need for common
    rules and language. *Oncology* **4,** 59–66.
Ahmedzai, S., Arrasas, J. I., Eisemann, M. et al. (1994) Development of an appropriate
    quality of lifemeasure for palliative care. *Quality of Life Research* **3,** 57–64.
Ahmedzai, S. (1993) Quality of life measurement in palliative care: philosophy, science or
    pontification. *Progress in Palliative Care* **1,** 6–10.
Bullinger, M. (1992) Quality of life assessment in palliative care. *Journal of Palliative Care* **8,**
    3, 34–39.
Carlsson, M. and Hamrin, E. (1996) Measurement of quality of life of women with breast
    cancer. Development of a Life Satisfaction Questionnaire (LSQ-32) and a comparison
    with the EORTC QLQ-C30. *Quality of Life Research* **5,** 265–274.
Cassel, E. J. (1982) The nature of suffering and the goals of medicine. *New England Journal
    of Medicine* **306,** 11, 639–645.
Cella, D. F. (1992) Quality of Life: the concept. *Journal of Palliative Care* **8,** 3, 8–13.
Coates, A., Gebski, V., Stat, M. et al. (1987) Improving the quality of life during chemo-
    therapy for advanced breast cancer: a comparison of intermittent and continuous treat-
    ment strategies. *New England Journal of Medicine* **317,** 24, 1490–1495.

Cohen, S. R., Mount, B. M., Tomas, J. and Mount, B. F. (1996) Existential well-being is an important determinant of quality of life. *Cancer* **1**, 77, 3, 576–586.

Cohen, S. R. and Mount, B. M. (1992) Quality of life assessment in terminal illness: defining and measuring subjective well-being in the dying. *Journal of Palliative Care* **8**, 40–5.

Cohen, S. R., Mount, B. M., Strobel, M. G.and Bui, F. (1995) The McGill Quality of Life Questionnaire: a measure of quality of life appropriate for people with advanced disease. A preliminary study of validity and acceptability. *Palliative Medicine* **9**, 207–219.

Crumbaugh, J. C. (1968) Cross-validation of purpose-in-life test based on Frankl's concepts. *Journal of Individual Psychology* **24**, 74–81.

Donnelly, S. and Walsh, D. (1996) Quality of life assessment in advanced cancer. *Palliative Medicine* **10**, 275–283.

Dudgeon, D. (1992) Quality of life: a bridge between the biomedical and illness models of medicine and nursing? *Journal of Palliative Care* **8**, 3, 14–7.

Dudgeon, D. J., Raubertas, R. F., Doerner, K., O'Connor, T., Tobin, M. and Rosenthal, S. N. (1995) When does palliative care begin? A needs assessment of cancer patients with recurrent disease. *Journal of Palliative Care* **11**, 1, 5–9.

Dush, D. M. (1993) High-tech, aggressive palliative care: in the service of quality of life. *Journal of Palliative Care* **9**, 1, 37–41.

Earl, H. M., Rudd, R. M., Spiro, S.G. et al. (1991) A randomised trial of planned versus as required chemotherapy in small cell lung cancer: a Cancer Research Campaign trial. *British Journal of Cancer* **64**, 566–572.

Editorial (1995) Quality of life and clinical trials. *Lancet* **346**, 8966, 1–2.

Ferrans, C. E. and Powers, M. J. (1985) Quality of life index: development and psychometric properties. *American Journal of Nursing Science* **8**, 15–24.

Finlay, I. G. and Dunlop, R. (1994) Quality of life assessment in palliative care. *Annals of Oncology* **5**, 13–8.

Fowlie, M., Berkeley, J. and Dingwall-Fordyce, I. (1989) Quality of life in advanced cancer: the benefits of asking the patient. *Palliative Medicine* **3**, 55–59.

Ganz, P. A., Lee, J. J. and Siau, J. (1991) Quality of life assessment: an independent prognostic variable for survival in lung cancer. *Cancer* **67**, 12, 3131–3135.

Gough, I. R. and Dalgleish, L. I. (1991) What value is given to quality of life assessment by health professionals considering response to palliative chemotherapy for advanced cancer? *Cancer* **68**, 220–225.

Hickey, A., Bury, G., O'Boyle, C. A., Bradley, F., O'Kelly, F. D. and Shannon, W. (1996) A new short form individual quality of life measure (SEIQOL-DW): application in a cohort of individuals with HIV/AIDS. *British Medical Journal* **313**, 29–33.

Higginson, I. J. and McCarthy, M. (1993) Validity of the support team assessment schedule: do staffs' ratings reflect those made by patients or theirfamilies? *Palliative Medicine* **7**, 219–228.

Hillier, R. (1988) Palliative medicine — a new speciality. *British Medical Journal* **297**, 874–875.

Hinton, J. (1975) The Influence of previous pesonality on reactions to having terminal cancer. *Omega* **6**, 95–111.

Kahn, S. B., Houts, P. S. and Harding, S. P. (1992) Quality of life and patients with cancer: a comparative study of patient versus physician perceptions and its implications for cancer education. *Journal of Cancer Education* **7**, 3, 241–249.

Karnofsky, D. A. and Burchenal, J. H. (1949) The clinical evluation of chemotherapeutic agents against cancer. *In Evaluation of Chemotherapeutic Agents*. C.M. McLeod (ed.) New York: Columbia University Press.

Kearney, M. (1992) Palliative medicine — just another speciality? *Palliative Medicine* **6**, 39–46.

Loew, F. and Rapin, C. (1994) The paradoxes of quality of life and its phenomenological approach. *Journal of Palliative Care* **10**, 1, 37–41.

MacAdam, D. B. and Smith, M. (1987) An initial assessment of suffering in terminal illness. *Palliative Medicine* **1**, 37–47.

MacDonald, N. (1992) Quality of life in clinical and research palliative medicine. *Journal of Palliative Care* **8**, 3, 46–51.

Maltori, M., Pirovano, M., Scarpi, E. et al. (1995) Prediction of survival of patients terminally ill with cancer. *Cancer* **75**, 10, 2613–22.

McMillan, S. C. and Mahon, M. (1994) Measuring quality of life in hospice patients using a newly developed Hospice Quality of Life Index. *Quality of Life Research* **3**, 437–447.

Morris, J., Suissa, S., Sherwood, S., Wright, S. M. and Greer, D. (1986) Last Days: A Study of The Quality of Life of Terminally Ill Cancer Patients. *Journal of Chronic Diseases* **39**, 1, 47–62.

O'Boyle, C. A., McGee, H. M., Hickey, A., Joyce, C. R. B., O'Malley, K. and Hiltbrunner, B. (1993) The Schedule of the Evaluation of Individual Quality of Life. User Manual. Department of Psychology, Royal College of Surgeons in Ireland, Dublin 2.

O'Boyle, C. A. (1996). Quality of life in paliative care. In: Managing Terminal Illness. G.Ford and I. Lewin (eds.). pp. 37–47. London, Royal College of Physicians.

O'Boyle, C. A. and Waldron, D. (1997). Quality of life issues in palliative medicine. *Journal of Neurology* **224**, (Suppl 4), S18–S25.

Presant, C. A. (1984) Quality of Life in cancer patients. Who measures what? *American Journal of Clinical Oncology* (CCT) **7**, 571–573.

Priestman, T. and Baum, M. (1976) Evaluation of quality of life in patients receiving treatment for advanced breast cancer. *Lancet* **i**, 899–901.

Rathbone, G. V., Horsley, S. and Goacher, J. (1994) A self-evaluated assessment suitable for seriously ill hospice patients. *Palliative Medicine* **8**, 29–34.

Rosenthal, T. (1973) How could I not be among you? New York: Avon Books pp. 69.

Roy, D. J. and Schipper, H. (eds). (1992) Quality of Life. *Journal of Palliative Care* **8**, 3, (Special Issue)

Rubens, R. D., Towlson, K. E., Ramirez, A. J., Coltart,S., Slevin, M. L., Terrell, C. and Timothy, A. R. (1992) Appropriate chemotherapy for palliating advanced cancer. *British Medical Journal* **304**, 35–40.

Salmon, P., Manzi, F. and Valori, R. M. (1996) Measuring the Meaning of Life for patients with incurable cancer: The Life Evaluation Questionnaire (LEQ). *European Journal of Cancer* **32A**, 5, 755–760

Saunders C (1993) Some challenges that face us. Palliative Medicine **7**(Suppl. 1), 77–83.

Schipper, H., Clinch, J., McMurray, A. and Levitt, M. (1984) Measuring the quality of life of cancer patients: the functional living index — cancer. Development and validation. *Journal of Clinical Oncology* **2**, 5, 472–483.

Schipper, H. (1983). Why measure quality of life? *Canadian Medical Association Journal*, **128**, 1367–1370.

Schipper, H. and Levitt, M. (1986) Quality of life in cancer trials: What is it? Why measure it? *In Assessment of Quality of Life and Cancer Treatment*. V. Ventafridda, FSAM van Dam, R Yancik and M. Tamburini (eds). Amsterdam: Elsevier.

Schipper, H. (1992) Quality of life: the final common pathway. *Journal of Palliative Care* **8**, 3, 5–7.

Slevin, M. L, Stubbs, L., Plant, H. J., Wilson, P. et al. (1990) Attitudes to chemotherapy: comparing views of patients with cancer with those of doctors, nurses and general practitioners. *British Medical Journal* **300**, 1458–1460.

Spangers, M. A. G. and Aaronson, N. K. (1992) The role of health care providers and significant others in evaluating the quality of life of patients with chronic disease: a review. *Clinical Epidemiology* **45,** 7, 743–760.

Spitzer, W. O., Dobson, A. J., Hall, J. and Chesterman, E. et al. (1981) Measuring the quality of life of cancer patients. a concise QOL-index for use by physicians. *Journal of Chronic Diseases* **34,** 585–97.

Sugarbaker, P. H., Barofsky, I., Rosenberg, S. A. and Gianola, F. J. (1982) Quality of life assessment of patients in extremity sarcoma clinical trials. *Surgery* **91,** 1, 17–23.

Taylor, K. M., Macdonald, K. G., Bezjak, A., Ng, P. and DePetrillo, A. D. (1996) Physicians' perspective on quality of life: an exploratory study of oncologists. *Quality of Life Research* **5,** 5–14.

Twycross, R. G. (1987) Quality before quantity — a note of caution. *Palliative Medicine* **1,** 65–72.

Waldron, D., O'Boyle, C. A., Moriarty, M., Kearney, M. and Carney, D. (1996). Use of an individualised measure of quality of life, the SEIQoL, in palliative care: results of a pilot study. *Palliative Medicine* **10,** 1, 56. (Abstract).

World Health Organisation. (1990) Cancer Pain Relief and Palliative Care. Technical Report Series 804. Geneva.

Yalom, I.D. (1980) Existential Psychotherapy. New York: Basic Books.

IV

FUTURE DIRECTIONS

16. INDIVIDUAL QUALITY OF LIFE: REVIEW AND OUTLOOK

C. R. B. JOYCE, HANNAH M. McGEE and CIARAN A. O'BOYLE

A discussion about quality of life that claims to be comprehensive must take account of three distinct aspects: the definition of the term; ways of studying and thinking about the subject; and the evolution of the concept itself (Joyce, 1996).

The claim that there have been almost as many definitions of quality of life as publications upon the subject is only to be dismissed as exaggerated because a large number of such publications offer no definition of their subject matter at all. This is clearly unsatisfactory, because it makes the valid comparison and compiling of information from different studies extremely difficult. The use of the rubric "individual quality of life" delimits a group of methods and their dependent investigations that observe the personal definitions of the individual, but it may be too much to hope that the term will continue to be restricted in this useful manner.

Individual quality of life assessment is important in medicine and health care because it places the patient rather than the disease at the centre of the process. Patients have a fundamental right to participate in decision making and to take into account the changes, both positive and negative, that their treatment brings about. Included in this are their own perceptions and reactions which are very often the most satisfactory indicators of outcome. A change for the better or slower deterioration is certainly the outcome of chief importance to the patient, as well as being of considerable interest to clinicians — who, of course, are also interested in the pathology.

The explosion of interest in measuring quality of life represents a welcome paradigm shift, some might say a revolution, in assessing the impact of illness and disease and the outcomes of treatment. The focus on evaluations by patients incorporates a biopsychosocial model of illness rather than a more traditional biomedical model of disease. However, in the majority of reports published during the first period of this "revolution" (dating from about 30 years ago until recently), the emphasis in studies of so-called "quality of life" has really been on health status, or on what might be called the epidemiology of individual quality of life — an oxymoron. Methods developed to look more closely at truly individual quality of life have been slow to move away from traditional medical emphases upon symptoms and signs, which the physician or surgeon can evaluate. Thus, most methods in wide current use are based upon standard questionnaires that, however carefully composed and exhaustively tested, represent an ideal set of responses, or one that is normalized, in the statistical sense, and allows no room for individuality. As Diane Johnson has pointed out, "we all know that

<none of> the choices in the dry language of a questionnaire (Not at all, Very Little, Somewhat, Pretty Much, Very Much, Don't Know)... capture the precise nature of our experience, which is more Sort of, or Pretty much some of the time but sometimes never" (Johnson, 1989).

One of the barriers to progress has undoubtedly been the view that, as many components of individual qualities of life inevitably differ from each other, their number is potentially enormous and consequently presents great difficulties to attempts at measurement: their full description would appear to require a prohibitively large number of dimensions for their analysis. Investigators are confronted with a problem that somewhat resembles that faced by those who wish to advertise virtual reality, holography or even 3-D high-fidelity colour television by means of the mere two dimensions that television has made available until now. Like Lucretius, "You may be able to hear the sound of someone talking in the next room when you cannot make out the meaning" (Lewis, 1990).

If it be accepted that quality of life is an individual phenomenon rooted within the unique experience of the individual and that any intervention may potentially influence it, it must also be accepted that some at least of the factors which influence quality of life will differ from one individual to another. To assess individual quality of life idiosyncratic factors must be fully taken into account — such factors as feelings about neighbours, pollution and pop music may be as important for some people as deterioration in health, anxieties about failing memory, relationships with one's partner or in working life are for others. This is no less true of interventions that make use of pharmacotherapy, where the importance of non-medical factors is systematically ignored, than of the treatment of patients suffering illnesses with important psychological or psychosomatic components.

Progress is being made in overcoming methodological impediments to the study of individual quality of life. A concluding chapter is the appropriate place to suggest ways forward, including the closing of lacunae in existing methods, as well as emphasising new directions and applications. A general area that could do with more attention than it has so far received is the ethical; the dangers and possible abuses of enquiries into quality of life (Joyce, 1995; Hayry 1991; Hunt 1996; McGee 1996).

THE NEED FOR A THEORY OF QUALITY OF LIFE

"Theory", "Model" and "Hypothesis" are concepts often used interchangeably and misused in other ways in all the sciences. In the present context, "theory" means a body of consistent knowledge at any level from the bio-physical to the sociological, that allows the effects of specified interventions to be observed and predicted. A theory of quality of life should integrate knowledge from other cognitive theories such as those of memory and information processing (Browne, McGee and O'Boyle, 1997; McGee and

Jenkinson, 1997). Thus, internal events must lead to biophysical changes in the organism, which reflect immediate effects and/or storage processes. Any stored information is at once subject to modification by previously recorded information, as well as by new or ongoing inputs. It is reconstructed by activation of a recall mechanism and brought to conscious attention in its current state, interpreted and reported. Any intervention, such as a stimulus to recall (for example, responding to a query about financial matters from one's partner, tax inspector or bank manager) may modify the individual's representation of his quality of life at any or all of these levels. The "record" itself, whether relatively stable or not, or any link between the levels, may be normal or healthy, or may have become pathological. On the other hand, a record although clearly pathological to an external observer may be treated by the individual owner as normal or become further "pathologized".

STATE, TRAIT AND FATE

It seems increasingly clear that there are different "depths" of quality of life. For example, most individuals' financial resources are relatively stable over a period of time, but an unexpected tax demand or (a less likely event) refund may very well produce a considerable effect upon quality of life. The effect of the basic financial situation as represented by income may be likened to a trait, whereas either specific event, a tax demand or refund, may acutely affect the individual's state. Congenital personality characteristics, such as a tendency to depression, or sexual preference, may influence basic quality of life more permanently and profoundly. For example, a patient may be suffering from irritable bowel disease or a bacterially induced dysentery. Similarly, he may suffer from an agitatedly depressive diathesis, or have lost a cufflink under the bed when already late for work. The kinds of enquiry described here and the philosophical approach to individual quality of life are contributing to the breakdown of what may be called the absolutist point of view: the hard-line distinction between "objective" and "subjective", between intellectual activity and emotion, between mood and personality.

The development of appropriate theory will help to make distinctions between state and trait factors that enter into quality of life. This is a matter of some importance, whether to the healthy individual or to the clinician advising an unhealthy patient (for example, the individual perception of the relative attractions of a guaranteed yearly income or unlimited access to a supply of high-quality cannabis). Not only do different factors enter into the picture at different times, but their relative importance changes, as well as the individual's assessment of their current power to satisfy. These aspects determine where on the trait-state continuum (for such it is) the factor in question momentarily lies.

Most health status assessments, purporting to be quality of life measures, assume that the identity and relative importance of an individual's quality of life cues are stable and it is the current assessment of a cue level which may change. Improved quality of life is therefore represented in improved ratings of function in these predetermined and pre-weighted cues. But an increase in such a score may be due either to a perceived improvement in one or more ratings, to a diminished importance of a cue that was earlier rated unfavourably, or to the entry of an entirely new cue or disappearance of an old one. A valid assessment of quality of life must combine such information in a consistent manner. Failure to appreciate that the manifestations of disease, the effects of treatment and the passage of time with its fresh experiences may each lead to change in cues, levels or weights will inevitably lead to failure to penetrate beyond "quality of life" to individual quality of life.

Examination of these relationships is important. It may be that measurements of health status in fact assess quality of life traits, and that measurements of so-called quality of life assess state; or it may be that traits are estimated by weights, whereas levels, or ratings, relate to state. The distinctions and relationships are unclear, and need further investigation.

It seems likely that there is a still deeper level, that has been called, by analogy with state and trait, quality of life "fate" (Joyce, 1998). This refers to the least changing aspects of all, that may be regarded as genetic or other congenital factors influencing quality of life in a relatively intractable manner. Aspects only relatively recently taken into discussion as additional dimensions — for example, attitudes to spiritual, religious and philosophical concerns and questions — may eventually come to be considered under the heading of quality of life "fate" as well.

The traditional reluctance of the medical profession in many countries to share all available information, often including the diagnosis, with the patient has meant that health status and so-called quality of life have often been assessed by proxy. Many clinicians and others, especially in Japan and Greece, for example, believe that patients with cancer should never be told their diagnosis. In such circumstances, individual quality of life cannot be meaningfully studied at all.

On the other hand, some of the most individual (or, so to say, "non-epidemic") diseases, such as schizophrenia and Alzheimer's disease, are those in which the quality of life of the individual either cannot be studied, or can only be studied with a degree of difficulty that increases with the progression of the disease. The use of a proxy is then often inevitable but, as discussed in Chapter 15, fraught with difficulty, and serious questions must be asked regarding the validity, reliability and sensitivity of such ratings in these circumstances.

THE NEED FOR ADEQUATE PSYCHOMETRIC INVESTIGATION

The psychometric criteria for establishing a new method as reliable, valid and acceptable for its intended (descriptive or evaluative) purposes are by now relatively well defined. The Medical Outcomes Trust has published to this end comprehensive guidelines and check-lists (Medical Outcomes Trust, 1995) and the selection of publications about methods for inclusion in the interactive On-Line Guide to Assessment of Quality of Life is made according to clear, published procedures (OLGA; Erickson et al., 1993).

The iterative and recursive steps generally considered necessary for adequate psychometric description of "traditional" methods of assessing quality of life can be schematized in a way that makes clearer differences that are not always clearly perceived as such between static, or descriptive, statistics, and the dynamic statistics needed for observations on time-series, or active processes. It is worth emphasizing that individual methods do not require, and indeed cannot be submitted to, all of these procedures (Table 16.1). Browne has approached the concept of validity in an interesting way, distinguishing between inner, "true" or "representative" and outer, "real-life" or "usable" validities (see Chapter 12).

Other important aspects not included in the scheme proposed above are acceptability (which involves comprehensibility, among other features), resource requirements for both training and application, as well as analysis and computation.

There is much lamentation that there are no "Gold Standards" against which results from new methods of assessing quality of life can be compared. This should surprise nobody. Gold standards are as absent from medicine as from subatomic physics and international finance. This is a matter for congratulation in the present case: low or zero correlations with existing measures are infinitely preferable, since they demonstrate that something different from the old is being estimated by the new instrument. The best validation appears to lie in a comparison of actual with predicted outcome.

Individual quality of life assessment is in its infancy. A great deal of work needs to be done on the influence of many as yet uninvestigated influences.

Table 16.1 Static and dynamic reliability and validity

Static	Dynamic
RELIABILITY	
Test-Retest	Stability
Split-half	
VALIDITY	
Face	
Discriminant	
Content	Predictive
Convergent	
Divergent	

These include, *inter alia*, the context (relaxed or formal, timed or uncon-
strained) in which the assessment is undertaken; the method of enquiry
(interviewer- or self-administration etc.); the scaling features (e.g., open vs.
closed) and the weighting procedures to be applied to the responses. Relative weights appear to be preferred (although they are not necessarily preferable) to absolute weights, probably because the psychometrics lend
themselves more readily to group statistics such as those required in clinical
trials. However, this is illogical when the individual is the focus of interest
and self-comparison is the most meaningful outcome variable.

Other psychometric concerns may be addressed by making an analogy
with the Beaufort and Richter scales. For example, the former is the less
reliably quantifiable of the two, but is closed; whereas although the latter is
based on harder seismographic observations, it is open. This does not
prevent comparisons between earthquakes. The Richter, rather than the
Beaufort, may in this respect be the model that quality of life scales should
emulate.

Some basic statistical problems are encountered as widely in quality of life
research as in psychology in general. They include the lack of justification
for intuitive (but perhaps misplaced?) satisfaction with such judgements as
that "a Cronbach alpha of 0.70 or more is taken as showing adequate
internal consistency" or the belief that "a multiple R^2 greater than 0.70
indicates that the judgement policy has been adequately modelled" (Nunally
1978; Streiner and Norman, 1995), not to mention the shibboleth of the 5%
significance level. Neither has the standing in natural law of the gravitational
constant, nor still less of the value of π.

FUTURE DIRECTIONS AND NEW APPLICATIONS

Improving Existing Measures and Developing New Ones

In studying quality of life, one can easily form the impression that there are
more instruments than topics for their application. Although there are
certainly some marked exceptions, such as the Sickness Impact Profile or the
Nottingham Health Profile, most methods seem to have been created to
answer a particular question that has arisen in a particular circumstance, and
their chances of ever being used again thereafter appear slim. Among the
reasons for this, one may suppose, are the greater joy in inventing a wheel
than in greasing its axle. Part of this may come from the increased likelihood
of securing a research grant that proposes to develop a new method of
transport.

The bibliographies in this book that cite many uses of the methods their
chapters describe show that this situation is changing. So far, few methods
have been found to be sensitive to change, and such sensitivity is essential if
they are to be used in studying the effects of clinical interventions — a major

driving force in quality of life research. The sheer volume of work in this field, the number of instruments available and the pace of development raise possible to compare, select and combine existing information, at least for choosing appropriate methods of investigation, if not for the analysis of results. There are now several specialised quality of life databases, but, with one exception, these are at best annotated bibliographies. The exception is the already mentioned OLGA (Erickson et al., 1993), a very comprehensive and consistent data-base, that makes use of interactive software to guide the enquirer through the decisions and choices that have to be made in designing a health status or quality of life protocol. The package is updated at least twice a year.

After this, it may seem inconsistent to propose that more instruments are needed. The carriage-house contains a large array of wheels, from the finer smithing and polishing of which others of even greater beauty and perhaps even utility will eventually arise. But the present concern, clearly, is with instruments for the assessment of individual quality of life, the prototypes for which are so far few in number. Among developments to be expected are further interactive computer programmes to economise in expensive and time-consuming one-on-one interviews. However, the possible loss of reliability and validity that may be caused by the absence of human interaction should be carefully considered.

The relative advantages of "provided" and "elicited" cues need to be similarly explored. The provision of standard cues is undoubtedly simpler than eliciting them from every individual patient, but to do this reduces an individual method to the application of a standard questionnaire. Yet important cues that are not presented spontaneously may have to be more actively sought because a cue not easily elicited is not necessarily unimportant. Weights given to provided cues may also be less reliable. Similar questions also arise in relation to changes in cue selection. It has been repeatedly shown that the individual's choice of cues, as well as the ratings and weights he attaches to them, are quite likely to change over time. These matters need to be explored in detail.

Utility to the Practitioner and Patient

Methods that evaluate individual quality of life should have considerable value in clinical practice. A sensitive method may facilitate diagnosis, especially if it is used as a screening device, for changes in quality of life may be early indicators of onset of disease or illness before symptoms or biological changes become obvious as, for example, in the onset of Alzheimer's disease or of an affective disorder. Although predictions of outcome from so-called quality of life assessments are being increasingly investigated (see Dancey et al., 1997), their basis is the group and not the individual.

Individual measurements will also broaden the basis of information upon which the choice of treatment is made ("horses for courses"), as well as allowing the development, in joint discussion, of a personal test battery that both clinician and patient agree is appropriate to their needs. The balance between a clinically useful effect that impresses the physician and an internal change of state that may inconvenience the patient will become easier to analyse when such methods are used in practice, but it will often require changes in clinical behaviour that at present do not always show the expected sensitivity. The problem is perhaps even more relevant to the policy-maker or manufacturer, though much harder to study at these levels. By this means, too, patients may come to share jurisdiction over their own medical care with their physician, thus regaining control from the statistician or bureaucrat.

Individual quality of life measures are already proving particularly useful as outcome measures in the evaluation of such unconventional therapies as homeopathy and chinese herbal medicine, and in the psychotherapies, including psychoanalysis and bioenergetics. In comparative trials of conventional and unconventional treatments, the creation of realistically comparable groups of patients, who frequently have strong preferences for one form of treatment or the other, may be more achieved by the use of quality of life assessments than by the use of conventional variables like age, sex and socio-economic class.

Utility to Administrative and Commercial Policy-Makers

Market research and product research in some ways resemble research upon health status and quality of life respectively in their use of such methods as "focus groups", for instance. The purpose of product research is to improve the product and that of market research to improve the market. Both are therapeutic, the first for the patient, the second for the manufacturer. A less sceptical viewpoint would hold that both kinds are of interest to pharmaceutical manufacturers: health status for obvious reasons and quality of life in the so far largely unrealised hope that this kind of information will differentiate a product (especially a "me-too" or "me-again") from its rivals when no conventional outcome measure has been able to do so. In any case, follow up of studies of clinical efficacy and tolerability should routinely include the assessment of quality of life and health status.

The end-results of product and quality of life research are of interest to the consumer, whether patient or clinician; market and health status research is of interest to the institutional policy-maker — politician, civil servant, local administrator, hospital superintendent, health insurer. At least, they should be.

Misuses and Abuses

The use of quality of life assessment is not free of potentially by undesirable effects. Although there are many seldom reported anecdotes about the therapeutic efficacy of individual methods ("No one ever took this amount of interest in me before !", patients sometimes comment) such evident transference may need skilled attention that the interviewer is either unequipped, or too busy, to provide. It may be therapeutically useful if it takes place in a secure clinical context, but it may interfere with the satisfactorily distanced collection of scientific information.

The quality of life is sometimes, perhaps increasingly, confused with its value. Sir Colenso Ridgeon might have found it easier to decide if Louis Dubedat or Dr Blenkinsop was to have his phagocyte stimulated had he had information about the quality of life of both, but even this would not have resolved the difficult, different question of their relative values (Shaw, 1906). This may be further confused by confounding the patient's capacity to function and his welfare (see Chapter 7).

These are some of many ethical questions that arise in regard to individual quality of life, and that must be explicitly confronted if research in the field is to be meaningful and responsible.

CONCLUSION

A particular attraction of the methodologies described here is that they pay more attention than is often usual in medical research to positive aspects of life, include positive reactions to illness ("crisis as opportunity"). There are many references in the literature of AIDS-related disease, as well as in that about cancer, to the strong feelings of support, attachment and love in the caregiver as well as in the patient that are occasioned by terminal illness.

Senn points out (Senn, 1993) that just as the statistician analysing clinical trials considers that "either no patient benefits or each does to the same extent", the treating physician that a patient is either a responder or a non-responder, and that no drug is useful for all patients, but that all are useful for some; whereas "the results of... individual study will be of little value for patients as a whole." The last statement is disputable. Groups are made up of individuals. Even though the calculation of group statistics sacrifices considerable quantities of information, attention to individual aspects, especially individual quality of life as both dependent and independent variable, will prove valuable to the group because of its value to the individuals who compose it.

The statistics of single cases studied over time have recently received simple treatments (for example, Morley and Adams, 1989) but, as Meehl pointed out 20 years ago (Meehl, 1978) and Pietschmann more recently (Pietschmann, 1995), it is not so much that "soft" science cannot produce observations that lend themselves to "hard" methods of analysis, as that hard analytical methods are all too frequently inappropriate even to hard science. Effect size is more important clinically and in other forms of real life than statistical significance (Sharelson, 1981). Studies of the individual will benefit from this recognition and studies of individual quality of life will benefit further whenever, unlike many everyday decisions (such as whether to buy, hold or sell stock, or to subject a child to state or private education), they do not require the controversial combination of facts and values (Hammond and Adelman, 1976), because they are able to concentrate exclusively upon the latter. Indeed, they represent a way of pressing a little further back the "ontological frontier" of enquiry which Pietschmann is unable to cross, as is at least one of the present editors — though with considerable ambivalence.

The methods and interests of those who research in health status, health-related quality of life and individual quality of life do not oppose but complement each other. As always, there is no chance of finding the best answer unless the appropriate question is carefully posed.

REFERENCES

Browne, J. P., McGee, H. M and O'Boyle, C. A. (1997) Conceptual approaches to the assessment of quality of life. *Psychology and Health* **12**, 737–751.

Dancey, J., Zee, B., Osoba, D. et al. (1997) Quality of life scores: an independent prognostic variable in a general population of cancer patients receiving chemotherapy. *Quality of Life Research* **6**, 151–158.

Hammond, K. R. and Adelman, L. (1976) Science, values and human judgment. *Science* **194**, 389–395.

Hayry, M. (1991) Measuring the quality of life: why, how and what? *Theoretical Medicine* **12**, 97–116.

Hunt, S. M. (1996) The problem of quality of life. *Quality of Life Research* **6**, 205–212.

McGee, H. M. and Jenkinson, C. (1997) Quality of life: Recent advances in theory and methods. *Psychology and Health* **12**(6) (guest editors: special issue).

Medical Outcomes Trust (1995) Instrument review criteria. *Medical Outcomes Trust Bulletin*, September p. 1–IV.

Meehl, P. (1978) Theoretical risks and tabular asterisks: Sir Karl, Sir Ronald and the slow progress of soft psychology. *Journal of Consulting and Clinical Psychology* **46**, 806–834.

Morley, S. and Adams, M. (1989) Some simple statistical tests for exploring single-case time-series data. *British Journal of Clinical Psychology* **28**, 1–18.

Pietschmann, H. (1995) Merits and limits of applying the scientific method to human society. *Proceedings, European Commission COST Conference on "Contribution of Science and Technology to the Development of Human Society"* Basel.

Senn, S. (1993) Suspended judgment: *n*-of-1 trials. *Controlled Clinical Trials* **14**, 1–5.

Sharelson, R. J. (1981) *Statistical Reasoning for the Behavioral Sciences*. Boston: Allyn and Bacon.

Shaw, G. B. (1946) *The Doctor's Dilemma*. London: Penguin (First performed 1906; first published 1911).

APPENDIX
THE RESEARCHER'S TALE: A STORY OF VIRTUE LOST AND REGAINED

SONJA M. HUNT

In 1978 I was offered a job as Lecturer in Community Health at the Queen's Medical School in Nottingham and declined. This foolish decision was influenced by the fact that one of the responsibilities of the job was leadership of a small team working on the second phase of what was then called The Nottingham Health Index. This was an attempt by Ian McDowell and Carlos Martini to develop a "quality of life population tool"; a self-completion questionnaire based on statements drawn from interviews with patients, which described how they felt. At that time I thought of myself as an empiricist, that is, I had more technical skill than common sense. My initial disdain for the project seems to have stemmed, not, as might have been more reasonable, from the vagueness of the undertaking but rather from the idea that such a project was not scientifically respectable.

However, poor innocent maiden that I was, I was seduced by the charms of Maurice Backett, the esteemed Professor of the Department. I changed my mind, threw away my principles and, having agreed to run the project, I tackled it like a true scientist. No-one seemed to have much idea what was meant by "quality of life", but we did find out that back in the 1930s an attempt to measure the quality of life of Americans had been abandoned when it was found that no consensus existed on its nature or components. Accordingly we changed the focus to "subjective health", a clearer if still questionable concept.

The Index was tested almost to destruction; face and content validity, discriminative and predictive validity, criterion and construct validity, on and on we went, every kind of validity we could think up. We tested reliability and the statements were weighted according to the seriousness with which they were perceived by lay people.

The original 132 statements on the Index were ruthlessly reduced to 38 and the Nottingham Health Profile (NHP) was born. This offspring of phenomenology and psychometrics could be compared to the babies in Huxley's "Brave New World", conditioned, monitored and subjected to strict control only to turn out seriously defective in the sensitivity department.

During the three years that it took to produce the final version, vague disquiet had troubled me, mainly related to the realisation that such intensive testing was in danger of removing many items of interest and the use of mean and median scores effectively eliminated individual values. In the effort to ensure a high level of reliability several less severe, but more commonly experienced items, had been eliminated. A decision had been made, based upon statistical analysis, to have only a Yes/No response system because it would make for fewer errors, without much loss of information, in the *mathematical sense*.

The initial interviews on which the questionnaire was based had contained little in the way of positive statements about health so the final content expressed only problems. The combination of these factors meant that many people who filled in the questionnaire had nothing to report and zero scores from a general population were as high as 60%. Nevertheless, the question-naire appeared to work well with certain groups, especially those who were chronically ill and it was sensitive to change, given that the change was sufficiently dramatic.

Meanwhile, unnoticed and unremarked, this attempt to objectify the sub-jective had led to the elimination of items which did not 'perform well', regardless of their relevance to some patients. The restriction of response categories forced respondents to make false accounting of themselves in the interests of statistical neatness.

Two issues did, however, impinge on our consciousness. First, the ques-tionnaire did not and could not measure subjective health because the focus of the original enquiry had been on illness and the items in the question-naire reflected only negative experiences. Second, the best use of the ques-tionnaire would not be as a "population tool" because of the seriousness of many items which led to a large number of zero scores from general populations. Eventually, it was agreed to describe the NHP as measuring "subjective distress". Papers were published, talks delivered, chapters written and a User's Manual prepared; it was time to launch the NHP. Immediately afterwards I left the country, as Martini and MacDowell had done before me.

On my return to England, three years later, I found that the NHP was in vogue. I, myself, had even acquired a certain fame in the narrow circles of academic health research. During this time and in the years to follow, it became apparent that our mind searching about how to describe the NHP had been wasted, since other researchers described the questionnaire in any way which was consonant with how they wished to use it, for example as a measure of perceived health, subjective health, health status, health, self-perceived illness, health problems, symptoms, quality of life and worst of all, health-related quality of life. Use of the questionnaire escalated alarmingly, often in ways which filled its authors with dismay.

Requests came from European countries to prepare translated versions. An early experience with an attempt to satisfy a request for an Arabic version of the NHP had given me immense pleasure and equal scepticism about the wisdom of cross-cultural adaptation. Most of the questionnaire items were regarded by our Egyptian samples as, variously, irrelevant, sacrilegious, obscene or laughable. Moreover, men refused to take part and women participated only because it gave them an opportunity to rest from their labours and meet their friends. Needless to say, the project was abandoned.

In spite of this early warning, and influenced by the idea that there were huge differences between Egyptian country folk and European rustics, Denis Bucquet and I formed *The European Group of Health Measurement and Quality of Life*, a loose conglomeration of fun-loving researchers from 10 countries.

A standard method was developed for translation and adaptation. A crucial part of this was input from monolingual lay people. One of the apparent advantages of the NHP, that the items were expressed in 'the language of the people', turned to disadvantage when it became increasingly apparent that the meaning of some items could not be satisfactorily represented in one or more other languages and substitutions had to be made. In some countries people had serious concerns which were not reflected in the English version and not all items in the English version were of concern to people in other countries. The further away items were from the physical domain and the closer they were to the emotional, the greater the problems. Nevertheless, versions of the NHP were finalised in most European languages.

Now, the phrase "quality of life" began to reverberate through many lands and researchers and clinicians alike began to ask to use the NHP in 'quality of life' studies in spite of the protestations of the authors and attempts to draw distinctions between notions such as subjective distress and quality of life. A similar lack of distinction was apparent with respect to other questionnaires such as the Sickness Impact Profile, the General Health Questionnaire, the SF-36 and even the Karnofsky Index. Indeed, there was a veritable epidemic of so-called quality of life studies which had as their outcome measures anything and everything from huge batteries of questionnaires to simple counts of diarrhoea frequency.

Clearly, on both technical and commonsense grounds none of these measured "quality of life". The positive aspect of the endeavours, that is that the patient's view of their situation should be elicited, was constantly undermined by the use of inappropriate measures. The lack of conceptual clarity was very striking and, obviously, had implications for the validity of instruments. How could validity be tested if no-one knew what was being measured?

So, I found myself engaging in discussion about definitions of quality of life and how to measure it. Alas, the years had not brought much in the way of wisdom and, still entranced more by technical challenge than philosophical enquiry, I became involved in developing questionnaires based upon the premise that quality of life was determined by the extent to which human needs, physical, social, psychological and existential were able to be fulfilled. The rationale for this approach was that a focus on needs would yield a content which would be applicable to all (unlike, say, items about work or sexual activity); the underlying conceptual model, where every item was related to the same concept, would yield a unitary measure, the instrument would based on patient's accounts of their concerns and reflect their perceptions. (Interesting to ponder here on the use of the term "instrument" to describe a few sheets of paper — it does give a kind of spurious medical respectability.)

This work involved intense in-depth interviews with individual patients since we had found that work with 'focus groups' often led to a misleading consensus growing out of a 'group ideology'. It covered topics such as depression, growth hormone deficiency in adults, genital herpes, migraine and gastro-intestinal problems.

Several of the resulting questionnaires were intended for cross-cultural use and in some cases interviews were held simultaneously in the participating countries. Since the questionnaires were required to be comparable across cultures, items which did not translate well or which were deemed inapplicable in some cultures were omitted from the final version. Once again psychometrics took precedence over meaning.

Although a willing participant in this orgy of thoughtless activity (not to mention my appreciation of the opportunities for travel), the processes in which I was involved exacerbated my pre-existing but suppressed uneasiness about the whole enterprise. By this time I had spent many hours with people who were ill with a variety of complaints, often in their own homes, meeting their families, and I had become familiar with individual, social, economic and cultural differences in the way individuals and their families reacted to the blows of Fate. Illness, even serious disease, was only a part of the complex dynamic of human existence.

In addition, there were two worrying trends in the wider world of national and institutional politics. One was the use of so-called quality of life studies to make economic and commercial decisions and the other was that, as large sums of money became available for "quality of life" research and applications, vested interests were promoting the use of one questionnaire over another regardless of its suitability for a study, the population under investigation or any respect for semantics. Instead of choosing the right tool for the job, it seemed that researchers were now pressured to use the same tool for every task, roughly comparable to conducting all surgery with a handsaw.

The appropriation of the term 'quality of life' by medicine, health services research and pharmaceutical companies seemed to imply a hidden agenda which went beyond the desire to incorporate the patient's viewpoint into outcome measures and monitoring. Moreover, the impression was given that the quality of a person's life was determined by that person's health status. This was known not be the case. Quality of life had become a "sound bite" which bore little relationship to the values of the people to whom it was applied.

Thus, an interrelated series of criticisms of my own work and that of others grew in my mind. Roughly, these criticisms fell into three categories: technical, philosophical and political. Often these are inseparable. Some of the issues are pertinent to the use of questionnaires for health measurement in general and some are particular to so-called quality of life assessment.

So, I've been asked to share with you dear reader, my thoughts on these matters and they are set out below, not necessarily in order of importance and many not fully worked out, as will, no doubt, become all too apparent.

Primarily there is the issue of definition — like Humpty Dumpty, researchers and practitioners alike seem to think that quality of life can mean anything they want it to mean, regardless the concerns of patients themselves. Yet what is in a name can have all kinds of reverberations and implications. Measurement requires precision and validity. These are inextricably linked. Strangely, although there is general acceptance that there is little agreement on the nature of quality of life and that a variety of conflicting definitions are in use, this does not prevent a large number of people from trying to apply measures. Imagine doing the same with blood pressure. Saying "Well I don't really know what it is but I'm going to say it is this and I'm going to measure it thus, even though others may disagree and then I'll make decisions about patients on the basis of what my measure tells me". A favourite strategy is to rationalise the choice of measures by writing, "there is general agreement that quality of life is..." although where this consensus came from and who participated remains a mystery.

Second, there are serious discrepancies between claims made by researchers and the content and psychometric properties of the instruments used. Many questionnaires have a strong emphasis on functional capacity and yet, discussions with patients and extensive material from sociological studies on the impact of illness show that adaptation to adversity is common. Impairments of function are often compensated for by substituting less strenuous for more strenuous activities so that feelings of well-being can be re-established. Human beings are reflective self conscious agents who interpret the world and events in a manner which is partly a consequence of social and cultural background and partly idiosyncratic. It is not the presence of symptoms or limitations of function which affect quality of life but rather the meaning and significance of them for individual patients. Thus, patients with an identical health status may experience a range of existential states from despair to happiness. In other words 'ordinary' people are much less obsessed by their health than health researchers seem to believe.

Third, most questionnaires have unfortunate normative overtones, implying that some states are necessarily more desirable than others. The content of questionnaires is not only, frequently, reflective of professional notions of 'normality', it is also forged out of statistical artefacts. Thus a good "quality of life" may become equated with optimal functioning defined within narrow confines of doubtful relevance to patients. Clearly, this is untenable and unethical. If we note that person A cannot walk as far as person B, it is a perfectly reasonable statement on the comparison of physical capacity. However, to extrapolate from this to imply that, **therefore**, person B has a better **quality of life** than person A is not only to discriminate against the physically disabled, the elderly and the chronically ill, but also to impose an arbitrary set of standards in relation to human experience which may well not apply outside the narrow confines of the professional and cultural world in which they were devised.

The meaning of "quality of life" has become firmly linked to health and disease. The coining of the term "health-related quality of life" even enabled old measures of health status to be presented, even promoted, in the guise of measures of quality of life, which they clearly were not. This might be regarded as a form of medical dominance or in Illich's terms the "medicalisation" of everyday life. Is it really possible to separate out effects due to health and those concomitant effects which are a consequence of changing patterns of finance, friendship, family life, responsibilities, expectations, occupations and so on? Surely, it is impossible to disentangle the strands of action and reaction, perception and misperception which are inextricably woven into the complex web of social and individual reality. (Or have I been reading too much Sartre?)

The content of questionnaires is derived from a limited set of people at fixed points in time, usually in a single cultural context. The composition of these groups often owes more to convenience than representativeness. In spite of this questionnaires are presented as having some form of universal applicability across people and time. The values held by human beings vary by cultural origins, over time and by sex, age, social class and geographical location at the least. But if one sets out to remove these differences in the interests of psychometric testing, the most important aspects of the human condition, as well as relevant individual differences, are obliterated.

Added to this is the ethnocentricity of assuming that a questionnaire developed in, say, the USA, or England, will be applicable (after adaptation) in pretty much any country or language in the world. A situation has arisen where notions of quality of life are assumed to have the same universality as physiology, that is, to transcend culture. Cross-culturally, even within some cultures, there is not always agreement about what constitutes a disease. How much more problematic is the definition for a construct such as "quality of life".

Culture determines, to a great extent, which features of existence are regarded as part of the human condition and which may be regarded as indicative of illness. Sorrow, anxiety, angst, melancholy may all, for example, be regarded as perfectly reasonable responses to less welcome events and not necessarily evidence of the need for treatment or counselling. This is a form of cultural dominance of, in Paolo Freire's term 'cultural invasion', the ethnocentricity of which is highlighted if one imagines the chances of a health questionnaire developed in Bali, Nigeria or Hong Kong, being deemed suitable for use in Newcastle, Newark or Nice. There may well be criteria with respect to health and disease which are not culture bound but the further we move into the subjective and phenomenological world the less likely this is to be the case and the greater the individual variation.

The aggregation of data across groups denies the very rationale upon which much health measurement and so-called quality of life assessment is based, that is, that the perceptions of the patient should be incorporated into outcomes and, possibly, decision-making. By summing scores from more than one person, individual values are effectively eliminated and what we are left with may well be the perspective of the non-existent Mr and Mrs Average and a distorted perspective at that.

It now appears to me with the clarity experienced by a reformed spirit that the technical aspects of measurement and the philosophical underpinnings of quality of life are inimical. The phrase "quality of life" has been largely appropriated by western medicine and health services research, both of which are embedded in western empiricism, where objective, quantitative and verifiable data have precedence over the subjective, the qualitative and the phenomenological. Yet, surely, if the term quality of life has any meaning it must be rooted in existentialism, the values of the individual and the fluid dynamics of human attempts to cope with the exigencies of life. The impersonal constructs of biomedical and social science are far removed from the inner life of fear, love and hope, an inner life which is, moreover, constantly in flux and, often, ambiguous.

Not only has the measurement of the so-called "quality of life" of individuals within medical settings isolated them from their cultural context, it has also ignored the social and material conditions within which they exist. For example, even though a particular treatment may alleviate or even eliminate the symptoms of a particular person, it is unlikely to affect their quality of life if they are sent home from hospital to an unheated apartment, no job, no prospects, no money and a dependent relative.

The vogue for quality of life studies in medical context has created the illusion that medical practitioners, health service decision-makers and, sometimes, pharmaceutical companies can directly influence quality of life. This is far from the case since they are unlikely to have any power with respect to the most important facets of the human condition and adaptation, or the spiritual and aesthetic values which give life (and death) its meaning, notwithstanding the fact that it is often possible for practitioners to improve function and to create or restore conditions under which a decent quality of life becomes possible.

Attention is also diverted from those material and political factors which constrict or enhance opportunities for a decent life, since the focus is solely on an aggregation of personal attributes. The use of QALYs to guide decision-making and health policy exemplifies the hidden political and financial agenda behind so-called quality of life measurement. In the guise of obtaining ratings of various states, and consulting lay people in a manner which bears no resemblance to a spirit of genuine enquiry, patients are made the unwitting dupes in their own disadvantage. QALYs are in the best victim-blaming tradition. If priorities have to be set then calling them patient-based puts the responsibility for what are political not health care decisions, on the backs of patients themselves.

Many of the foregoing points raise serious ethical questions, not the least of which is implying that "quality of life" will be improved by care, or not adversely affected by treatment, when it is not the quality of a person's life which is being addressed at all.

I believe that the existential and variable nature of quality of life makes it unsuitable for measurement and the relatively small impact of health status on quality of life makes it a problematic concept for medical practitioners. There appears to be no particular reason why outcomes research should continue to focus on quality of life with all the attendant difficulties and equivocal results. Why is the notion of quality of life now so important within the medical arena? Is it not enough to save lives, patch up wounds, relieve symptoms, mend broken bones, restore chemical balances and alleviate pain? Are these no longer honourable pursuits?

In my view (which I must say was not arrived at lightly), the role of medical practitioners and decision-makers should be to provide those conditions, as culturally appropriate, which optimise the chances of a good quality of life and not to dabble in the ineffable and unmeasurable depths of the human spirit. Quality of life is the domain of the individual and should not be attributed on the basis of a culturally biased view of normality.

There is certainly a case for obtaining the views of a patient and giving them serious consideration, but as David Mechanic argued recently, decisions about individual care should be taken by doctor and patient equally, based upon an extension and deepening of the clinical interview, not upon some doubtful statistical artefact. There is also a need to improve the measurement of disability and dysfunction and to widen enquiry about patient's lives to include the material and financial aspects of their situation. If hard decisions need to be taken about the rationing of health care, politicians and economists should take full responsibility and not pretend that they are, somehow, taking the wishes of the public into account having their well-being at heart. Nor should "quality of life" claims be used to sell pharmaceutical products.

Well, thank you for your patience. It's taken me a long time to change my mind and move back on to the path of virtue. I believe my years of work on health measurement and quality of life have probably benefited me far more than they have benefited any single patient. It was certainly a lot of fun. There's a lot to be said for sin!

INDEX